The Witness of Preaching

The Witness of Preaching

Thomas G. Long

Westminster / John Knox Press
Louisville, Kentucky

Unless otherwise indicated, Scripture quotations are from the Revised Standard Version of the Bible, copyrighted 1946, 1952, © 1971, 1973 by the Division of Christian Education of the National Council of the Churches of Christ in the U.S.A., and are used by permission. Any divergence in text reflects the author's translation.

Grateful acknowledgment is made to the following:

For permission to reprint copyrighted material—Abingdon Press, for excerpts from Fred B. Craddock's *As One Without Authority* and *Preaching;* Augsburg Fortress Publishers, for excerpts reprinted by permission from *Homiletic: Moves and Structures* by David Buttrick copyright © 1987 Fortress Press and from *Preaching in the Witnessing Community* by Herman G. Stuempfle copyright © 1973 Fortress Press; Harper & Row Publishers, Inc., for excerpts from *The Church in the Power of the Spirit* by Jürgen Moltmann, copyright © 1977 by SCM Press Ltd., reprinted by permission of Harper & Row, Publishers, Inc., and SCM Press Ltd.; and Paulist Press, for excerpts from *Sir, We Would Like to See Jesus: Homilies from a Hilltop,* by Walter J. Burghardt, S.J., copyright 1982 by Paulist Press.

For permission to quote from unpublished material—Cynthia Jarvis, Barbara K. Lundblad, Henry Mitchell, Mrs. Edmund Steimle, John Vannorsdall, William Willimon, and Patrick Willson.

Book design by Gene Harris

First edition

Published by Westminster/John Knox Press
Louisville, Kentucky

PRINTED IN THE UNITED STATES OF AMERICA

9 8 7 6 5 4 3 2 1

Library of Congress Cataloging-in-Publication Data

Long, Thomas G., 1946–
The witness of preaching / Thomas G. Long. — 1st ed.
    p.   cm.
Bibliography: p.
Includes index.
ISBN 0-8042-1571-5

1. Preaching.   I. Title.
BV4211.2.L67 1989   89-32570
251—dc20   CIP

For my brother Bill,

maker of good music

and rich laughter

Contents

Introduction

Because I am a seminary professor and not the pastor of a congregation, most of the preaching I do these days is as a "guest preacher." Guest preachers, because they are—well, guests, unfamiliar with the local customs, are almost inevitably given an elaborate list of instructions before the service begins. Sit here, stand there, speak directly into the microphone, say "trespasses" instead of "debts" in the Lord's Prayer, go to this door—that sort of thing. Strangely enough, one of the most important pieces of information we guest preachers receive is a set of directions for entering the sanctuary. Church floor plans are notoriously complex, and a wrong turn can easily send an embarrassed visitor into the choir loft or a broom closet instead of the chancel.

FINDING THE ENTRANCE

My experiences as a visiting preacher have prompted me to do some thinking in a more general sense about this matter of how ministers and priests make their entrances into the sanctuary. Admittedly, this is not one of the burning liturgical issues of our time. Most Christian congregations have never given a second thought to whether their worship leaders enter by the back door, through a window, or on a swinging vine. Indeed, why should they? How, and from where, the clergy enter seems to be one of those routine behind-the-liturgical-scenes matters, like turning on the sanctuary lights, making sure the hymnals are in place, greeting people at the door, or setting the thermostat. Such things must be done, of course, but *how* they are done is apparently of little consequence. The ones who will lead the service and preach must somehow get into their places; they must travel the distance from the study or the vestry to the chancel, and one way of getting there is seemingly as good as another.

As a matter of custom, clergy make this journey to the chancel in a wide variety of ways. In some churches, the minister appears, almost unnoticed, through a side door during the playing of the prelude, unobtrusively moving to a seat near the pulpit. In other churches, the minister joins the choir in a processional down the aisle during the opening hymn. In still others, the entrance of the clergy is a moment of high ceremony, marked by prayers of confession and declarations of commitment. The practices vary, but, no matter how it is done, demurely or with great visibility, informally or as a matter of ritual, the entrance of the one who will preside at worship and preach the sermon follows a pattern so often repeated it tends to blend indistinctly into the liturgical background.

Routine or not, this matter of where clergy come from to lead worship deserves some scrutiny. Notice that in almost every instance, the clergy come from somewhere *outside* into the place where the congregation waits. This makes a certain logistical sense, of course, since ministers typically spend the last few minutes before the service in the study fiddling with their sermon notes or in the sacristy pulling on vestments or in the music room meeting for prayer with the choir or in the hallway being tugged on the sleeve by someone who wants a quick word before the service begins. Pragmatically, then, the clergy must come from wherever they have been to the place of worship and make some kind of entrance, fancy or plain.

If we look at this theologically, though, rather than logistically, another picture appears. Regardless of where the worship leaders emerge physically and architecturally, theologically they come from *within* the community of faith and not *to* it from the outside. Whether they use this door or that one, process down the center aisle or modestly glide to their chairs, it is of little import as long as they remember that though they will now preside at worship, they proceed from the midst of the community of faith.

If we were putting this theological conviction into strict practice, worship leaders would not enter from outside the sanctuary at all. They would come from the pew to the pulpit, from the nave to their place in the chancel, from the middle of the congregation to the place of leadership. For most church settings it may seem somewhat far-fetched to imagine a minister rising from a pew to give the call to worship or to preach the sermon, but this is precisely the picture of the Christian church at worship portrayed by Jürgen Moltmann in *The Church in the Power of the Spirit:*

> [W]e can take our bearings from the simple, visible procedure: the community gathers to hear the proclamation, or for a baptism, for the common meal, for the feast and to talk together. Then one person or more gets up in front of the congregation in order to preach the

Gospel, to baptize, to prepare the meal, to arrange the feast, and to make his contribution to the discussion. These people come from the community but come forward in front of it and act in Christ's name. It is not they as "office bearers" who "confront" the congregation; it is Christ. What they do and say is in the name of the triune God. How, then, are we to understand the position of these people with their particular charges or assignments? They come from God's people, stand up in front of God's people and act in God's name.[1]

What is at stake here is not a liturgical quarrel over the mechanics of how worship leaders get into place. Local circumstances and traditions will always dictate different patterns for that. What is at stake is the more urgent matter of how worship leaders, including preachers, understand themselves and their leadership roles in relationship to the whole community of faith. This is a book about preaching, and we will soon turn our attention to that particular ministry and to the many tasks involved in creating sermons. It would be a mistake, however, to jump immediately into that undertaking, as if sermons had no context and preachers no community. Preachers come to the pulpit from *somewhere,* and unless we can name that place, we risk misunderstanding who we are and what we are supposed to be doing in the pulpit. When we who preach open the sanctuary door on Sunday morning and find a congregation waiting there for us, it is easy to forget that we come *from* these people, not *to* them from the outside. We are not visitors from clergy-land, strangers from an unknown land, ambassadors from seminary-land, or even, as much as we may cherish the thought, prophets from a wilderness land. We are members of the body of Christ, commissioned to preach by the very people to whom we are about to speak.

FROM THE PEW TO THE PULPIT

Whether we realize it or not, most of us who preach do, in our own ways, act out this business of coming to the pulpit from the midst of the congregation's life. Regardless of how we navigate those last few steps into the sanctuary, we come fresh from engagements with the community of faith. We may enter the sanctuary having spent the previous hour in prayer for ourselves and for the others who will worship, or with a blue pencil, still trying to find just the right sermon words for these people on this day. We may have attended a church school class or taught one, listened caringly to a person in distress or been listened to ourselves, met with the church officers as they made a decision about the budget, drunk a cup of coffee with some people in the fellowship hall, been given a last-minute an-

nouncement about the pancake breakfast or heard the choir rehear
the anthem. Whether we have been praying, talking, teaching, pr
paring, or listening, we have been immersed in the lives of the
people to whom we will speak, which is another way of saying tha
symbolically at least, we rise to the pulpit from the pew.

Moreover, we have been involved with these people, in minist
to and with them, throughout the week, in hospital rooms and livi
rooms, in town halls and school auditoriums, in kitchens and fact
ries. Perhaps our work has strengthened the faith of others; perha
we have found our own faith strengthened. Even if we do not do
literally, we stand up to preach from our place in the middle of th
community's life, not from a point above it or at its edge. Moltmar
has it right; preachers "come from God's people."

Preachers "come from God's people" in another and more bas
sense as well. Those who preach are baptized Christians. Becau
preachers are people who have been baptized into Christ, they a
members of Christ's body, the church, before they are its *leader*
Sometimes we tend to think of "the call to preach" as a rath
isolated event which happens to a few select persons. The finger
God somehow falls upon these people, summoning them to preac
and sending them into pulpits to perform this task. Some preache
have indeed had dramatic experiences of personal calling, but it
simply misleading to speak of the preacher's call apart from God
calling of the church as a whole. "What matters," writes Moltmar
in another place, "is that public preaching and the preacher shou
not be isolated from the simple, everyday and matter-of-course la
guage of the congregation's faith, the language used by Christians
the world."[2]

God calls the whole church to proclaim the gospel, and eve
disciple of Jesus Christ is a part of this calling. The whole churc
proclaims the gospel, and the preaching of sermons is but one pa
of this larger ministry. When a church school teacher gathers a grou
of children to teach them the stories of Jesus, the gospel is pr
claimed. When a congregation opens its fellowship hall on wint
nights as a shelter and provides hospitality for the homeless, it bea
witness to the gospel. When, in the name of Christ, members of tl
congregation bring words of comfort and encouragement to the sic
and those in prison, pray for and with those in distress, and welcon
the stranger, they announce the good news of the kingdom. So wh
a preacher stands in the pulpit, reads the scripture, and preaches tl
sermon, this action is but another form of the one common minist
to which the whole church is called.

Those who preach not only participate in the church's commc
ministry, they are also shaped by it. Seminaries are sometimes jo
ingly called "preacher factories," as if it were the task of theologic

schools to take people and fabricate them into ministers. This is not
he case at all. Ministers are not "made" in seminaries. Seminaries
rain ministers; ministers are made in and through the church. People come to seminary to gain deeper knowledge of the Christian
tory, but they were first taught that story by Christian people in the
church. They come to seminary to acquire the skills of guiding,
eaching, counseling, and speaking, but they come because the
church, in some way, has already discerned in them gifts for leadership. They leave seminary not to create the church but to take their
places of service in its ongoing ministry. People do not stand up to
preach because they needed a job and have answered a want ad in
he newspaper but because the church prayerfully set them apart for
his ministry. They have been entrusted with a ministry which does
not belong to them but which belongs to Christ and is given to the
whole church.

A LONELY PLACE

Despite this brave talk about the church, every honest preacher
knows something of the loneliness of the pulpit too. As Moltmann's
picture implies, we who preach get up from our place in the midst
of the congregation, and then we walk to the pulpit and stand in front
of the people. There is a distance between *us* and *them,* and often
we feel this distance keenly. We want to speak the gospel to them,
he gospel of grace and demand, and yet we are standing there
looking out at people who could hardly seem less receptive. Because
we come from them, we know them, know their apathies and divi-
ions, know their broken places and their dull ears. We stand there
and look out at the man who is even now cheating on his wife, the
parents who are pressuring their children into lives of frenzied su-
perachievement, the couple who just purchased a new home to es-
ape an integrated neighborhood, and the merchant who recently
pulled a fast one on the Internal Revenue Service. As we stand there,
we see the restless teenagers on the back pew passing notes to each
other, the church officer who is doing her best to undermine our
ministry, the man who is already asleep, and the place where we
stand feels like a lonely place.

Part of this feeling comes because we allow our theology of the
church to grow slack. We know better, of course, but it is always
empting to hold the gritty reality of the church up against some
omantic image of the community of faith, vibrating in perfect pitch
with the music of the Spirit. We adjust our carefully prepared sermon
notes, clear our throats to begin, look up at the odd assortment of
people out there who dare to call themselves a congregation, and
wonder, "Can this be the church of Jesus Christ?" A realistic theol-

ogy of the church must always begin with the frank acknowledgment that, as Craig Dykstra has claimed, "a basic reality of congregational life is that we are engaged in socially acceptable (indeed, socially celebrated) patterns of mutual self-destruction."[3] Dykstra goes on to say:

> Furthermore, the mere presence of the story, vision, and language of the faith is no guarantee that these powerful patterns will be overcome. The patterns easily survive in congregational life, no matter how much that life may be filled with talk about sin, crucifixion, the love of God, or the grace of the Lord Jesus Christ.[4]

This is where our theology of the church must begin, but it is not where it may end because there is more to the story. It is true that the church is tarnished by the same failings that stain every human organization, but congregations continue to say and do things that point to another truth about themselves; namely, that what is most important about their life does not spring from within but from God who calls the church into being. Worship, as Dykstra has observed, is the central event by which the church points beyond itself to God. "In worship," he states, "the congregation is a congregation. Through worship, patterns of mutual self-destruction become redemptively transformed."[5]

What does it look like for a congregation to point beyond its own institutional life in worship? One place we can see this happening is in prayers of confession. These prayers may seem at first to be rather unremarkable features of the liturgy, but they are quite remarkable indeed when we contrast them to the rituals of the rest of society. Lofty words are spoken at the dedication of a civic center or a country club, but no one confesses sin. Prayers uttered before football games and corporate banquets are devoid of confession. In Christian churches every week, though, people say in one form or another, "We have erred and strayed from Thy ways like lost sheep. ... O Lord, have mercy upon us." Week after week Christian people repeat words like these, and by them they celebrate the freedom that belongs to those who know that what is truly good in human life does not finally depend upon our capacity to manufacture it.

One can also see a congregation pointing beyond itself as they share the bread and wine at the Lord's Table, as they gather to witness the marriages of one another's sons and daughters, as they sing songs of the resurrection at graveside, and as they pray for the needs of people all over the world. By doing so, they confess that they belong to a fellowship larger and deeper than their own making, greater even than their own desires. They testify that they have been made brothers and sisters to people they might otherwise pass by with a shrug of indifference. Through the words of worship, they are beckoned to speak, however haltingly, the language of a world that transcends self-interest and self-reliance; and even their children, just learning the rhythms of this language, begin to sense the difference between "When you wish upon a star" and "Now I lay me down to sleep; I pray the Lord my soul to keep."

The fact that the church in its worship points to, hopes for, and expects the reality of God beyond itself is the reason that William Willimon has insisted that the church, in its worship, retreats *to* the real world and not *from* it. "This is the 'function' of the delightfully nonfunctional world of Sunday worship," he writes, "*—to withdraw to the real world where we are given eyes to see and ears to hear the advent of a Kingdom that the world has taught us to regard as only fantasy.*"[6]

This is also the reason why the preacher rises from the pew and then stands in front of the people to preach. The preacher comes from God's people and thus is not outside the people or above them. But the preacher stands in front of the people because what the preacher is about to do is not of the people's own making or, despite all the work of sermon preparation, of the preacher's own making. As Moltmann puts it, "It comes from their God, in whose name they speak and act. After all, the commissioned and commissioning community does not want to listen to itself and project its own image of itself; it wants to hear Christ's voice, celebrate his fellowship, and have the assurance of his commission."[7]

So there we stand, we who somehow find ourselves in the pulpit with the commission to preach. We know, now, from where we have come, and it is from the congregation of Christ's people, both faithful and faithless, of which we are a part. They have taught us the "old, old gospel story" and have sent us now to this place to tell it anew to them; to recount its cherished word of hope; to remind them, because they have often forgotten, of its power; to call them, because they are prone to resist its claim, to take on once again its yoke which is easy and its burden which is light; to comfort them, because they are frightened and doubting, with its unfailing grace; and to reassure them that, no matter how far they have strayed from home, it is still, and ever will be, the story of God with and for them.

A SENSE OF MYSTERY, A SENSE OF HUMOR

No discerning person can stand in this place in front of the community of Christ without a deep sense of awe and responsibility. It is also true that no one should stand in this place without a deep sense of humility and a healthy sense of humor. We come to the place of preaching, we have been insisting, from the congregation, and we share their faith, but we also share their failings. We have no more right to be in the pulpit than anyone else in the congregation; indeed, we have no "right" to be there at all. As fully as anyone present, we have our doubts and our disobediences about the very gospel we are to proclaim. It is good to be there in the pulpit, but we are not there because we are good. That the group of people from which we come could be called the body of Christ, that we, of all people, could stand before them to preach the gospel in Christ's name is humbling and, in its own way, humorous. As Barth once remarked concerning those who speak of God:

> We can and must act as those who know. But we must not claim to be those who know. . . . [The power of God's self-revelation] consists in the divine act of majesty in face of which those who really know will always find and confess that they do not know. The attitude of those who know in this power can only be one of the greatest humility. . . . It is just because they can have no doubt as to the liberation which is quite outside their own control that those who are really free to know this matter can never lose a sense of humor in relation to themselves.[8]

"Never lose a sense of humor about yourself." Perhaps that line ought to be engraved on a plaque and placed on the back of the pulpit alongside the traditional quotation from John, "We would see Jesus." The Johannine quote would remind us to take the task of preaching the gospel of Christ seriously; the other phrase would encourage us not to take ourselves too seriously while we are doing that task. Moreover, a sense of humor in worship is not only a sign of humility but also of the gospel's liberating power. "With Easter," states Moltmann, "the laughter of the redeemed . . . begins."[9] Because God in Christ has broken the power of sin and death, Christian congregations and their preachers are free to laugh at themselves, and they can also laugh at the empty gods of pride and greed. They can mock hell and dance on the grave of death and sin.

When I was a child, my family and I worshiped in a small clapboard church set in the red-clay farming land of rural Georgia. We were a congregation of simple folk, farmers and schoolteachers mainly, and our ministers led worship wearing inexpensive and ill-fitting dark suits, believing that robes were a sign of ostentation.

The heavy summer heat of that region settled in at sunrise and gathered intensity through the day, so that Sunday worship in the hot months was punctuated by the waving of funeral-home fans and the swatting of gnats. All the windows of the sanctuary, and the main doors as well, were opened wide to accept whatever merciful breezes might blow our way. On some Sundays, however, it was not a draft that blew in the church door but a neighborhood dog, a stray hound of indecipherable lineage who somehow found our service irresistible. He was not there every Sunday by any means, but his summer appearances were frequent enough that some joked he had a better attendance record at worship than many of the officers.

The ushers knew better than to try to run him off, the one and only attempt at that having driven him bounding toward the pulpit. So, while we sang the hymns, the cur would sniff curiously at the ankles of the worshipers. Deacons would step around him on their way to take up the offering, and during the pastoral prayer the dog would wander aimlessly around the room. He was an endless source of mirth for us children, and he occasionally served as a handy and spontaneous sermon illustration in such references as "no more sense of right and wrong than that dog over there."

Looking back on it now, I realize what a trial it must have been for our ministers to attempt to lead worship and to preach on those Sundays when this mongrel was scampering around the building and nuzzling the feet of the congregation. I readily confess that I do not covet similar circumstances for myself, but there was something wonderful about those times as well. Whatever else it may mean, a dog loose in worship unmasks all pretense and undermines false dignity. It was clear to us all that the grace and the joy and power present in our communion, and these were present in abundance, were not of our own making. We were, after all, people of little worldly standing who could not keep even our most solemn moments free of stray dogs. I want to believe that even our dark-suited, serious-faced ministers were aware of the poetic connection between a congregation of simple farmers and teachers in their Sunday best with a hound absurdly loose in their midst and a gathering of frail human beings astonishingly saved by the grace of God, grace they did not control but could only receive as a gift. If so, then in some deep and silent place within them they were surely taken with rich and cleansing laughter—and if they were, they were better preachers of the gospel for it.

1

What Does It Mean
to Preach?

I don't understand preaching, but I believe in it deeply.
—**Ian Pitt-Watson,**
Preaching: A Kind of Folly

One might assume that anyone who enters a seminary is eager to take on the work of preaching. After all, being a "preacher" is one of the most striking and public of all ministerial roles, and, in the popular mind, anyone who would respond to a call to the ministry must surely be the sort of person who is ready and willing to preach and who earnestly covets this "preacher" role. The truth, however, is that the preacher's mantle rests more comfortably on some shoulders than it does on others. Preachers, regardless of whether they happen to be seminarians preparing to preach their very first sermons or experienced ministers who have preached more often than they can recall, approach the work of preaching with a wide spectrum of attitudes and feelings, from zestful anticipation to downright reluctance, from enthusiasm to paralyzing fear.

GETTING STARTED

Some ministers come to preaching eagerly. In fact, some come to preaching almost too eagerly. Because they relish the exposure of the pulpit or overlook the complexities involved in preaching the gospel or mistakenly indulge themselves in visions of the "authority" of the preacher or possess a naïve confidence in their ability to stir up a congregation, they stride into the pulpit without heeding its dangers, unmindful of its profound responsibilities. "I used to preach better," one minister said facetiously, "before I understood the issues." He was pointing to the truth that the more one understands about the task of preaching, the more respectful one becomes of its challenges and the more aware one becomes of one's limitations. Preaching is a wild river, wide and deep, and one of the goals of this book is to encourage the modesty and caution needed by all who navigate its currents.

Other ministers, however, find preaching to be a heavy and at times unbearable burden. Simply standing up and speaking to a group can be a fearful experience for some people. Despite the prevalent assumption that all ministers are free from the terrors of stage fright, this is clearly not so. Also, many ministers find themselves worn down by the unrelenting schedule of regular preaching. "Sundays come toward the preacher," quipped Ernest T. Campbell, "like telephone poles by the window of a moving train." Week after week the pressures to be solidly prepared as well as interesting and creative take their toll.

At an even deeper level, perceptive ministers can feel the weight of preaching because they know how essential it is for the larger mission of the community of faith. Congregations *want* to hear well-executed preaching; they desperately *need* to hear thoughtful and faithful preaching of the gospel. Ministers with a clear understanding of the power of preaching in the life of the Christian community, ministers who have seen the people sitting there in the pews hungry for a truthful word which clarifies and compels, know that preaching is serious and urgent business. These same ministers, however, are pushed and pulled by the many demands of ministry, and they wonder where they will find the time, the energy, the courage, the powers of insight necessary for the task. "I confess," a minister admitted, "that sometimes I wish they weren't listening. I can tell you, as a preacher, that I bear a terrible burden when people listen, really listen, from the depths of their souls."[1] Such ministers understand well why the respected student of preaching Joseph Sittler would have entitled one of his books *The Anguish of Preaching.* They also know why Karl Barth once wondered, "Who dares, who can, preach, knowing what preaching is?"

Nevertheless, it is another of the aims of this book to present preaching as a ministry of exceptional joy. To discover joy in the work of preaching does not mean whittling down its sizable demands, minimizing its perils, or even eliminating its anguish. What it does mean is strengthening our grip on the truth that the announcing of the good news of Jesus Christ in human words is an inestimable gift from God. To have our own lives, our own work, our own words, our own struggles and fears gathered up in some way into that event is an occasion of rich and joyful grace. To be a preacher is to be entrusted with the task of speaking the one word humanity most urgently and desperately needs to hear, the glad tidings of God's redemption through Jesus Christ. To be a preacher is to be a midwife. We do not create the word; we do not establish the time of its arriving; we cannot eliminate the labor pains that surround it; but we serve with gratitude at its coming and exclaim with joy at its birth.

As we begin our journey toward understanding what preaching is and how it is done, we must ask ourselves a very practical educational question: "Can preaching really be learned?" The more dynamic preachers, the ones people seem most to admire, often appear to have a certain innate flair, a knack for preaching that seems more like a gift than a set of skills. Some of these preachers have never taken a class in preaching, never read a manual on homiletics. Even if they have been formally trained in preaching, they seem more born to the task than instructed in the craft. We admire their abilities, but we wonder for ourselves if the capacity for effective preaching is within our reach. Can we really *learn* how to preach, or must we be born with the gift?

It is true, of course, that some preachers have a rare measure of talent and charisma and are readily identified as "naturally" and extraordinarily gifted, but it would be wrong for the rest of us to envy them and theologically shortsighted to set them up as the standard of effective preaching. The church is blessed by the occasional preacher of exceptional ability, but the church is nourished most of all by the kind of careful, responsible, and faithful preaching that falls within the range of most of us.

Such preaching requires study, practice, and hard work, but this does not mean that preaching is merely a matter of acquired technique. Preaching is, in fact, an alloy of art and craft, gift and training—something like playing the piano. People must have at least some raw ability to play the piano, but most of all they must be willing to master the scales, study the appropriate techniques, learn the music, and practice resolutely. There is simply no denying that the church has looked for certain qualities of mind and spirit as prerequisites for preaching, but it is important to know that these essential gifts are not the same as those of the polished orator or the electrifying speaker. Preaching requires such gifts as a sensitivity to human need, a discerning eye for the connections between faith and life, an ear attuned to hearing the voice of scripture, compassion, a growing personal faith, and the courage to tell the truth. These qualities cannot be taught in the traditional sense of classroom instruction, but those who possess them can learn much in the classroom about how to exercise them in preaching. There are lessons to be mastered, skills to be honed, processes of sermon development to be explored. In short, there is much about preaching that can be, and must be, learned.

An additional goal of this book is to assist this learning by presenting as much good information as possible about how sermons are created and delivered. Along the way we will make use of the insights of many writers in the field of homiletics. Almost as long as Christians have been preaching, there have been others who reflected on this activity, tried to understand what makes for responsible preaching, and sought to make available for preachers the best wisdom from rhetoric, psychology, sociology, and other pertinent disciplines. As a result, books and articles in the field of homiletics are plentiful. Not all of them are good, of course. Homiletics has suffered its share of fads and gimmicks, but much that is solid and fruitful as well has been learned through the years. As you read this book, you will recognize that my own voice and views form the main threads of the discussion, but others will frequently be brought in as conversational, sometimes as debating, partners. There are many good ways to approach preaching, and there are often disagreements over which is the best tack to take on certain matters. So you will have choices before you and decisions to make for your own preaching ministry.

THE EVENT OF PREACHING

What is preaching? That sounds like a simple question, but the more we think about it, the larger and more complex it becomes. Indeed, we will never be able to answer that question fully, but until we can arrive at some response, some general understanding of the nature of preaching, it makes no sense to talk about the practical steps we must take to create a sermon. We cannot really know whether a piece of advice about some aspect of our preaching is good or bad, wise or foolish, until we have a standard of measurement, a fairly clear picture of what it is that we are attempting to do when we preach.

One possible way to answer this question is to formulate a concise, dictionary-style definition of preaching, but such a definition would inevitably disappoint us because it would miss much of the richness and mystery of preaching. A better approach is to look with a probing and theologically discerning eye at the *event* of preaching, at what actually takes place in the worship of the Christian community. Moltmann's description, given in the Introduction, is again helpful: "One person or more gets up in front of the congregation in order to preach the Gospel. . . . These people come from the community but come forward in front of it and act in Christ's name."[2]

The crucial ingredients of preaching are all present here. There is the *congregation,* who will, of course, be the hearers of the preaching. There is the *preacher,* who arises from the congregation but now stands to preach in front of the community. This means that the preacher is no longer simply one among the many. Something has changed, and the preacher is in some new relationship to the others in the community. There is the *sermon,* which we must be careful to say is not what the preacher has written down beforehand but rather what the preacher says. The preacher may employ notes or a manuscript, of course, but the sermon is not something written on paper. It is an action, a spoken event, that the preacher performs in Christ's name. Finally, there is the *presence of Christ,* for to say that the preacher acts in Christ's name is to say more than the mere notion that the preacher is an agent for a distant authority. Christ is present in and with the church, and all ministries, including preaching, are expressions of this presence. Preaching does not cause Christ to be present. It is possible only because Christ is already present, and to speak in Christ's name is to claim Christ's own promise, "The one who hears you, hears me" (Luke 10:16).

So the pieces are all here—congregation, preacher, sermon, presence of Christ. What is missing is an understanding of how these aspects of the total event of preaching work together. What sort of relationship, for example, does the preacher have to the congregation? Is the preacher a peer or a leader? Is the preacher their counselor, their teacher, their prophet, or simply a good friend with a word of comfort? Or, again, how does the sermon relate to the other realities of the preaching event? Is it proper to speak of the preacher's sermon, or is it better to talk of the church's sermon, of a dialogue between preacher and hearer, or even of the sermon belonging to Christ alone? The act of preaching possesses an inner dynamic; its parts are arranged into an active system. Even though we have named the main elements, we have not yet described its inner coherence, and we do not yet know how these elements are related to each other.

We have to stand somewhere in this solar system of preaching in order to be able to see the positions of the other planets. One vantage point is potentially as good as another, but the obvious place for us to be is in the preacher's spot. If we can stand where the preacher stands and describe the role of the preacher in a comprehensive manner, we will, as a matter of necessity, also describe all the other relationships and dimensions of preaching. In other words, we are going to begin to answer the question, What is preaching? by focusing our attention on a related question, Who is the preacher?

IMAGES OF THE PREACHER

Most ministers have in their minds a general understanding of who they are and what they are doing as they go about the work of ministry. In other words, we do not just go out and do ministry. We carry with us, as we go, pictures of what we think ministers ought to be and do, pictures of who we believe ourselves to be as ministers.

Sometimes the picture we have is vague (occasionally even incoherent), and often the minister is not fully conscious of its presence, but it is there nonetheless, exercising a high degree of control over the patterns and practices of ministry. If ministers picture themselves as "shepherds" or "prophets" or "enablers" or "evangelists" or "wounded healers," these guiding images of ministry will prompt them to emphasize certain tasks of ministry and to minimize others. They will speak and act in the ways demanded by those images. Woven into these organizing metaphors of ministry are not only convictions about the nature of the ministry but also key understandings of the mission of the church, the character of the world, the nature of the human situation, and the content of the gospel.

The same is true, in a more particular sense, about preaching. When a preacher delivers a sermon, that act is embedded in some larger framework of ministerial self-understanding. In other words, preachers have at least tacit images of the preacher's role, primary metaphors that not only describe the nature of the preacher but also embrace by implication all the other crucial aspects of the preaching event. In recent years homiletical scholars have identified many of these controlling images, but the vast majority of these pictures of the preacher can be clustered around three "master" metaphors: the *herald,* the *pastor,* and the *storyteller.* At some points these three images share values about the ministry of preaching, but at other places they are rivals, embodying quite different and competing beliefs about who a preacher is and what a preacher should do. If we explore each of these images, we can begin to grasp some of the possibilities they contain for a larger understanding of preaching, and we can also make some assessment of their respective strengths and weaknesses.

The Herald

The herald image was the most prevalent metaphor advanced by homileticians of the last generation when they sought to describe what they believed the role of the preacher ought to be, though it has probably not been the most influential metaphor in terms of the actual practice of preaching. The image is a biblical one, derived from one of the several Greek terms used in the New Testament to describe preaching *(kerusso).* The herald metaphor received its modern homiletical impetus not merely because it is a biblical term but also because of the prominence given to it by the neo-orthodox theological movement, especially among those who sought to be followers of Karl Barth. Barth himself employed this image in his definition of proclamation, a term that is larger than preaching but which includes it:

Proclamation is human language in and through which God Himself speaks, *like a king through the mouth of his herald,* which moreover is meant to be heard and apprehended ... in faith as the divine decision upon life and death, as the divine judgment and the divine acquittal, the eternal law and the eternal gospel both together.[3]

Obviously, the herald image contains a very high theological view of preaching since it implies that, though the preacher is the one who speaks the words of the sermon, God is actually doing the proclaiming. The purpose of preaching is not to provide a forum for the preacher—giving moral advice, expressing opinions on important topics, or listing religious "principles for living"—but rather to be the occasion for the hearing of a voice beyond the preacher's voice—the very word of the living God.

Built into the herald image, then, is the conviction that preaching is far more than it appears to be on the surface. Suppose a rhetorician and a theologian (who happened to be committed to the herald perspective on preaching) were to hear the same sermon. The rhetorician would name the sermon as a speech about some passage from the Bible and would then go on to describe the preacher's use of language, the structure of the sermon, and so on. The theologian would agree with the rhetorician's assessment but would then make a larger claim. The theologian would assert that the human language of the sermon was, by the free and gracious act of God, the occasion for the speaking of the divine word. The theologian would insist, of course, that the preacher did not in any way control this action of God; God freely chose to speak in and through the preacher's words.

For the rhetorician, then, preaching is a human language act, and therefore we can consider ways to make it even better. Perhaps the structure could have been tightened, more effective words could have been chosen, or the illustrations could have been clearer. For our theologian, however, the important thing about the sermon is that it was the vehicle for the word of God, and this conviction places a strict limit on all talk about making the sermon "more effective." It would be a strange, even a blasphemous, idea to think that the preacher could rearrange a few words in the sermon and thereby enable God to speak more clearly. Herald preachers, then, do not strive to create more beautiful and more excellent sermons; they seek to be more faithful to the message they receive in scripture. Heralds do not aspire to be artists; they aspire to be servants of the word.

How does a preacher do this? We can explore this question by examining three additional facets of the herald image.

1. In the first place, what becomes truly important about preaching, viewed as an act of ministry, is the message, the news the herald proclaims. A herald has but two responsibilities: to get the message

straight and to speak it plainly. The king tells the herald what to proclaim, and the herald is obedient only to the extent that the king's word is delivered faithfully and without alteration.

In the case of Christian preaching, the message is the good news of Jesus Christ, as entrusted to the herald through the scripture; and the task of the preacher is to announce that news to those to whom the herald is sent. We must make a careful distinction here between the words of scripture and sermon, on the one hand, and the dynamic word of God, on the other. The herald image does not rest on the claim that the preacher, by repeating or explicating the words of the Bible, actually speaks God's word. God's word is not a set of *words;* it is an event, the very presence of God in Christ addressing the hearers. The claim of the herald image is rather that God has promised to be present as we faithfully proclaim the scripture in preaching. The herald preacher does not possess the word of God; the herald preacher possesses a command—to preach the scripture—and a promise—that as the scriptures are faithfully preached, God will speak through scripture and sermon.

So the herald preacher has one clear task with two parts: to attend to the message of the Bible and to proclaim it plainly. The preacher does not invent this message, nor should the preacher attempt to add anything to it. The preacher is not sent to evaluate the message, to try to make it more palatable, or to debate its relative merits—only to announce it faithfully. Preaching, wrote D. W. Cleverley Ford, "is not to be confused with lecturing, nor with diagnosing a situation, nor with providing homiletical advice. Preaching is being a herald because what it proclaims is the word of God which in itself is dynamic."[4]

It should come as no surprise, then, that those who encourage the herald image are suspicious of communication strategies or any attempt by the preacher to make the message more attractive or "relevant" to the hearer. It is an act of arrogance for the preacher to modify the message of God or try to find some way to make it more "reasonable" to the hearers, even in the interest of gaining wider appeal. As Barth once wrote:

> I have the impression that my sermons reach and "interest" my audience most when I least rely on anything to "correspond" to the Word of God already "being there," when I least rely on the "possibility" of proclaiming this Word, when I least rely on my ability to "reach" people by my rhetoric, when on the contrary I allow my language to be formed and shaped and adapted as much as possible by what the text seems to be saying.[5]

Dietrich Ritschl, writing in his book *A Theology of Proclamation,* is even more adamant on this point:

The lack of trust in the absolute priority and dependability of the Word is the main reason for the increasing interest of the Churches and their "experts" in the techniques of speech, communication, illustration, and rhetoric. . . . It is not the business of the preacher to try to force [the sermon's] result or even to speculate about it.[6]

Herald preachers, then, do not attempt to defend Christian doctrine or to persuade people that what they are preaching is true. They only speak the message. They do not say things to themselves like, "Now my hearers will resist this idea, so I must give reasons for it to soften their resistance." To do that would be to mistrust the message, to try to add some power to it because they fear it is weak.

2. If the herald image emphasizes the importance of the message, it correspondingly deemphasizes the personality of the preacher. Heralding is a derivative activity. The task of the herald is not to *be* somebody, but to *do* something on another's behalf and under another's authority. A herald preacher, for example, would probably be hesitant to relate a personal experience in a sermon, lest attention be drawn to the person of the preacher and away from the message. The preacher's dynamic personality, personal opinions, religious experiences, or colorful anecdotes are not truly important. Only the message is important, and once the message is spoken, the herald is thoroughly dispensable.

3. The herald preacher has a paradoxical relationship to the congregation, the church. One the one hand, a herald comes to the people with news from the king. The herald preacher proclaims the biblical message, which always comes to the hearers as a word from beyond them, a word from God. On the other hand, those who hear this word from God in faith and obedience constitute the church, and God entrusts to the church the ongoing ministry of preaching. Preaching is one of the ministries of the church, and the preacher is called to preach both by God and by the church. Again, as D. W. Cleverley Ford put it:

Wisdom counsels that the word of God as the Bible, the word of God as preaching, and the Church be seen as belonging together in a relationship which if broken can only distort the true nature of each of the separate parts. So preaching is proclaiming Christ from the scriptures, a ministry of the word specifically entrusted to the Church and which operates for the wholeness of the Church itself, but is also an instrument for the furtherance of God's will to reconcile [the world] to himself.[7]

What we have here is the idea that the Bible is the church's book, preaching is the church's ministry, and the preacher is the church's servant, but that something happens in biblical preaching that is not

of the church's own making or doing. Within the reciprocal relationships among Bible, preacher, and church, an event occurs in which
God freely speaks. Thus the herald metaphor underscores the conviction that the primary movement of preaching is *from* God
through the herald *to* the hearers.

There is clearly considerable strength in the herald image. Its
focus upon the mandate for the preacher to remain close to the
scriptural message presents a picture of a preacher with something
to say, news of vital importance to announce. It reinforces preaching
that possesses a vigorous biblical and theological character, over
against the thin gruel of moralisms, popular wisdom, bits and pieces
of advice for creative living, and encouragements to positive thinking
derived from the culture, which are found in all too many sermons.
Such sermons, wrote Gene Bartlett, remind one of what was once
said of the speeches of a certain politician; they

> left the impression of an army of pompous phrases moving over the
> landscape in search of an idea; sometimes these meandering words
> would actually capture a straggling thought and bear it triumphantly,
> a prisoner in their midst, until it died of servitude and overwork.[8]

Moreover, the herald image refuses to allow the vain paradings of
preachers who substitute charm and style for the substance of the
gospel. Rhetorical ornament and flourish in sermons, as well as the
personality-powered preachers who build congregations around
their own charisma, are exposed not simply as excessive but as the
products of a fundamental distrust of the power of the gospel itself.

The main value of the herald image, though, lies in its insistence
upon the transcendent dimension of preaching. If the power of
preaching is limited to the preacher's strength, if the truthfulness of
preaching is restricted to the preacher's wisdom, it is ultimately too
little to stake our lives on. "After all," we have heard Moltmann say,
"the . . . community does not want to listen to itself and project its
own image of itself; it wants to hear Christ's voice."[9]

But there are also weaknesses in the herald image. To begin with,
its disdain for matters of rhetorical form and communication runs
counter to what we now know, through literary approaches to biblical interpretation, about the character of the scriptures themselves.
Much of the Bible was in oral form before it was scripture. In other
words, much of the Bible was preaching before it was scripture, and
the biblical writings still show evidence of considerable attention to
rhetorical dynamics and to what Robert Tannehill has called "forceful and imaginative language."[10] Biblical writers themselves were
concerned, in other words, not only with what they were saying but
also with how they were saying it. Those critics (like Ritschl) who
warn preachers away from being concerned about style and method

must reckon with the fact that we already find in the Bible a concern for the very things they so disparage: techniques of speech, communication, illustration, and rhetoric.

Moreover, New Testament scholar Amos Wilder, among others, has reminded us that the rhetorical dimensions of the gospel were not mere ornaments designed to make the message more pleasing and attractive; they were forms called forth by the nature of the gospel itself; "the coming of the Christian Gospel was in one aspect a renewal and liberation of language. It was a 'speech-event', the occasion for a new utterance and new forms of utterance."[11]

In sum, the biblical writers were about the business of creating effects with words, and they were doing so not as ornament or merely to create interest but because these effects were extensions of the impact of the gospel itself.

Pushing the same theme a bit further, the herald image, taken alone, not only downplays what the preacher can do in the areas of language and form but, ironically, tends to undermine almost all serious theological thinking about every practical aspect of creating sermons. The herald image so stresses that preaching is something which God does, insists so firmly that preaching is divine activity rather than human effort, that the role of the preacher is almost driven from sight. Another remark by D. W. Cleverley Ford can serve as an example of this view: "The preacher cannot control the word of God, he cannot even forecast what his preaching of it will accomplish. . . . [I]n a sense he is not responsible for his preaching."[12]

There is a measure of truth here, of course, but taken at full and face value such a perspective finally dissipates the preacher's true sense of responsibility. A preacher cannot, of course, "control" God, but a preacher does exercise considerable control over what is actually said in the sermon and is responsible for the quality of that control. Moreover, it is plainly true that what a preacher decides to say and how the preacher decides to say it enormously influence the impact of the sermon. It is one thing to be careful not to equate God's activity and the preacher's actions; it is another thing to disconnect them so completely that they do not even touch.

In addition, the herald image fails to take adequate account of the context of preaching. Preaching does not occur in thin air but always happens on a specific occasion and with particular people in a given cultural setting. These circumstances necessarily affect both the content and style of preaching, and if we think of preaching as announcing some rarefied biblical message untouched by the situation at hand, we risk preaching in ways that simply cannot be heard.[13]

Plus, the personal character of the preacher and the quality of the relationship between the preacher and the hearers are factors of more importance than the task-oriented herald image normally allows.

Whether or not the congregation believes and trusts the preacher, whether or not the preacher is perceived to have integrity, undeniably affects to some degree the receptivity of the hearers. These circumstances shape the event of preaching; and the herald image, with its accent upon the unilateral movement from God to the hearers, along with its emphasis on the purity and the integrity of the message, can give the impression of preaching as an anonymous message dropped into a box. Commenting on this element in Barth's theology of preaching, Heinz Zahrnt remarked: "On the one hand, without [Barth's theology] present-day preaching would not be so pure, so biblical, and so concerned with central issues, but on the other hand, it would also not be so alarmingly correct, boringly precise, and remote from the world."[14] And again: "Not sufficient account is taken, in this theology of the word, of the fact that the situation to which the word of God has to speak possesses theological relevance, and that, as Martin Buber once expressed it, 'situations have a word to add as well.' "[15]

The irony here is that Barth himself, in his actual preaching, was vitally aware of the ways in which the context of his preaching and the needs of his hearers shaped the development of his sermons. Indeed, when he gave some more informal and practical advice on sermon construction, the herald metaphor diminished and a much more dialogical process emerged:

> One should . . . make every effort to ensure that one's sermon is not simply a monologue, magnificent perhaps, but not necessarily helpful to the congregation. Those to whom he is going to speak must constantly be present in the mind of the preacher while he is preparing his sermon. What he knows about them will suggest unexpected ideas and associations which will be with him as he studies his text and will provide the element of actuality, the application of his text to the contemporary situation.[16]

Most of the excesses of the herald image cannot be attributed to Barth but rather to his overzealous disciples in the homiletical field. Not even the prime advocates of the herald image, though, would press it beyond the point that the sermon is no longer "helpful to the congregation." On the other hand, if the aim of being helpful to the congregation is allowed to govern preaching, to become the dominant motif, the herald metaphor must be abandoned in favor of another image of the preacher. It is to this alternative image we turn.

The Pastor

The second image employed to describe the identity of the preacher is that of the pastor. Built into this image is the idea of preaching which, as J. Randall Nichols put it, "deliberately sets out to touch and involve people's personal concerns."[17] Sometimes other terms have been used to describe this understanding of preaching: "priestly," "therapeutic," or even, taken in the broad sense, "educational." In all these terms, the underlying assumption about the purpose of preaching is the same: Such preaching seeks to enable some beneficial change in the hearers, attempts to help them make sense of their lives, and strives to be a catalyst for more responsible living on the part of those who hear. In short, the pastor wants something good to happen to and for the hearers as a result of the sermon.

For the preacher as pastor, the needs of the hearers (not necessarily their wants) take on much more prominence than they do for the herald. The preacher discerns these needs, we may even say diagnoses these needs, and then strives to be of help by intervening with the gospel, by speaking a word that clarifies and restores. Clement Welsh, former warden of the College of Preachers in Washington, D.C., articulates this image in *Preaching in a New Key:*

> The preacher, standing in his special place . . . asks the complex question: "What shall I do to help [the hearer] grow? How shall I enable him to perceive, to understand, and to act: to do the human thing with the aid of those who have been most human before him?" . . . [The preacher's] function is partly therapeutic, partly educational. He does not drop a "message" into a box ready made for it. He hopes to adjust, delicately, some elements of [the hearer's] receiving mechanism to help it function more adequately.[18]

We can quickly see that with the image of "pastor" comes a whole ground-shift in the understanding of the preacher's responsibility. The herald is charged with the responsibility of remaining faithful to the message, but the pastoral preacher must develop a communicational strategy designed to provoke change in the hearers. In sum, the pastoral preacher must know more than a set of messages; the pastoral preacher must also know people and how they listen to messages. The pastor in the pulpit must always be asking, "What is it like to hear?"[19]

Let us examine two other implications of the pastor metaphor for the nature and practice of preaching.

1. For the herald, the most important dimension of preaching is the message. For the pastor, the crucial dimension of preaching is an event, something that happens inside the hearer. Whether this event is described using psychodynamic, ethical, or evangelistic language, the sine qua non of good preaching, for the pastor, is that, when the sermon is over, the hearers are different and better people than when the sermon began. A chapter title in a recent homiletical textbook

concisely states the pastoral preacher's goal: "Healing Is the Point."[20]

The preacher who perhaps did more than anyone else, in the American context, to formulate and popularize the therapeutic approach to preaching was Harry Emerson Fosdick, the well-known and controversial minister of the Riverside Church in New York City. Edmund Linn, whose book on Fosdick's method is entitled *Preaching as Counseling,* describes the aim of Fosdick's preaching as follows:

> The supreme purpose of a sermon, [Fosdick] decided, is to create in the listener no less than the thing which is being spoken. A sermon on joy must rise above a mere dissertation on the subject of joy by producing a congregation which goes out with deeper joy than it had before. . . . The preacher's task is to create in the listener whatever he is preaching about.[21]

What this means is that, with the image of pastor, we have moved 180 degrees away from the understanding of preaching as communication that we found in the herald. The herald disdains communicational concerns and strategies for changing the hearers; the pastor specializes in them. The herald starts with the Bible as source; the pastor starts with the human dilemma as experienced by the hearer and turns to the Bible as resource. For the pastor, the primary question is not "What shall I say?" but "What do I want to happen?"

2. If the herald image deemphasized the person and presence of the preacher, the pastor image implies that the preacher's relationship to the hearers—in terms of style, personality, character, previous experiences, and so on—is a crucial dimension of the pastoral and therapeutic process. As a healer, counselor, and caretaker, the pastor must be seen as competent, authoritative, compassionate, and trustworthy. Homiletical books that develop the pastoral theme, such as Gary D. Stratman's *Pastoral Preaching,* [22] typically spend much time and space discussing the personal virtues (e.g., sensitivity, vulnerability, empathy) and professional skills (e.g., diagnostic insight, ability to listen) required of the preacher. In other words, the pastor must *be* a certain kind of person in order to establish the sorts of relationships with hearers necessary to *do* the therapeutic pastoral task.

The strength of the pastor image comes from the attention it gives to the inner dynamics of preaching and to the active role played by the preacher in causing them to occur. The pastoral preacher is an active and responsible agent for change, and there is room in this image to think critically about which approaches and strategies for preaching are more effective than others. Language and form are taken seriously, and the context of preaching (at least in terms of the inner needs of the hearers) is allowed to influence the shape and content of the sermon.

The pastoral image also contains a more historically based understanding of the scripture as the record of the interaction of the gospel with the concrete realities of human situations. In the Bible, real people laugh, cry, steal, praise, lie, discover wonder, repent, rebel, come to faith, commit adultery, and strive in hundreds of very particular ways to figure out who they are and what they are called to do in the light of God's claim on their lives. In short, the Bible describes people trying by the grace of God to be human, and it can serve as a resource for contemporary people attempting to do the same. "The human conflicts and dilemmas one encounters in the Bible and in the tradition of the church," states Nichols, "are already 'ours' in the sense that they are givens in the created order and human situation."[23]

The pastor image also carries with it a keen and immediate sense of the gospel as good news *for us.* Something *happens* in pastoral preaching; the needs, hungers, and torn seams in the hearers' experience are not irrelevant, nor are they simply distractions to the preaching of the gospel. They are, instead, the very places where the grace of God may be discovered. For the pastoral preacher, then, boredom becomes a homiletical deadly sin. Pastoral preachers are not content with sermons that do not engage and enliven the hearers; they are constantly striving to preach the gospel in such a way that the hearers say, "This is good news for *me* . . . for *us!*"

There are, however, some weaknesses in the pastor image as well.

1. To begin with, to think of the preacher as pastor almost inevitably views the hearers of sermons as a collection of discrete individuals who have personal problems and needs rather than as a group, a community, a church with a mission. The public, corporate, and systemic dimensions of the gospel are often downplayed in favor of more personalistic themes.

Moreover, pastorally oriented sermons tend to focus upon those situations in human life where people are hurting and need help. What can be forgotten in all this is that people bring their strengths as well as their weaknesses to church. It may be true that a church, to use the popular phrase, is "a hospital for sinners," but that is not all that it is. A church is also a community of faith where people come to offer their commitment, energy, and intelligence for the mission of Jesus Christ. Pastoral preaching, to be sure, is not by definition compelled to ignore people's strengths, but as a matter of practice it usually does. As Joseph Sittler stated:

> It has recently been remarked that whereas we have a gospel for the alienated, the hurt, the depressed, the defeated, we have not a gospel

for the well, the effective, the joyous, busy, engaged [people] of this world. And while, to be sure, a gospel that has no word to desolation is no gospel at all, it is more and more widely true that a gospel whose scope does not address [people] in [their] joyous, creative, constructive, and effectual operations is unchallenging because uninteresting.[24]

2. Another related difficulty with the pastor image is its tendency to overwork the notion of relevance. The fullness of the gospel may be reduced to those aspects that are seen to be useful in the present moment. While it is true that preaching should always connect to the situation at hand, it is also true that the gospel is larger than the questions, issues, and needs contained in any particular moment. Preaching, like the gospel to which it seeks to be faithful, has a past tense and a future tense as well as a present tense. Preaching must do more than help people cope successfully with the challenges of the here and now. The Christian community is not at a resting place, it is on a journey. In addition to facing the challenges of the present, the task of preaching is to evoke the memories of where we have been and to articulate the vision of where we are going. The language of the gospel is the language of a kingdom land toward which we are traveling. We are learning the vocabulary of that language, celebrating the customs of that land, and trying to obey its laws, even though we are not yet there. The pastor's question, "How are we to live through the day?" must always be held in tension with another question, "How can we live toward the tomorrow of God's promised future?" Here the herald image corrects the pastoral one. The gospel message contains elements that must be proclaimed, even though, for the moment, they do not fully connect to present possibilities and therefore must be held in trust.

This is an important theological point for preaching. Whenever preaching presents human dilemmas and then says, "Here is how the gospel can speak to those problems," the inevitable conclusion is that the gospel is a finished and ready resource requiring only that we apply it to our circumstances. The truth is, the promised victory of God is not yet fully present or realized. Some tragic human suffering remains, for the time being, unintelligible and meaningless to us. Some conflicts are for the moment beyond resolution. Some illnesses have no available cure, some problems contain no ready answer. There are, to be sure, places in our experience where healing does take place, where the dividing walls of hostility are broken down, where justice emerges out of oppression, but these are "signs and wonders" pointing toward the future triumph of God. The faithful preacher cannot always speak a pastoral word that makes life healthier and more manageable but may only declare the trustworthiness of Christ, celebrate the signs and wonders in the present, and point to the future, which belongs to God.

3. The herald image also corrects the pastoral image in another way. The message of the herald is primarily news about what God in Christ has done, is doing, and will do on our behalf. The pastor runs the risk of reducing theology to anthropology by presenting the gospel merely as a resource for human growth. If the herald image created a one-directional model of preaching, the pastoral preacher is tempted simply to reverse the flow by moving from the experience of the hearer toward the gospel, with a resulting constriction of the gospel agenda. The gospel is true even when we are unable or unwilling to believe it, trust it, and live it out in our experience, and the adequacy of preaching cannot be fully measured by how much immediate change it effects in the hearers.

All this calls into question the way in which pastoral preaching typically uses the Bible. The critical question is whether preachers are supposed to help people "find their stories in the Bible" or are supposed to call the hearers, as George Lindbeck has suggested, to "make the story of the Bible their story."[25] This is a helpful distinction (even if it is possibly too sharply stated) because it highlights two quite different ways of connecting the Bible and contemporary human life. The pastoral preacher, as we have noted, assumes that the people in the pages of the Bible were, in important ways, much like the people now in the pews. We can begin, then, with some circumstance in contemporary life, explore it at some depth, and go to the Bible to see what insight is available to help us. What we understand about life, thus, becomes the key used to unlock the claims of scripture.

The second approach moves down the same highway, but in precisely the opposite direction. In this view, the people in the Bible may be seen as people like ourselves, but what makes them critically different is that their lives became absorbed into the narration of God's action in the world. They have become, in other words, characters in a larger story that is not primarily about them but about God. If this is so, we do not go to the scripture to gain more information about life as we know it but, rather, to have our fundamental understandings of life altered. The task of preaching is not to set out some reality in life and then to go to the Bible to find extra wisdom. It is instead to tell the story of the Bible so clearly that it calls into question and ultimately redefines what we think we know of reality and what we call wisdom in the first place. The Bible becomes the key to unlock the true nature of life, not vice versa. "It is the text, so to speak," writes Lindbeck, "which absorbs the world, rather than the world the text."[26]

It is this concept of telling the story of the Bible, or, more properly, the whole idea of storytelling, that governs the third major image of preaching, to which we now turn.

The Storyteller

This image differs from the previous two in that it tells us *who* the preacher is by describing *how* the preacher preaches: by telling stories. The storyteller image has received increasing attention in the literature of homiletics, and the storytelling style has become more and more popular in ministerial practice. "We are trying," say the authors of a recent textbook on preaching,

> to find that formative image that could both articulate what preaching is and free people to do it. Is there an image adequate to shape the form, content, and style of preaching? If we had to say, in a word or two, or in a picture, what preaching is and how it is done well, what would that phrase or picture be? . . . Let us consider the storyteller.
> . . . If we were pressed to say what Christian faith and life are, we could hardly do better than *hearing, telling, and living a story.* And if asked for a short definition of preaching, could we do better than *shared story?* . . . Perhaps the image of storyteller can move us toward . . . a holistic theory of preaching.[27]

Can we do better at defining preaching than "shared story"? Herald preachers would surely respond, "Yes, we certainly can!" The picture of a preacher gathering people around for a time of story sharing would be, in their view, far too soft, too immanent, too anthropologically oriented. As Peter Berger once said, "Ages of faith are not marked by dialogue, but by proclamation."[28] Pastoral preachers would perhaps object less, but even for them the notion of preaching as storytelling would lack the surgically sharp purposiveness usually associated with pastoral intervention.

Proponents of this image, however, would counter that the storyteller preacher actually blends the best traits of both the herald and the pastor without bringing along their most serious faults. The storyteller, they would say, can be just as attuned to the biblical message as the herald and, at the same time, just as sensitive to the human situation as the pastor. What enables the preacher to combine these virtues is the use of narrative as the sermonic form of choice.

Storytelling preachers do not choose the narrative form arbitrarily but because they believe that narrative is superior theologically and communicationally. Theologically narrative is superior because, at its base, the gospel itself is a narrative. One must finally respond to the question "What is the Christian faith?" by telling a story. "I believe in God," we say. Which God? "Well, the one who made heaven and earth, the God we meet in Jesus Christ, who was born of the virgin Mary, suffered under Pontius Pilate . . . ," and off we go narrating the essential story of the faith.

The Bible itself, when taken as a whole, can be described as a story, "a vast, loosely-structured, non-fiction novel."[29] What about those parts of the Bible that are clearly not narrative—epistles, proverbs, poems, doctrinal argumentation, and the like? This material fits, the argument goes, into the larger and primary narrative framework of the Bible. In fact, the non-narrative material grows out of this larger narrative, making little sense apart from the overarching biblical story which frames it. When Paul, for instance, is discussing the question of whether Christians should be free to eat meat previously used in pagan religious ceremonies (1 Corinthians 8), he does not tell stories to score his points, but the narrative of the life of Jesus stands in the background of his argument. His case grows out of this story, appeals to this story, and is unintelligible apart from the narrative framework of the story of Jesus.

The communicational case for storytelling can be made in a sophisticated manner—and some have done this—but we really need look no further than our own experience. What do listeners like in sermons? We like stories. Not only do we like stories, we live our lives out of them. We remember in stories, dream in stories, shape our values through stories. Long after the rest of a sermon is forgotten, many hearers can still recall the stories told. It is no accident that it is said of Jesus that "he did not speak to them without a parable," a story (Mark 4:34). "Given the power of narration," writes David Buttrick, "is it surprising that through most of the Christian centuries preaching has been discursive, [that is to say] best described as storytelling?"[30]

So a persuasive case can be made for the preacher as a storyteller, and in some ways this image has suffered because it is such a good one. So many people have saluted the storytelling flag in the name of so many different causes, it has become difficult to pin down its meaning. The understandings of "story preaching" are, it seems, almost as numerous as the homileticians who use the phrase.

Some advocates of the storyteller image, for example, are simply after a more critical and effective use of what has been traditionally called sermon "illustrations." Preachers should tell stories in their sermons about human experience not merely to make their sermons clearer or more interesting but also because such stories show how the Christian faith can be embodied in the actual circumstances of life. The gospel, they argue, is not a set of abstract concepts or principles to which we give assent but a total way of being in the world, a way which only narrative can embrace. If the preacher, for example, simply announces, "We can trust the goodness of God even in the midst of tragedy," the hearers may understand this idea—indeed, they may even believe it—but it may remain nonetheless remote from their experience. If, on the other hand, the preacher relates the story of a family that struggled with the meaning of God's love in the midst of the death of a child, the hearers participate vicariously in that struggle and have new possibilities opened up for their own lives.

Other advocates of this image move beyond the notion of stories *in* sermons to the more expansive concept of shaping the whole sermon in a storylike way. Sermons are not just lists of ideas placed one after the other like beads on a string. They are shaped according to some logical pattern. The typical speech is arranged around a major idea, or thesis, with subpoints serving this main thought—one, two, three, and so on. What if it is true, though, that people listen and learn most deeply not when the ideas come at them in one, two, three fashion but when the ideas flow along like the episodes of a narrative? Sermons, then, would be most powerful when shaped according to such patterns. This is, in fact, the claim of some homileticians. Sermons, they argue, may or may not contain actual stories, but they should be designed to move in the listeners' consciousness like stories. Sermons should have *plots* rather than *points*, and they should flow along according to the logic of narrative rather than the more linear logic of a philosophical argument.[31]

Still others have been attracted to the "open-endedness" of stories, the fact that the best stories, the ones most faithful to real experience, have enough ambiguity built into them to force the hearer to make a decision about the story's meaning and application. The idea is that a story listener cannot be passive but must participate with the narrator in creating the world of the story. This emphasis upon the activity and responsibility of the listener—what textbook authors called "shared story"—is clearly quite appealing, since it undergirds a dynamic and interactive understanding of Christian preaching. What these advocates of storytelling preaching are after is a sermon that is open-ended: that is to say, not quite finished. The listeners have to roll up their sleeves and get involved in the project of making meaning in the sermon.

People mean different things by the picture of the preacher as a storyteller, and they present varied reasons in defense of this image, but there are commonalities as well in these positions. We can spell these out more clearly by examining some additional implications of the storyteller image for preaching.

1. Like the herald, the storyteller metaphor places stress upon the message of preaching but with an important difference. The herald seeks to discover the content of the gospel; the storyteller refuses to divorce that content from the rhetorical form in which it is found.

The storytelling image, as we have seen, grows out of a conviction that the fundamental literary form of the gospel is narrative. "I am convinced," claims Stanley Hauerwas, "that the most appropriate image . . . for characterizing scripture, for the use of the church as well as morally, is that of a narrative or a story."[32]

For the storyteller, then, narrative is not merely one way to proclaim the gospel, it is the normative way. The gospel is essentially narrative in shape and, consequently, so is the expression of the church's faith in that gospel. As H. Richard Niebuhr stated: "The church's compulsion [to confess its faith] arises out of its need—since it is a living church—to say truly what it stands for and out of its inability to do so otherwise than by telling the story of its life."[33]

2. Like the pastor, the storyteller is deeply concerned about communication and the listening process. The pastor wants to know, What is it like to hear? The storyteller wants to know, What is the process of hearing? and is persuaded that the dynamics of listening are narrativelike to some degree. Stories that are well told both enable and demand a high level of involvement on the part of those who hear them. Stories "create a world" and invite the listeners to enter into that world and participate in it. In a sense, the storytelling image establishes a middle ground and a meeting ground between the concerns of the herald and the pastor, since the storyteller can both honor the integrity of the gospel message and take full cognizance of the life situation of the hearer. Preaching does not move unidirectionally but from both the gospel and the context toward the center. Those who advocate this image speak of the goal of preaching as creating, in the sermon, an intersection between the gospel story (or God's story) and the hearer's story.

3. The storyteller image places an emphasis upon the person of the preacher, not as pastoral expert but as one skilled in the narrative arts. Good preaching demands good storytelling. Moreover, while the herald would be reluctant to employ a personal anecdote in a sermon, the storyteller is convinced that the preacher's own life story is an indispensable resource for preaching. The preacher does not stand outside the community of hearers but in the middle of it—indeed, as a member of it. The story of the preacher's own experience of the gospel (in both positive and negative ways) can be participated in by the hearers and, to some degree, be recognized as like their own experiences.

4. The storyteller image, like that of the pastor, places a premium upon the experiential dimensions of the faith. The goal of the storyteller is for something eventful to happen to the hearer in a sermon. The pastor hopes for healing and transformation, but the storyteller has an even broader range of experiential goals. The listeners may see life and themselves in a new way, identify with a character in a

biblical story, feel the presence of God, or understand more fully the intersection between faith and routine experience.

The storyteller image thus possesses many strengths. It balances the concern for the objective truth of the gospel with a passion for religious experience. By weaving the stories of human experience into the biblical narrative, and by naming the theological dimension of those experiences, the storyteller announces, "Today this scripture has been fulfilled in your hearing." In addition, the storyteller image is attentive to the rhetorical craft of preaching without forcing the gospel into an alien rhetorical mold. The concern for narrative is not developed apart from the character of the gospel but rather on the basis of the gospel's own narrative shape.

The capacity of narrative to create a common world allows the storyteller to go a long way toward overcoming the dichotomy between individual and community in preaching. In listening to stories we are willing, to an extent, to suspend our own concerns in favor of the experience we are having together. Moreover, there is a vigorous view of the church implied by the storyteller image. The church is not only gathered by the story, it participates actively in the telling and finishing of the story.

Finally, the effective storyteller creates sermons that are popular in the best sense of that word. Good stories demand our attention, receive our interest, generate our involvement, and remain in our active memories.

As strong as this storytelling image is, though, it is not without weaknesses.

1. First of all, it tends to underplay the non-narrative dimensions of scripture and to narrow the communicational range of preaching to a single method. Despite the value of claiming that the gospel is essentially narrative and that every scriptural text fits somehow into the overarching biblical story, the fact of the matter is that there *are* non-narrative texts, and for good reason. The biblical writers do not always tell stories, because the communication of some aspects of the faith is best done in a poetic or didactic or proverbial voice and not always through narrative. Even if the basic narrative shape of the gospel is always standing in the background, there comes a time when preaching must speak in another voice, drawing out concepts, singing songs, speaking of the logical character of belief, talking about practical ethics, and so on. These tasks of preaching may rest upon a narrative base, but a narrative form is not necessarily the best means to accomplish them.

2. The same warning sounded about the experiential dimension of the pastoral image applies to the storyteller as well. There is a deep theological danger in measuring preaching by its capacity to generate religious experience. Theologian Hendrikus Berkhof has reminded

us that, in the Old Testament, one of the reasons why Israel was continually abandoning Yahweh for Baal was that Baal was always more available, more visible, providing blessings that were more predictable.[34] One could always count on Baal for a religious experience, but not so Yahweh. Yahweh tended, on many occasions, to have a hidden face, to be absent in those times when the people yearned for a more readily available God. In sum, God does not always move us when we desire to be moved, and everything that moves us deeply is not God.

The herald image places an emphasis upon the biblical message or, to use the language of narrative, upon "God's story" as disclosed in scripture. The storytelling preacher, on the other hand, recounts both God's story and our stories, seeking to weave our stories, the narratives of contemporary life, into the framework of God's story. The result can be a powerful interplay between the Bible and life, but we must admit that it can also produce simply a confusion of stories. People have many ways of narrating the story of their lives. They can tell the "Christian story" of their lives, but they can also relate their family story, their national story, their racial story, their vocational story, the story of their psychosocial growth, and so on. Ideally, the Christian story serves as the normative center of this narrative universe, critically informing all lesser stories. The danger, of course, is that this process gets reversed and the lesser story erodes or replaces the gospel story.

Herald, pastor, storyteller—these master images depict the ways in which the preacher has been described in the recent literature of homiletics. As you have read about them, you may have been comparing and contrasting these pictures with your own understanding of preaching, finding aspects of each to admire and forming your own criticisms of them. Most of us, I suspect, would resist being tagged with any of these three labels, preferring to see ourselves as a creative blend of them all. We can imagine circumstances in which it would be better to be a herald than a pastor or a storyteller, but we can probably also think of situations when the opposite would be so.

I want to suggest yet another image for the preacher. I do this not simply to add one more figure to an already crowded landscape but because I believe this new image is more suited than any of the others to disclose the true character of Christian preaching. Indeed, this new image gathers up the virtues of the others and holds their strongest traits in creative tension. Also, this picture of the preacher, and the implications for preaching it contains, expresses the convictions about preaching that will guide our discussion throughout the remainder of this book. I refer to the image of the Christian preacher as *witness.*

PREACHING AS BEARING WITNESS

Seeing the preacher as a witness is not a new idea. It has deep roots in the Bible, appearing in such passages as Acts 20:24, where Paul is reported to have said, "I do not account my life of any value nor as precious to myself, if only I may accomplish my course and the ministry which I received from the Lord Jesus, to witness to the gospel of the grace of God." The New Testament concept of witness grows out of Old Testament precedents. Consider the following passage from Isaiah 43:8–13:

Bring forth the people who are blind, yet have eyes,
who are deaf, yet have ears!
Let all the nations gather together,
and let the peoples assemble.
Who among them can declare this,
and show us the former things?
Let them bring their witnesses to justify them,
and let them hear and say, It is true.
"You are my witnesses," says the LORD,
"and my servant whom I have chosen,
that you may know and believe me
and understand that I am He.
Before me no god was formed,
nor shall there be any after me.
I, I am the LORD,
and besides me there is no savior.
I declared and saved and proclaimed,
when there was no strange god among you;
and you are my witnesses," says the LORD.
"I am God, and also henceforth I am He;
there is none who can deliver from my hand;
I work and who can hinder it?"

Commenting on this passage in an important essay, Paul Ricoeur identified four claims about the witness made by this text:[35]

1. The witness is not a volunteer, not just anyone who comes forward to give testimony, but only the one who is *sent* to testify.
2. The testimony of the witness is not about the global meaning of human experience but about God's claim upon life. It is Yahweh who is witnessed to in the testimony.
3. The purpose of the testimony is proclamation to all peoples. It is on behalf of the people, for their belief and understanding, that the testimony is made.
4. The testimony is not merely one of words but rather demands

a total engagement of speech and action. The whole life of the witness is bound up in the testimony.

One can quickly see the relationship between preaching and the idea of witness, and in this light it may seem curious that the witness image has not been more prominent in homiletical literature. There are reasons for this, however. To begin with, the terms "witnessing" and "giving a testimony" have often been associated with some of the more aggressive forms of evangelism. Homileticians have sniffed the odor of manipulation around these words and thus have stayed far away from them. As such, "witness" is a good word that has gotten into some trouble through no fault of its own.

More significantly, homileticians have not been greatly attracted to the witness image because it seems out of place. Witness is a legal term; a witness appears in the courtroom as part of a trial. An aura of law and judgment surrounds the witness idea, and this appears to be at odds with the grace and freedom associated with preaching the gospel. It is important to keep in mind, though, that the image implies that the preacher is the one bearing witness, not the lawmaker, the police officer, or the judge, and in that light it is precisely the lawcourt origin of the witness metaphor that gives it power as an image for the preacher.

Consider what happens in a court trial. The trial is conducted in a public place because what happens is a public matter. A trial is designed to get at the truth, and the people have a vested interest in the truth. In order to get at the truth, a witness is brought to the stand to testify. Now this witness is in every way one of the people, but he or she is placed on the stand because of two credentials: The witness has seen something, and the witness is willing to tell the truth about it—the whole truth and nothing but the truth. In one sense, the personal characteristics of the witness do not matter. The court is interested in the truth and in justice, not in the witness per se. In another sense, however, the character of the witness is crucial. If the witness lies—bears false witness—the ability of the people to discover the truth will suffer a grievous blow. "False testimony," writes Ricoeur, "is a lie in the heart of the witness. This perverse intention is so fatal to the exercise of justice and to the entire order of discourse that all codes of morality place it very high in the scale of vices."[36]

The court has access to the truth only through the witness. It seeks the truth, but it must look for it in testimony of the witness. The very life of the witness, then, is bound up into the testimony. The witness cannot claim to be removed, objectively pointing to the evidence. What the witness believes to be true is a part of the evidence, and when the truth told by the witness is despised by the people, the witness may suffer, or even be killed, as a result of the testimony. It is no coincidence that the New Testament word for "witness" is *martyr.*

What happens to our understanding of preaching when this image of witness is taken as a guide?

1. The witness image emphasizes the authority of the preacher in a new way. The preacher as witness is not authoritative because of rank or power but rather because of what the preacher has seen and heard. When the preacher prepares a sermon by wrestling with a biblical text, the preacher is not merely gathering information about that text. The preacher is listening for a voice, looking for a presence, hoping for the claim of God to be encountered through the text. Until this happens, there is nothing for the preacher to say. When it happens, the preacher becomes a witness to what has been seen and heard through the scripture, and the preacher's authority grows out of this seeing and hearing.

Does this mean that the preacher is authoritative because the preacher has more Christian experience than the people in the pews? No, of course not. There may well be many in the congregation whose faith is richer, more mature, and more tested than the preacher's. In addition, there will probably be people in the congregation who have more education or more common sense, who have a firmer grasp of human nature, or maybe even know more Bible and theology than does the preacher. To call the preacher an authority does not mean that the preacher is wiser than others. What it does mean is that the preacher is the one whom the congregation sends on their behalf, week after week, to the scripture. The church knows that its life depends upon hearing the truth of God's promise and claim through the scripture, and it has set the preacher apart for the crucial activity of going to the scripture to listen for that truth. The authority of the preacher, then, is the authority of ordination, the authority of being identified by the faithful community as the one called to preach and the one who has been prayerfully set apart for this ministry, the authority that comes from being "sworn in" as a witness.

Accordingly, the church prepares and trains its ministers, including sending them to seminaries, not because ministers are better or smarter than other Christians, but because the church needs workers equipped to help the church to know the truth and to live in its light. If the preacher is to be the one sent to listen for God's truth in the Bible, the preacher not only must be willing to listen to the Bible but also must know how to listen. If the preacher is to be sent on behalf of the congregation, the preacher must also know how to listen to *them.* These activities require a right spirit, but they also require special preparation. Seminary training does not equip one to be a professor in the church but, rather, a trustworthy witness. An unreliable witness does not make the truth any less true, but the community's quest to encounter the truth is undeniably damaged by false or unreliable witnesses.

2. The witness image embodies a way of approaching the Bible. Witnesses testify to events, and the event to which the preacher testifies is the encounter between God and ourselves. This event is the same one proclaimed in Isaiah, "that you may know and believe me and understand that I am [God]." One of the essential ways that we come to "know" God is through the scripture, not because the Bible speculates about the nature of God in a metaphysical sense but because the Bible is itself the faithful witness to the interactions of God with the whole creation. We come to know God as the central "character" in the story, as a "Person" in relationship with human beings, as One who creates, judges, saves, loves, destroys, builds, forgives, and renews. "The primary focus [of the Bible] is not on God's being in itself," claims Lindbeck, "for that is not what the text is about, but on how life is to be lived and reality construed in the light of God's character as an agent as this is depicted in the stories of Israel and of Jesus."[37]

We go to scripture, then, not to glean a set of facts about God or the faith that can then be announced whenever and wherever, but to encounter a Presence, to hear God's voice speaking to us ever anew, calling us in the midst of the situations in which we find ourselves to be God's faithful people. The picture of the preacher sitting alone in the study, working with a biblical text in preparation for the sermon, is misleading. It is not the preacher who goes to the scripture; it is the church that goes to the scripture by means of the preacher. The preacher is a member of the community, set apart by them and sent to the scripture to search, to study, and to listen obediently on their behalf.

So, the preacher goes to the scripture, but not alone. The preacher goes on behalf of the faithful community and, in a sense, on behalf of the world. Their questions and needs are in the preacher's mind and heart. The preacher explores the scripture, faithfully expecting to discover the truth of God's claim there and always willing to be surprised by it. Those who have sent the preacher have questions and concerns, and sometimes the text will speak directly to those questions. The text may, however, call those questions into question. The truth found there may resolve a problem, and then again it may deepen that problem. The truth found there may generate a religious experience, but it may also create the experience of God's absence. Whatever needs of church and world have been brought to the text by the preacher, when the claims of God through the scripture are seen and heard, the preacher turns back toward those who wait—and tells the truth.

3. The witness image carries with it guidance about the rhetorical form of preaching. The witness is not called upon to testify in the abstract but to find just those words and patterns that can convey the event the witness has heard and seen. One can even say that the truth to which the witness testifies seeks its own verbal form, and the responsibility of the witness is to allow that form to emerge. Most often the witness is invited to "tell your story"; thus the prominence given to narrative in the storytelling image is also implied in the image of witness. On other occasions, though, the truth will demand another form. Preaching, in other words, will assume a variety of rhetorical styles, not as ornaments but as governed by the truth to which they correspond. The shape of the witness's sermon should fit the character of the testimony.

4. The witness is not a neutral observer. The truth is larger than the witness's own experience of it, and the witness is always testifying to a gospel larger than the preacher's personal faith, but the witness preacher *has* experienced it at some depth and is thereby involved in it. This is especially true of the New Testament concept of witness, in which witnessing takes on an acted as well as a verbal form. The witness often testifies to hard truths, unpopular truths, and sometimes at great risk. As Paul Ricoeur has commented, "This profession [of a witness] implies a total engagement not only of words but of acts, and, in the extreme, in the sacrifice of a life."[38]

The witness is also not a neutral observer in the sense that where one stands influences what one sees. The location of the witness, in other words, is critical, and the preacher as witness is one who stands in and with a particular community of faith, deeply involved in the concrete struggles of that community to find meaning, to seek justice, and to be faithful to the gospel. If the community of faith to which the witness belongs and from which the witness comes is urban or rural, black or Asian, rich or poor, powerless or powerful, these circumstances firmly shape the character of the preaching. We have recognized, through the work of liberation and feminist theologians among others, that a "disinterested" reading of the gospel is neither possible nor desirable. Effective preaching has an invested local flavor because the preacher as witness participates in the mission of a specific community of faith, goes to the scripture on behalf of that community, and hears a particular word for them on this day and in this place.

5. The witness image also underscores the ecclesiastical and liturgical setting of preaching. Though it is not always apparent, the worship of the church is a dramatic enactment of a great and cosmic trial in which the justice of God is poised against all the powers that spoil creation and enslave human life. In this trial Christ is the one true and faithful witness. "For this I was born, and for this I have

come into the world, to bear witness to the truth" (John 18:37). All human testimony is authentic only to the extent that it remains faithful to the witness of Christ. "You also are witnesses, because you have been with me from the beginning" (John 15:27).

"It is only with the day of the Lord," writes Richard Fenn, "that all accusation ends, and the trial is over." He goes on: "It is for that reason on the Lord's Day that the people of God celebrate a mock trial, in which the law is read, confession and testimony obtained, and the verdict once again given as it was once before all time."[39]

"I give thanks to God always for you," wrote Paul to the Corinthians, speaking of the relationship between witness and the life of the Christian community, "because of the grace of God which was given you in Christ Jesus, that in every way you were enriched in him with all speech and all knowledge—even as the testimony to Christ was confirmed among you" (1 Cor. 1:4–5).

PREACHING AND WORSHIP

Christian preaching bears witness to Christ both in the church and through the church to the world. Preaching occurs in the context of the Christian community gathered for worship, but it also takes place "out there" in the world—on street corners, in prisons and hospitals, on campuses, and in public assemblies. Preaching in the church and preaching in the world are not fundamentally different kinds of preaching but different settings for the same activity of bearing witness to Christ. Preaching, as David Buttrick has observed, continues "the work of Christ who gathered a people to himself and, by death and resurrection, set them free for new life in the world."[40]

Preaching and the community of faith, then, are reciprocal realities. Those who hear and believe the witness to Christ in preaching are thus gathered into the community of faith that continues to tell, to teach, and to celebrate that witness. "The proclamation of the gospel," Moltmann maintains, "always belongs within a community, for every language lives in a community or creates one."[41] And it is this very community that continues to bear witness to Christ in and for the world through every aspect of its life, including preaching.

For most of us, the majority of our preaching will occur in the context of the community of faith at worship. This means, in part, that preaching becomes woven into the dramatic structure of the larger service of worship, which itself is a witness to the gospel. This has many practical implications, of course, regarding the relationship between the sermon and the other parts of worship. More basically, however, it indicates that preaching is not merely a deed performed by an individual preacher but rather the faithful action of the whole church.

2

The Biblical Witness in Preaching

Whoever listens to the text and converses with it opens . . . the possibility that a word will be heard. This "hearing" goes beyond understanding. A word that is heard is compelling; it grasps us and our imagination; it causes us to reassess other words, values, and the web of assumptions and trusts that make up our lives. . . . All sorts of surprises can occur when the preacher takes the Bible seriously.
—**Leander E. Keck,**
The Bible in the Pulpit

Bearing witness to the gospel means engaging in serious and responsible biblical preaching. Preaching is biblical whenever the preacher allows a text from the Bible to serve as the leading force in shaping the content and purpose of the sermon. More dynamically, biblical preaching involves telling the truth about—bearing witness to—what happens when a biblical text intersects some aspect of our life and exerts a claim upon us. Biblical preaching does not mean merely talking about the Bible, using the Bible to bolster doctrinal arguments, or applying biblical "principles" to everyday life. Biblical preaching happens when a preacher prayerfully goes to listen to the Bible on behalf of the people and then speaks on Christ's behalf what he or she hears there. Biblical preaching has almost nothing to do with how many times the Bible is quoted in a sermon and everything to do with how faithfully the Bible is interpreted in relation to contemporary experience. "A sermon that begins in the Bible and ends in the Bible," Edmund Steimle once observed, "is not necessarily a biblical sermon."

BIBLICAL PREACHING AS NORMATIVE

Biblical preaching is the normative form of Christian preaching. That statement can be taken in two different ways. When we call a

48

certain practice "normative" we may mean either that it is what is usually done (the normal, customary practice) or that it is the standard (the norm, the rule) by which all other practices are measured. When we say that biblical preaching is normative, we mean both.

Historically, biblical preaching has been normative in the sense that it is the most common practice, the customary pattern. Here and there challenges have been made to the notion that preaching should be biblically based, but throughout the centuries the relationship between scripture and sermon has remained firm. When the Lutheran scholar Yngve Brilioth surveyed the history of Christian preaching, he discovered that the linkage between the sermon and a biblical text has been a consistent feature of Christian preaching from its origins. The Christian sermon, Brilioth pointed out, is patterned after synagogue preaching, and as such has "its roots in the exposition of a [biblical] text."[1] When Jesus preached in the synagogue at Nazareth (Luke 4), he spoke from a text, and for the most part Christian preachers ever since have done the same.

Biblical preaching is also normative in the more vigorous sense that it serves as the standard over against which all other types of preaching are measured. Does this mean, as George Buttrick once claimed, that "there is no true preaching except biblical preaching"?[2] Not exactly. Over the years many strong and effective sermons have been preached that were surely gospel sermons even though they were not linked explicitly to any particular passage in the Bible. Sermons of this kind, often called "topical" sermons, usually appeal to general theological themes, doctrines, creedal statements, and the like, rather than to specific biblical texts. Even so, these sermons are really only one step removed from direct encounter with the Bible, since the doctrinal sources to which they appeal are themselves the result, to some degree, of biblical interpretation. To the extent that these sermons can be called "gospel" sermons, then, they presuppose an encounter with scripture having taken place somewhere, sometimes, since the Bible provides the framework in which the church conceptualizes its understanding of the gospel and formulates its theology. All gospel preaching, then, is in some sense biblical preaching, since biblical interpretation stands in the background even when it is absent from the foreground.

When we call biblical preaching "normative," though, we are stating something stronger than the mere claim that the Bible stands in the background of all Christian preaching. We are saying that biblical preaching, in the strict sense, should be the rule and not the exception.

Why should this be so? Biblical preaching—the kind of preaching that produces sermons formed through engaging particular texts in the Bible—is, and should be, normative because it alone embodies the primary way in which the church discerns the will of God for its life. Biblical preaching not only announces the gospel, it also reenacts the essential way in which the church has come to know that gospel.

When the church seeks to discover God's presence and will, it looks in many places—its own life and worship, the world, theological traditions, and so on—but it primarily and essentially looks to scripture. The doctrine of the inspiration of scripture has a history of divisive controversy and marked disagreements, but even though theological parties may disagree about what the Bible is and what it means to call it "inspired," there is a surprising consensus about what the Bible *does*. Throughout its history, the church has discovered that when it goes to the scripture in openness and trust, it finds itself uniquely addressed there by God and its identity as the people of God shaped by that encounter. A biblical sermon, in its very form, models this primal and radical action of discernment, and therefore, when it is responsibly done, it is the basic and paradigmatic form of Christian preaching.

To put this another way, the church listens to scripture because it recognizes that it is addressed there by Christ. This does not imply that the Bible itself is perfect, inerrant, completely consistent, or historically precise or that the words of the Bible were somehow dictated by God. What it does mean is that the church has discovered that when it goes to the scripture in faith, it finds itself encountered by Christ in ways that serve as the keys for understanding its encounters with Christ everywhere else. "Christian faith," writes James Barr, "is not faith in the Bible, not primarily: it is faith in Christ as the one through whom one comes to God, and faith that through the Bible we meet him, he communicates with us."[3] When the church goes to the Scripture, it finds that there, unlike anywhere else, its life is nurtured and empowered by Christ and its identity is re-formed.[4]

So, week after week, in sermon after sermon, this action of going in faith to the meeting ground of scripture is reenacted, the inner dynamics of the sermon corresponding to the pattern of the church's basic manner of coming to know the gospel. Thus biblical preaching in the strict sense, while not the only form of Christian preaching, is the form regularly and urgently needed by the community of faith.

SCRIPTURE, THEOLOGY, AND CONTEMPORARY EXPERIENCE

The preacher goes on behalf of the church to the Bible, but the preacher does not go with a blank tablet. The preacher comes from the community of faith, a community with its own theological traditions, social location, and prior understandings of the nature of both the Bible and the Christian gospel. Thus the preacher goes to scripture with a set of categories and expectations already in place. The actual encounter with scripture may upset these expectations, confirm them, or both, but the preacher brings them nonetheless, and they are vital aspects of the process of interpretation. It would be impossible to describe everything that a preacher brings to the interpretation of a text, but at least three of these important frames of understanding deserve our special attention.

1. A Critically Informed View of Scripture

We know that the Bible contains a set of writings produced by human beings caught up in the circumstances of particular times and places, people who wrote both with a faithful vision and a culturally conditioned mind-set. This means that the church must not only listen obediently to the words of the Bible, it must also interpret those words as the human products of their own age. As Barr states, "Our recognition that the Bible provides an essential and God-given meeting-ground for our encounter with God in faith does not alter the fact that we have a right, and indeed a duty, to use the Bible *critically.*"[5]

J. Christiaan Beker has described the aim of biblical interpretation as obtaining a "catalytic reading" of scripture, a reading that distinguishes between, on the one hand, the enduring claim of a text and, on the other hand, both the features of a text that are bound to the culture of the text's origin and those aspects of our own culture that we may wish to force upon a text. He writes:

A catalytic reading of Scripture intends to listen to the claim of the text on us, but it resists a literalistic and anachronistic transfer (as if, for instance, its culturally conditioned admonitions about submission of slaves and women to the rule of men and its prevalent androcentrism must directly apply to our time and culture). A catalytic reading of Scripture also resists modernist prejudices, as if twentieth-century perspectives can be imposed on a first-century text. A catalytic claim of the biblical text, therefore, means that the text undergoes a necessary change in its transferral to our time and yet is not altered in its "substance." In other words, a catalytic view of a text's authority distinguishes between a variety of its components, especially between its abiding character (its coherence) and its time-conditioned interpretations (its contingency).[6]

It would be convenient, of course, if there were some method, some careful step-by-step process, by which we could separate the abiding gospel in a biblical text from the time-conditioned material, but no such procedure exists. Because the Bible is in human language, and the texts of the Bible were written both for and in social situations, everything about the Bible is culturally conditioned. Because the ultimate referent of biblical texts is God, everything about the Bible is infused with gospel.

Any preacher, for instance, who happened to preach a sermon on Ephesians 6:5ff and simply repeated the text's message, "Slaves, be obedient to those who are your earthly masters," would be worthy of ridicule. This preacher would, at best, have presented the gospel as a foolish, obsolete word and, at worst, as a hateful, oppressive word. It is tempting, then, to write off a text like that one as "culturally conditioned" and to pass on to other texts that seem free of social bias, like Ephesians 2:8: "For by grace you have been saved through faith; and this is not your own doing, it is the gift of God." It is not that simple, however. A careful and attentive reading of the passage from Ephesians 6 will yield much cultural material that must finally be emphatically rejected by Christians today, but it will also disclose another spirit at work in the text. Breathing through that passage is an underlying claim about the freedom from worldly structures found in one's relationship to God in Christ, who shows no partiality. In Ephesians this claim modifies the institution of slavery, and eventually the truth of this claim destroys that institution.

Moreover, Ephesians 2:8, which seems so universal and timeless, actually contains concepts, such as "grace," "saved" and "faith," that are not ideas dropped from heaven. They are rather concepts with a long and varied cultural and theological heritage.

The point is that texts which scream cultural bias are also gospel texts, and texts which shout the gospel are also culturally conditioned. There is no surgical procedure for separating the tissues, no guaranteed way to separate the wheat from the chaff. Hearing the claim of God in and through a biblical text always demands an act of faithful imagination, a refusing to let a text go until it has blessed us, a listening and a probing until the text becomes, in Walter Brueggemann's words, "a live memory always pressing into the present as a demand and a resource."[7]

2. A Theological Heritage

Preachers go to the scripture not only with a critically informed understanding of the Bible but also with prior understandings of the Christian faith embodied in rich theological traditions. A theological tradition is a complex, often ambiguous, but somewhat systematic way of seeing the Christian faith as a whole, built up slowly over time and deeply influenced by the social circumstances of the people who participated in its formation.

Brazilian Pentecostals, for example, have different ways of describing the Christian faith than do Scottish Presbyterians, African Methodist Episcopalians in Georgia, Spanish Roman Catholics, or Wisconsin Lutherans. These differing theological traditions affect not only large matters, such as creeds and liturgies, but also show up in less significant places, like the organizational structure of hymnbooks. In one denominational hymnbook, for instance, the hymns are arranged according to a classical systematic doctrinal scheme: Hymns about God are followed by hymns about Christ, then hymns about the Holy Spirit, hymns about the church, and so on. The hymnbook of another denomination, however, arranges the hymns according to the worship life of the church, especially the seasons and festivals of the church year—Advent, Christmas, Epiphany, Lent, and so on. Yet another denomination's hymnal is ordered around stages in the experience of the Christian believer. A hymnbook is a product of a theological worldview, and though these hymnbooks contain many of the very same hymns, the hymns are grouped differently because the traditions that the hymnbooks serve organize the faith in different ways.

Even within denominational groups, there is considerable theological diversity. All Christians recite, confess, sing, and preach the same gospel story, but with their own characteristic styles and places of emphasis. They all share a basic commitment to the Christian faith, but they have different patterns for "seeing it whole," of understanding what aspects of the faith form the centers around which all else is organized.

Preachers go to the Bible, then, not as "universal Christians" (there is no such thing) but with a particular theological heritage and viewpoint. We may wish that we were free of these theological presuppositions so that we could go to a biblical text with a completely fresh and open mind, devoid of expectations or prior understandings, ready for the text to inscribe its pure message on our unblemished minds. Not only is this not realistic, it is actually not desirable. When the preacher goes to the scripture, new ground is not being broken. The church has been to this text before—many times—and a theological tradition is, in part, the church's memory of past encounters with this and other biblical texts. A theologically informed interpreter of scripture enters the text guided by a map drawn and refined by those who have come to this place before. Coming to a text from a theological tradition, the interpreter arrives not as a disoriented stranger but as a pilgrim returning to a familiar land, recognizing old landmarks and thereby alert for new and previously unseen wonders.

A theologically informed interpreter is also steered away from the distortions of the gospel that can result when a single text is heard in isolation from all others. Since a theological tradition is a way of seeing the Christian faith whole, it provides a means for placing the word of one text into the larger pattern of the witness of the whole

Bible. Some New Testament passages, for example, refer to the Jews in ways that could lead to a harsh anti-Semitism, were these texts not seen in the brighter light of the whole of the Christian faith, with its affirmation of the God who keeps promises and who, as Paul wrote, has by no means rejected Israel.

Our theological traditions guide us, then, in the conversation with scripture, but theological traditions can be dangerous as well. They are vantage points, and we need a vantage point to be able to see something, but we cannot see everything from a single perspective. Theological traditions serve as means for the church to remember, organize, and comprehend what has been discerned of the gospel over time. They are, as we have said, ways of seeing the gospel whole, but they do not see the whole gospel. This is why ecumenical conversation among the various traditions in the larger church is so crucial. Church unity is at stake in these discussions, but so is the fullness of the gospel. As preachers, we are called to humility about what we can see and know of the gospel. We can see, and we do know, but we must be content to see and know only in part, for, as Paul said, "our knowledge is imperfect and our prophecy is imperfect" (1 Cor. 13:9).

Theological traditions can also become hard of hearing. They tend to become fixed systems no longer open to listening to any new claims of scripture. Whenever a church or a preacher hears in scripture only that which has been heard before, finds there only a confirmation of what is already known and believed, be assured that the theological tradition has ossified and is being employed not as a means for hearing the living word of scripture but as a replacement for it.

It is important for preachers to go to scripture illumined by a theological tradition larger than their own personal creeds, more comprehensive than their private theological opinions. All of us are changing and growing in regard to our own theological views. We do not believe the same things in the same ways when we are fifty years old that we did when we were sixteen or thirty-six. The preacher's own faith and beliefs are important for preaching, of course, but the church's theological heritage is always larger, more enduring, and less privatistic than anyone's set of personal convictions. As we prepare to preach, we go to scripture not just as individual believers but as practicing theologians on the frontlines of the church, seeking to hear the gospel today in continuity with the theological memory of the whole church.

How can preachers become acquainted with their theological traditions? This is really a complex and lifelong task, since theological traditions are not lists of beliefs but comprehensive ways of living, worshiping, serving, and believing. A good way to begin, though, is to make a list of every important feature you can think of that characterizes your theological tradition. What would you include? My own theological heritage is the Reformed tradition, and I would write down such convictions as "an emphasis upon the sovereignty of God," "a radical understanding of salvation by grace," "an understanding of the church as covenant community," "a clear distinction between the Creator and the creation," "a respect for order in church life and worship," among other things. What would you list? Would you name "a focus upon the sacramental life" or "an emphasis upon the new birth of the Christian believer" or "a seeking after the gifts of the Spirit" or "a firm peace ethic"?

Whatever we may claim as central to our theological worldviews, once we have named them, the next step is for us to consider every emphasis we have named to be a slogan, a formula, even a cliché, and to push deeper. Only when we have dug underneath the mottoes of our tradition and grasped the historical and theological forces that gave them birth can we claim to know our own heritage. Only when we perceive what was—and is—at stake in these affirmations, only when we know what is gained and what is lost by making them, do we begin to have a working understanding of our theological tradition.

3. An Awareness of the Circumstances of the Hearers

The biblical word does not come as a disembodied word, speaking timeless verities to all people everywhere. The Bible speaks to particular people in the concrete circumstances of their lives. It speaks "a word on target," illumining our situation from within. The word of God we encounter in the scripture does not attack idolatry in general; it dethrones *our* idols, severs the bonds of *our* old and crippling loyalties. It is not the word of God in the abstract but of God who is for us, of God who is against us in order to be truly for us. The living word that comes to us in the Bible does not hum generically about concepts like "salvation" and "hope"; rather, it divides the seas that churn around us, saves our lives, and beckons us to follow toward a new and hopeful land.

When preachers go to the scripture, then, they must take the people with them, since what will be heard there is a word for them. How does the preacher do this? In part, we do this by heightening the awareness of our own struggle to be faithful. The more honest we are with ourselves about our own lives—the places of strength and trust, the crevices of doubt, the moments of kindness, the hidden cruelties—the more we find ourselves on common ground with the others who will hear the sermon. Eventually we will be the preacher of the sermon, but we must not forget that we will also be one of its hearers as well. When we go to the scripture seeking not what "the people ought to hear" but hungering ourselves for a gospel word, we will hear a word for them too.

It is not enough, though, to go to the Bible only with our own lives in view. We must self-consciously embody the needs and situations of others, especially those who are different from ourselves. Some preachers find it helpful, as a part of the process of interpreting the scripture, to visualize the congregation that will be present when the sermon is preached. They survey the congregation in their mind's eye, seeing there the familiar faces and the lives behind them. They see the adults and the children, the families and those who are single, those who participate actively in the church's mission and those who stand cautiously on the edges of the church's life. They see those for whom life is full and good and those for whom life is composed of jagged pieces. They see the regulars sitting in their customary places, and they see the stranger, the newcomer, the visitor, hesitating and wondering if there is a place for them. They see the people who are there, and they see the people who cannot be there, or who choose not to be there. When preachers turn to the scripture, all these people go with them.

Other preachers invite members of the congregation actually to participate with them in exploring the biblical text, gathering a small group early in the sermon development process to listen to the text, to study it together, to raise questions about it, and to name the concerns it evokes. This may be a general group, or it may be a group of people who have a special relationship to the issues in the text. Suppose, for example, a preacher—in this case a man—is preparing a sermon on the passage in John 16 that includes these words of Jesus:

> You will be sorrowful, but your sorrow will turn into joy. When a woman is in travail she has sorrow, because her hour has come; but when she is delivered of the child, she no longer remembers the anguish, for joy that a child is born into the world. So you have sorrow now, but I will see you again and your hearts will rejoice, and no one will take your joy from you.
>
> John 16:20–22

Now the preacher, as a man, can certainly understand the birthing image in this passage, but there are obvious limits to his ability to know its full depths. Time spent exploring this text with women who have experienced childbirth, who know from their own experience its fearful anguish and its even more intense joy, would almost surely open up the richness of the image and disclose connections with human experience that otherwise would simply not be available to him

Many other methods are available to bring the questions, needs, and insights of the congregation into the preacher's awareness as the text is encountered, but what we are talking about is larger than strategy and technique. Going to the Bible on behalf of the people is a priestly act. As an exercise of the priestly office, the preacher represents the people before the text as a way of representing them before God. Leander Keck has aptly compared this priestly view of biblical interpretation to the pastoral prayer in worship. "To pray on their behalf," he says, "one must enter into their lives to the point that one begins to feel what they feel, yet without losing one's identity as a pastor."[8]

What is brought to expression in the pastoral prayer? The urgent pleas of the congregation? Yes, but not only the cries of the faithful. The pastor prays on behalf of the world too, seeking to speak the words the world would speak to God if it could find them and if it could feel the unfailing embrace of God's love.

Just so, the preacher goes to the biblical text as a priest, carrying the questions, needs, and concerns of congregation and world, not as an agenda to be met but as an offering to be made. And then the preacher listens to the text. The word heard there may be one of comfort, but it may also be one that judges. It may answer our questions, but it may call our questions into question. It may be a word that brings us joyfully home, or it may call us deeper into the wilderness. Whatever that word may be, the preacher must tell the truth about it. The priest must now become the witness.

IN THE BEGINNING

At first glance it would appear that the study of the biblical text ought always to be the starting place for a biblical sermon, and most of the time this is so. Preachers usually begin developing sermons by first going to biblical texts. When we do this, we do not yet know what the sermon will be "about." We only know that the sermon will be based on a passage from Genesis or Isaiah or John or Romans, and beyond this we look to the text to form the focus of the sermon. Theological traditions and the life situations of the hearers are, as we have said, already present as we go to the scripture, but it is the text that will initiate the conversation and name its topics.

On other occasions, however, biblical sermons begin with a concern generated outside the Bible. Sometimes the starting point will be a line from a creed, like "I believe in the holy catholic church"; a historic doctrine, such as the Trinity; a question from a catechism; a theological and ethical issue, like abortion or ecology; or a theological theme, such as "grace" or "discipleship." At other times an event in the community (a wedding, a funeral, the dedication of a church building, the closing of a plant, the ending of a war) or a concern among the people (grief, family life, conflict, work) initiates the discussion.

When the sermon originates outside the text, we know from the beginning what the sermon will be *about*, but if it is truly to be a biblical sermon, we must not decide in advance what the sermon will *say*. The text must be allowed to surprise us, even to violate our expectations. Suppose, for example, that a preacher finds that the issue of personal self-esteem has become a concern of some people in the congregation. Pastoral conversations often come around to this topic, paperback books on self-esteem are being read and discussed, television talk shows on the issue are watched with interest, and the time has come to address the matter from the pulpit. The preacher who goes to the Bible digging around for material for a sermon on "Christian self-esteem" will be disappointed. Self-esteem, as defined by the paperbacks and the talk shows, is a psychological phenomenon peculiar to modern culture and unknown to the biblical world. The preacher can, of course, force the Bible to march to the cultural drumbeat, but then the sermon will only be a word from the culture to itself.

Underlying the contemporary quest for self-esteem, however, is a more basic hunger to know what it means to be human, and about this the scripture and theology have much to say. The preacher begins, then, with the cultural issues and questions but goes in a theologically informed manner to the text, prepared for those issues to be redefined and for those questions to be both answered and overturned. The preacher not only has a critical understanding of the Bible but also gains a critical understanding of the culture. The resulting sermon will be about self-esteem, but the engagement with the biblical text will provide a new way of seeing what is truly at stake in that concern.

Regardless of the sermon's starting point, then, preaching is biblical when the text serves as the leading force in shaping the content and purpose of the sermon.

THE EXEGETICAL HABIT

Responsible biblical preaching does not come easily. It requires time, study, and hard work. The time required for the study of scripture is not spent apart from ministry; it is not even done in preparation for ministry. It *is* ministry, and as such it should be cherished and protected. There are ways to use study time wisely and efficiently. There are even shortcuts we can take in the process of biblical interpretation, but there are no short circuits.

Presented in the next chapter is a description of a brief exegetical process for biblical preaching. Every responsible preacher will engage in a process something like this one, but no preacher will do it exactly the same. However we perform the task of biblical study toward preaching, though, it must become a habit, a routine carved so deeply into our schedule and our way of doing ministry that it becomes second nature.

3

Biblical Exegesis for Preaching

When your head droops at night, let a page of Scripture pillow it.
—St. Jerome
Letter 22

Blessed is the one who reads aloud the words of the prophecy, and blessed are those who hear, and who keep what is written therein; for the time is near.

—*Revelation 1:3*

Broadly speaking, exegesis is a systematic plan for coming to understand a biblical text.[1] The brief, step-by-step process outlined in this chapter is, in some ways, a condensed, less technical version of the sort of exegetical scheme typically encountered in a seminary course in biblical studies. In other ways, however, this is distinctly a *preacher's* exegetical procedure. When we interpret a biblical passage for preaching, it changes not just what we do with the results of the exegesis but the *way* we go about the exegesis in the first place. To a great extent, the exegetical methods of strict biblical scholarship operate independently of local circumstances.[2] A Pauline scholar working on a passage in Galatians, for instance, would go about business in the same manner regardless of whether or not the local auto plant was out on strike or the couple next door were getting a divorce. Preachers, though, cannot—should not—filter out such local circumstances from the interpretation of scripture. The whole aim of a preacher's study of a biblical text is to hear in that text a specific word for *us,* and who "we" happen to be at this moment makes a considerable difference in how the preacher approaches the text. If families in the congregation are in crisis, if some who will hear the sermon are unemployed, these circumstances bring new questions and concerns to the encounter with scripture.

The exegetical process outlined here is designed to be thorough

60

enough to provide a solid engagement with the text but brief enough to become a regular part of a minister's weekly schedule. Each step is explored in some detail, and consequently the procedure given in this chapter may appear hopelessly protracted for the busy pastor. Once the process becomes familiar, though, it can be accomplished in a reasonable length of time. For some, this will mean setting aside (and guarding) a single undisturbed block of time for textual study and sermon preparation. Most preachers, however, will divide the process into smaller strands, weaving them into the weekly mix of constant tasks and unexpected demands that compose a minister's life.

Again, this set of exegetical steps must be tailored to the individual preacher and to the particular biblical text being studied. Indeed, the goal should be eventually to move beyond the notion of biblical interpretation as a sequence of steps and toward an instinctive way of dwelling critically, attentively, and faithfully with the text. "A method will be most fruitful," claims Fred Craddock, "when it has become as comfortable as an old sweater."[3]

Outline of a Brief Exegetical Method for Preaching

group on notes by outline

I. Getting the text in view
   A. Select the text
   B. Reconsider where the text begins and ends
   C. Establish a reliable translation of the text

II. Getting introduced to the text
   D. Read the text for basic understanding
   E. Place the text in its larger context

III. Attending to the text
   F. Listen attentively to the text

IV. Testing what is heard in the text
   G. Explore the text historically
   H. Explore the literary character of the text
   I. Explore the text theologically
   J. Check the text in the commentaries

V. Moving toward the sermon
   K. State the claim of the text upon the hearers
      (including the preacher)

A BRIEF EXEGETICAL METHOD FOR PREACHING

I. Getting the Text in View

A. Select the text

There are four basic ways for a preacher to select the biblical text for a sermon.

1. Lectio continua. This ancient method of textual selection involves preaching through the Bible, book by book, text by text. Preachers of an earlier era would read as much scripture as time would allow and then preach on the portion read, often blending the preaching and the reading into a single action. The ending spot would be marked, and the preacher would pick up at that point the next time the community gathered for worship.

Not much pure *lectio continua* preaching exists now. Sixteen weeks marching seriatim through the Levitical laws would be a desert experience for most congregations. The clear advantage of this approach, though, is that the congregation hears each book of the Bible as a unified whole. The hearers would not, for instance, receive just a snippet from Romans every now and then; they would get *Romans.*

In most settings, *lectio continua* preaching could best be an occasional exception to the normal pattern of text selection and would take the form of a series of sermons on a single book of the Bible.

2. A lectionary. A lectionary is a list of biblical passages assigned to the various days in the church calendar. Some lectionaries have readings only for Sundays and the other major festivals and holidays; other lectionaries designate texts for every day in the year. In some traditions the use of a lectionary is already the established practice, but the use of "consensus" and ecumenical lectionaries is growing in many circles where a generation ago lectionaries were scarcely ever employed. .

In general, the use of a lectionary is a superb plan for obtaining sermon texts. The readings are set to the rhythm and seasons of the church year, which provides an opportunity for coordinated planning of the sermon, music, prayers, and other aspects of worship. The wide range of readings included in the major denominational lectionaries ensures that preachers and congregations will encounter the breadth of the biblical witness, and these lectionaries share enough common readings that many fine and relatively inexpensive lectionary-based preaching commentaries have appeared. The recent increased use of lectionaries has encouraged groups of preachers, sometimes from several denominations, to study the Bible together as a part of sermon preparation.

Lectionaries have their limitations, however. A wide range of biblical texts is included in a good lectionary, but many texts are omitted, including some entire books of the Bible. Moreover, since a particular set of readings always appears in relation to a certain time in the church calendar, the interpretational deck gets somewhat stacked. It makes sense, of course, for a text about the crucifixion normally to be preached on Good Friday, as the lectionary provides, and not, say, during the Christmas season. As a matter of fact, though, the crucifixion has much to speak to the Christmas season, and the story of Jesus' birth cannot really be understood apart from the account of his death. The story of the crucifixion belongs on Good Friday, but not only then. In addition, since lectionaries are designed, for the most part, around the texts from the four gospels, there is a subtle built-in pressure to preach on those passages rather than from the Old Testament or the rest of the New Testament.[4] The result can be a practical constriction of the canon of scripture in the preaching of the church.

3. Local plan. Sometimes the preacher and the others who plan for worship create, in effect, a local church lectionary. The seasons of the Christian year, the denominational program of special days and emphases, and the congregational calendar of events are all combined to produce a schedule to which biblical texts are matched. As long as a wide spectrum of biblical texts is included, the advantages of this plan are the same as those of the regular lectionary, minus the ecumenical support and resources.

4. Preacher's choice. This means that the preacher selects the texts based on whatever are the pressing needs of the moment, usually on a week-to-week basis. The only real advantage of this process is flexibility, which can also be a liability. Obviously, if the church burns down or a riot erupts in the town, no preacher will feel bound to a lectionary or any other prior program for selecting a text. Also, when sermons are intended to present doctrines, public issues, pastoral themes, and the like, the preacher will begin with the issue and search for an apt text (note the cautions about this discussed in chapter 2). To go on a search mission every week for a text, though, is not only time-consuming, it also invites a haphazard and episodic relationship to the Bible. Flexibility can create serendipity, but it can also be mere randomness.

This method of selecting a text is the only one of the four that depends entirely on the personal choices of the preacher. It is sometimes claimed, therefore, that a lectionary, or other systematic plan, is a superior method because it keeps a preacher from riding personal hobby horses. Actually, any preacher unwise enough to use the pulpit as a private forum can manage to throw a saddle over any text, no matter how it is selected. The personal-choice method, however, does tend to favor biblical passages that the preacher already knows well, and, when it is used, care must be taken to ensure that the preacher and the congregation encounter the richness present in less familiar texts.

B. Reconsider where the text begins and ends

A biblical text is an artifical creation. The Bible does not come to us in little texts, or pericopes. It comes as a canon, a set of documents that are themselves letters, legal writings, historical narratives, and so on. A text taken from the Bible is like a small piece cut out of a roll of wallpaper with a very large pattern. Once we have removed it, we may no longer be able to see how it fits into the overall design.

We should look, then, with a slightly suspicious eye at the way we—or the lectionaries—have cut our text. Examine what comes before the text, and after it, to see if the surgical incision has taken place at a responsible place. Take as an example a text assigned in one lectionary to a Sunday in the season of Easter: 1 Peter 2:19–25. This passage is about the relationship between human suffering and the suffering of Christ. If we look at verse 18, though, which has been left on the cutting-room floor, we quickly see that this whole text is a part of a larger set of instructions to *slaves,* a fact we would have missed if we had begun reading only at verse 19. Knowing this larger context changes our understanding of the social setting of the text and makes a difference in how we hear its claim upon us now. Another lectionary includes as one of its texts Leviticus 19:1–2, 15–18. This is a passage about the call to God's people to be holy. The curious preacher, though, immediately wonders about those verses chopped out of the middle and discovers upon reading them that they are specific laws relating to the doing of justice in society. Without these verses, the passage could be read in an exclusively private and inward manner, but when they are included they give the notion of "holiness" some social bite.[5]

Sometimes a text will give us clues that it is explicitly connected to the material which surrounds it. Watch especially for connecting phrases, such as "there were some present at that very time who . . ." (*what* time?) or "while he was still speaking . . ." (speaking *what?*).

What we are looking for in a text is not a passage that can stand alone—all texts are linked to their surroundings—but rather a text that can stand as a reasonably coherent unit of thought. At this point in the exegetical process, we should make only a tentative decision about the limits of our text, since what we discover through the rest of the exegesis may cause us to change our minds.

C. Establish a reliable translation of the text

The best way to do this, obviously, is to work with the original language of the text, examining the textual variants, and comparing our own translation with well-established translated versions of the Bible. If we cannot do translation ourselves, we can select a reliable modern translation, like the Revised Standard Version, and compare the wording there to two or three other good translations. Since our goals are accuracy and reliability, we should at this point stay away from paraphrase versions, such as *The Living Bible*. We can find clues by checking the footnotes in the translations, since the translators often indicate there a reading that was a close second choice to the one in the text. Whenever we find a difference in wording that is more than stylistic, we should make a note of it. Perhaps the commentaries, which will be consulted later in the process, can be of help in making a judgment about the best translation.

II. Getting Introduced to the Text

D. Read the text for basic understanding

There is nothing fancy about this step. We are not trying to pry loose hidden meanings or perform theological analysis at this point. We are simply trying to make sure that we understand the straight-forward meaning of the words and syntax of the text. This is the time to look up any unfamiliar terms, like "ephah" or "zealot" or "phy-lactery," in a Bible dictionary. The punctuation of the text can be a good guide to syntactical meaning, but we should be warned that punctuation marks are later additions to the text and are therefore already interpretations of a sort.

E. Place the text in its larger context

In good commentaries or reliable Bible encyclopedias, we can find two or three outlines of the book of the Bible in which our passage appears. By examining how our text fits into the larger structure, we can obtain a sense of where our text comes in the overall flow and development of the book.

Suppose our text is the story of Zacchaeus (Luke 19:1–10). The outline of Luke in one major commentary places this story in a section called "Jesus' Journey to Jerusalem," and the commentator indicates that this section describes Jesus' "exodus" to the Father, a movement that culminates in the ascension. Another commentary titles this section of Luke "The Road to Jerusalem: Discipleship and the Rejected King."[6] The first commentary, then, calls us to be alert to the potential christological emphasis of our text, and the second signals the possible presence of a discipleship theme. The Zacchaeus story functions, in fact, to describe both the mission and destiny of Jesus and the nature of discipleship.

Some biblical passages, especially certain sections of the gospels, appear in more than one place in the Bible. If a version of our text appears elsewhere, a careful comparison of the text with its parallels can reveal differences—sometimes small, sometimes large—that often show how the writer has fit the text into the flow and emphases of the larger context.

III. Attending to the Text

F. Listen attentively to the text

The art of biblical exegesis, put very simply, involves learning how to ask questions of a biblical text.[7] Two major problems can cause this to go awry: We can ask the wrong questions, and we can refuse to listen to the responses that the text gives to good questions. When we ask only those questions to which we believe we already possess the answers, we have asked the wrong questions. When we resist being surprised or troubled by the text, we have shut our ears to its voice.

At this step in the exegesis, the preacher begins the interrogation of the text by asking of the text every potentially fruitful question that comes to mind. Some of the questions we ask of a text will inevitably turn out to be misdirected or loaded questions, and our results will need to be checked. Indeed, most of the remaining steps in this exegetical process are designed to test the validity of the questions we have asked and the responses we believe we have received. If we genuinely attend to the text, however, and ask every question we are provoked to ask, the chances are increased that we will hear the text's voice and receive its claim upon us.

Where do our questions come from? Some of them will be generated by the theological tradition of the preacher, some by the emphases of the church year,[8] others by the contemporary situation, and still others by puzzling or intriguing aspects of the text itself. Most of the time, though, the questions will emerge from the interaction among these conversational partners: that is, from the totality of our situation as we stand before the text. If the text, for example, is the prophet Amos's word from the Lord (Amos 5:21, 24):

> I hate, I despise your feasts,
> and I take no delight in your solemn assemblies. . . .
> But let justice roll down like waters,
> and righteousness like an ever-flowing stream.

The preacher may ask such questions as:

Is the text claiming that God rejects all religious assemblies, feasts, and ceremonies, or is there a more complex dynamic at work? If so, what is it?

Theologically, are justice and righteousness two separate qualities, or are they two faces of the same issue?

Is there anything about *our* worship that God "hates"? What would it be? Why?

Are there places in our religious life where church and civil government become cozy coconspirators against the needy as they did in Amos's day?

Is the empty ceremony of the church the only target of this text, or are there other "sanctuaries" in the culture where ceremonies take place that undermine justice and righteousness? If so, where are they?

Can worship be infused with justice? Can justice be infused with worship? What would these look like?

This text sounds like bad news. When is bad news the "good news"? Can it be bad news and good news at the same time? For the same people?

What about those people in the congregation who are hanging on to their church life by a thread, people who approach worship and the Christian faith warily, wondering if there is anything here for them? Is there a word in Amos's prophecy for them? A word against them? No word at all?

It is tempting to leap over this free-flowing time of questioning and go directly to the commentaries, the books written by the expert interrogators of texts. It will be important later to consult the biblical experts, but it is a mistake to do so too early. Commentaries can provide many valuable services, and they can check and guide our exegesis, but the one thing they cannot do is tell us what the text is saying this day to the particular situation of the hearers. The preacher, not the commentator, is the one sent by these people at this moment to the text, and only the preacher truly knows the full range of questions to ask. The commentator's interrogation of the text can assist the preacher's exploration, but it cannot replace it. Commentaries were made to serve the preacher, and not the preacher to serve the commentaries.

Questioning a text is a creative, imaginative activity—something like brainstorming. The main difference is that we are not trying to expand the range of our own creativity; we are trying to knock the barnacles off our assumptions about the text so that it can speak to us anew. No one can prescribe or predict how such a free-form activity takes place, but here are some suggestions for getting a fresh look at the text.

1. A number of homileticians encourage the writing of a paraphrase of the text. If we attempt to rephrase every line of the text in contemporary language, questions of meaning are quickly brought to the surface. Another good approach to the paraphrase is to set the text completely aside at some point and then write the passage as you remember it, in your own words. Now, compare what you have written with the text itself. What, if anything, did you leave out? Were the omissions minor, or were they left out because they are troublesome in some way? What, if anything, did you emphasize in your paraphrase? Was it underscored because it connects to some concern you brought to the text?

2. If the text is a narrative, stand in the shoes of each of the characters and experience the story from these varied perspectives. For instance, if the text is the story of the healing in the synagogue in Mark 3:1–6, move through the narrative taking the role of Jesus. Then go back through the story from the point of view of the man with the withered hand, as a member of the Sabbath congregation gathered for worship, and finally as one of the Pharisees present. As much as is possible, suspend judgment about who is the hero and who is the villain. Identify with each character and take a sympathetic view of that character's understanding of the world. Try to experience, for instance, what is truly at stake for a loyal Pharisee as the action unfolds in the synagogue that Sabbath.

3. Explore the text looking for details that appear, at first glance, to be unusual or out of place. Why, for example, does Mark tell us that the grass was *green* out in the desert where the five thousand were fed by Jesus (Mark 6:39)? It seems to be a random bit of graphic detail in an otherwise straightforward description. Perhaps so, but it may also be that Mark is linking this story to Isaiah's vision of the desert in blossom. Or again, Mark has told us that the crowd that day was "like sheep without a shepherd" (Mark 6:34). The prophet Ezekiel employed the same image and went on to announce the promise of God: "I myself will search for my sheep, . . . and I will feed them on the mountains of Israel. . . . I will feed them with good pasture . . . ; there they shall lie down in good grazing land" (Ezek. 34:11,13,14). Mark also told us that Jesus "commanded them all to sit down," on the green grass (Mark 6:39), and that command echoes the language of Psalm 23: "He makes me lie down in green pastures"

(Ps. 23:2). Is Mark's "green grass" an Old Testament allusion? If so, what does this say about the feeding of the five thousand?

4. Ask if the text has a center of gravity: that is, a main thought around which all other thoughts are organized. To illustrate, I can remember hearing many sermons in my youth on the phrase, "all have sinned and fall short of the glory of God" (Rom. 3:23). The thrust of these sermons was, of course, the universal sinfulness of human beings. "*All* have sinned," the preacher would boom, his accusing finger roaming across the guilty congregation. Now the verse does say that, to be sure, and it *is* a truth that deserves to be proclaimed, but if we look at the larger passage we will quickly see that sin is not the main event. This single phrase about human sin is spoken in the service of a more central theme: the righteousness of God. Romans 3:21–26 is built like a folk dance, the phrases spinning out toward concepts like law and prophecy, sin and redemption, but always returning to circle the main theme of God's righteousness. The center of gravity of this passage is not you and me and our sin, but rather God who is mercifully righteous. When we preach this text, then, our fingers may point for a moment at ourselves and our sinfulness, but ultimately the hand of the witness stretches out toward the gracious and righteous God.

5. Look for conflict, either in the text or behind it. Human communication is a force that implies the presence of opposing forces. A command ("Clean up your room!") implies the presence of inaction or counteraction. A question ("Do you love me?") arises from the struggle between knowledge and uncertainty. A declaration ("Marilyn is a fine lawyer") attempts to sweep aside other, less flattering possibilities.

Sometimes conflict clearly occurs *in* a biblical text. "Get behind me, Satan! For you are not on the side of God," said Jesus to Peter (Mark 8:33), making the conflict plain. "O foolish Galatians! Who has bewitched you?" said Paul (Gal. 3:1), fanning the flames of the debate. In other texts, the conflict lies *behind* the text, and the passage stands as a response to the conflict hidden in the situational context.[9] Even the cymbal-crashing exuberance of Psalm 150 stakes its claim over against the implied presence of a less celebrative view of worship.

Conflict can be present both in the text and behind it. When Jesus said, "Render therefore to Caesar the things that are Caesar's, and to God the things that are God's" (Matt. 22:21), it was in the midst of conflict with the Pharisees, but it may well have been remembered and cherished by the early church also because it illumined a debate among them about conflicting loyalties.

6. Look for connections between the text and what comes before

and after it. Mark 8:22–26, for example, relates the story of a blind man who is healed by Jesus. The story is unusual in that Jesus' first touching of the man's eyes brings only partial vision. It is only with a second touch that the man sees clearly. If we examine the material surrounding this story, we discover accounts of Jesus' interaction with the disciples which make it apparent that they, too, are only gradually coming to "sight." The story of the growing awareness of the disciples and that of the growing vision of the blind man serve as mutually interpreting narratives.

7. View the text through many different "eyes." How would this passage appear to a man? A woman? A child? To a rich person? A poor person? A homeless person? To a farmer? A city dweller? A prisoner? To a feminist? To an employer? A worker? An unemployed person? To a homosexual? To a parent? To a person outside the church? To a Jew or a Buddhist? To a person of a race different from our own?

Sometimes, as we noted earlier, exegesis takes place in a group setting, and the preacher can actually hear the reactions of a variety of people. Much of the time, though, preachers will need to imagine the presence of a diverse group. Preachers cannot, and should not, presume to know how all these people would respond and must therefore always be reading, studying, and listening to voices of people unlike themselves.

Here is the place for the preacher to survey the congregation in the imagination's eye. Picture the people who are likely to hear the sermon; call to mind what you know of their lives. Go to the text on behalf of the young family in the third pew, the teenager in the back row, the young woman just beginning a career, the man whose father has recently died, the eight-year-old girl sitting there with her mother and new step-father. Ask the text questions they would ask. Ask, on their behalf, the questions they may not dare to ask. Be their pastor—their advocate—and then listen to the text, hoping for a word for them.

8. Think of the text, as J. Randall Nichols suggests, "as someone's attempt to reflect on the answer to some important question,"[10] and then try to discern what that question could be. Nichols cites as an example the text in the book of Esther where Mordecai challenges Esther to use her position as queen to speak a courageous (and illegal) word to the king on behalf of the Jews: "Who knows whether you have not come to the kingdom for such a time as this?" (Esth. 5:14):

> On the surface, it looks like an anguished, but provincial, issue largely unrelated to anything we might face these days. To try to find a point of contact on the surface of the text would be ludicrous—rather like

saying that the text teaches us we ought to get out and vote for the reform candidate even at the risk of pneumonia on a bitter November day.[11]

When the text is explored beneath the surface, though, as a response to questions such as, When is it more critical to be faithful than to save one's own skin? or, Are we more defined by the circumstances we find ourselves in or by those things we are willing to die for? then, claims Nichols, "there is a point of contact, several in fact, with the modern hearer."[12]

9. Ask, as Fred Craddock suggests, what the text is *doing*.[13] Is it commanding, singing, narrating, explaining, warning, debating, praying, reciting? The words "Praise the Lord!" mean one thing if they are the opening lyrics of an exuberant anthem, quite another if they come as a rebuke to inattentive worshipers. In each case we have the same words, but because they are sent out to perform different tasks, they mean quite different things.

One way to get at this matter of what a text is doing is to imagine that the text is to be set to music and then to decide what sort of music would fit. Mark's announcement that "Jesus came into Galilee, preaching the gospel of God" (Mark 1:14) may call for a bright trumpet flourish, while Lamentations' cry "How lonely sits the city that was full of people!" (Lam. 1:1) calls for a melancholy violin, and the thunderous hymns of the multitudes in Revelation will demand a full orchestra complete with throbbing tympani and crashing cymbals.

At this point in the exegetical process curiosity and freewheeling inquisitiveness are virtues. The preacher bombards the text with questions, even with bold challenges, and listens eagerly for responses, faith to faith. The preacher should fill a blank sheet with the resulting insights and ideas, no matter how farfetched some of them may seem at the moment. Like the maidens in the famous parable, some of these insights will turn out to be foolish and some will be wise, but for the moment every possibility from the text should be preserved.

When this is done, the preacher begins the task of testing these insights by placing them into the crucible of scholarly and critical exegesis. Actually, the step of listening attentively to the text and the subsequent steps of critical testing form a repeating loop in exegesis. We listen, then we test, but the testing sharpens our ears to listen again. Both the open listening and the rigorous testing are important, since, ironically, critical exegesis is better at warning the preacher about what the text does *not* say than it is at telling the preacher what the text *does* say. So we listen to the Bible faithfully, but if we do so uncritically, we will often mistake the whispers of our own inner voices for the biblical word. If we only perform the critical analysis and not the attentive listening, we will gather data *about* the Bible rather than hearing the living word that comes *through* the Bible.

IV. Testing What Is Heard in the Text

G. Explore the text historically

Biblical texts often speak of events in history, such as the reign of a king or the destruction of Jerusalem. Biblical texts also *have* a history, in the sense that they were written in particular moments in history and sometimes modified as they were passed along from generation to generation. It is possible, then, maintain John Hayes and Carl Holladay, to speak of both "the 'history *in* the text' and the 'history *of* the text.' "[14]

The book of Daniel, for example, describes events set as early as the sixth century B.C.E., but the best evidence indicates that the book itself was composed in the mid-second century B.C.E. The interpreter, therefore, needs to know about both the period depicted in the book and the period in which the book was written.[15]

Fred Craddock has noted that the interpreter of 1 Corinthians 10:1–5 needs to be aware of not one or even two levels of history, but several. In this passage Paul refers to a Jewish interpretation of the exodus, and at least four historical levels are implicitly present: (1) the exodus event itself, (2) the narrative description of this in the book of Exodus, (3) the later Jewish interpretation, and (4) Paul's use of the story in the context of the situation at Corinth.[16]

In *The Living and Active Word,* O. C. Edwards, Jr., compared the historical levels in a biblical text to the architecture of an ancient cathedral:

> Perhaps you have had the experience of visiting an English cathedral that includes in its structure almost the entire history of English architecture. The crypt may be Saxon and the nave Norman, the choir Decorated and the sanctuary Perpendicular, while the rood screen is Jacobite and the baptistry Victorian. The same kind of indications of period in a gospel story are obvious to a trained eye. One can detect which elements go back to the ministry of Jesus, which were added during the time the story was handed down by word of mouth, which came from the hand of Mark, and which from a later gospel writer.[17]

The goal of the preacher is to discover as much as possible about all the historical levels of the text. It would take a lifetime to do this thoroughly, of course, but much can be learned about a text's authorship, date of composition, social setting, and so on in Old and New Testament introductory textbooks, or in the opening sections of a good commentary. More recent reference works are especially helpful because they are likely to include sociological and political perspectives on the text's history often missing from older historical analyses.[18] The historical environments in which biblical texts were created were as highly charged politically as our own, and no biblical text is, as Walter Brueggemann insists, socially "innocent or disinterested."[19]

H. Explore the literary character of the text

Here the preacher examines the text to determine both its literary character and function. A laundry list is different from a short story, a poem, or a political essay. Each of these types of literature has its own stylistic features and pattern of construction. A letter in our mailbox and a letter to the editor in the newspaper are both letters, but they serve quite different functions.

Walter Brueggemann has grouped biblical texts into six broad categories in regard to their literary type and purpose:[20]

1. The primal narrative. These texts are in story or storylike form, and they recite the elemental narrative that undergirds the rest of the Bible. Embracing such passages as the song of deliverance (Exod. 15:1–18), the liturgical confession of Deuteronomy 26:5–9, and the summary of the Christian *kerygma* in 1 Corinthians 15:3–8, the primal narrative confesses without ornamentation or elaboration those mighty acts of God that shape the identity, faith, and life of the believing community. The primal narrative is the vine to which all other biblical texts are attached as branches.

2. The expanded narrative. These texts are also narratives, and they elaborate and expand upon the primal narrative. The stories of the wilderness wanderings and the entering of the promised land, and the stories that relate the details of Jesus' birth, ministry, trial, death, and resurrection appearances, are examples of expanded narrative texts. These stories constitute "an *epic* derived from the *credo*."[21]

3. Derivative narratives. These narratives are found in those texts that describe the history of the community of faith as it struggled to live out its identity formed by the primal and expanded narratives. In the Old Testament, this covers the books from Judges through Nehemiah and, in the New Testament, the book of Acts.[22]

4. Literature of institutionalization. Such books as Leviticus and the Pastoral Epistles include texts that provide instruction and guidance on matters of leadership, community order, ritual, discipline, combating heresy, and the other internal "maintenance" concerns of the enduring community.

5. Literature of mature theological reflection. The Bible contains no systematic theology as such, but some books, like Deuteronomy and Romans, do include serious and deep reflection upon the coherence of theological claims and values implied by the basic story of the faith.

6. Literature of instruction and vocation. These texts attempt to assert the claims of the faith for a particular situation. Sometimes these passages are didactic in form, such as Proverbs, the epistle of James, or the ethical sections of Paul's letters; sometimes they are lyrical, such as the psalms or the poetry of prophetic oracles; and occasionally they are visionary, such as in apocalyptic literature. What holds these texts together is their common function: relating the power of the primal narrative to a specific circumstance in the community.

Obviously, these are not airtight categories, and not every text can be neatly placed in one of these boxes. They do help us, however, to perceive the literary functions of individual texts and the interrelationships among texts. The primal narrative forms the heart of the Bible, with the expanded narratives growing directly from it. The derivative narratives are the next layer, and they make sense only in relationship to the more basic narratives. The other literary categories, generally non-narrative, grow in turn out of the narrative core of the scripture.

We can see something of these interrelationships in Paul's injunctions about worship in 1 Corinthians 14. This text definitely belongs to the literature of instruction and vocation, but, as such, it depends on the unstated background of the primal and expanded narratives. The text asserts, for example, that clear prophecy is to be preferred in worship to speaking in tongues, not merely because it is more "orderly" but because, through prophecy, the stranger in worship can come to know and declare "that God is really among you" (1 Cor. 14:25). In other words, liturgical practice is connected to the confession of God's presence and action among the faithful. The preacher needs to see the particular instructional function of this text, but the preacher also needs to discern the ways in which these instructions spring from the more basic kerygmatic confession of the church.

In addition to fitting into these broad literary categories, texts also embody specific literary genres, such as lament psalm, parable, proverb, epistle, and the like. Each of these genres follows its own conventions of form and construction. Lament psalms, for example, are quite different on the surface, but they are typically built according to a basic literary blueprint and thus have similar structures. The same is true for miracle stories, epistles, pronouncement stories, and so on. Moreover, the biblical writers often employ literary conventions, such as parallelism, chiastic forms, irony, and the like. The preacher should become familiar with the literary features of the text to determine how they affect the reading and interpretation.[23]

I. Explore the text theologically

Critical theological exploration of the text involves pulling out of the textual fabric a single thread already glimpsed, through historical analysis, as a part of the pattern. We are trying to discover what specific assumptions and claims are present in the text regarding God-in-relation-to-humanity. J. Randall Nichols reminds us that we are not trying "to shoehorn a text into a theological mold or to lay an interpretive template over it." Rather, we are attempting "to connect the narrative or poetic or historical content of a text with the ways of thinking the Christian tradition has used to make sense of itself."[24]

The introductory background material recommended in step 6 will help in naming major theological themes and issues present in each book of the Bible. Another key factor is the theological vocabulary employed in the text. Words like "faith," "grace," "Lord," "covenant," "flesh," "glory," and "savior" are powerful and rich theological concepts that vibrate with memory and meaning wherever they are used. When Paul uses the word "law," he means both the same thing and something different than the psalmist does in Psalm 1. The preacher must maintain the tension between understanding a theological word in a text as a musical chord with harmonies throughout the Bible and grasping the explicit meaning of that same word as it is used in *this* text. The preacher can often find help in theological wordbooks and in commentaries that include discussions of a book's significant theological vocabulary.

As we examine our text historically, literarily, and theologically, we should review the insights we have written down in step 5 and put them to the test. On the basis of what we have learned, can we eliminate any of these ideas? Are there any that should be underscored? Should any new ideas be added?

J. Check the text in the commentaries

Now that we have done our own exegetical work, the time has come to explore the text in biblical commentaries. "Why should one turn to a commentary, anyway?" asks Old Testament scholar

Bernhard W. Anderson. "Reaching for a commentary is not the first step in interpreting a text," he acknowledges, and, indeed, "one should turn to a commentary only as a last resort." Nevertheless, commentaries are important resources for the preacher, and "in the final analysis," Anderson claims, "one ought to turn to a commentary." The reason? He puts it this way: "The reason is that we do not, or anyway should not, interpret the text individualistically but within a larger circle of interpretation, a community of discrimination where private views are checked, enriched, corrected, deepened."[25]

What is implied in Anderson's statement is that by pulling commentaries off the shelf the preacher can create a scholarly seminar on the biblical text. Here is yet another way to avoid the perils of doing biblical interpretation in an isolation ward. Through the commentaries a community of scholarship is fashioned; by the exchange of ideas and viewpoints, the preacher's understanding of the text is both challenged and enhanced. Because we have waited until now to consult these commentaries—that is, until we have done our own homework on the text—we are prepared to moderate the discussion and to contribute to the conversation ourselves.

Obviously the greater number of responsible voices we can gather at the table, the richer and more interesting the conversation will be. Recent commentaries will bring us the latest word in critical textual interpretation, but older "pre-critical" commentaries should not be neglected, because they are in touch with textual issues filtered out by the refracting lenses of modern criticism. Some modern commentaries also include discussions of how the text has been interpreted throughout the church's history. Ancient interpreters, precisely because they are not products of our time, can often help us discover treasures in the text otherwise hidden to our modern eyes.

Moreover, as biblical scholar Elisabeth Schüssler Fiorenza warns, preachers ought not to depend entirely upon the "established" biblical scholars at this point.[26] Only by listening to scholarship that springs from less traditional perspectives—liberationist, feminist, ethnic, poetic, psychoanalytic, and so on—can the "vested interests" of all interpretation be exposed (even that which falsely presents itself as "neutral" and "objective"),[27] our own unstated presuppositions be challenged, and the fullness of the text be explored.

Most good commentaries will cover the same historical, literary, and theological ground we have traversed, and they can refine and challenge our findings at each point along the way. The commentators are not the ones, though, who bear the responsibility of preaching, and eventually we must leave the seminar and cross the bridge ourselves from the text to the place where our congregation waits to hear the sermon. The commentators can, at best, go only halfway across with us. Most of them, in fact, bid farewell much sooner, and we must go alone to the final step of the exegesis.

Moving Toward the Sermon

K. *State the claim of the text upon the hearers (including the preacher)*

Good exegesis can point us in the right direction, and it can eliminate wrongheaded interpretations of the text. It can provide essential information about the text, and it can uncover issues in the text we would never have seen at first glance. Exegesis can help us in many ways, but it finally cannot do what is most important: tell us what this text wishes to say on this occasion to our congregation. The preacher must decide this, and it is a risky and exciting decision.

Getting to know a biblical text is much like getting to know another person in a profound way. It takes time and energy to get to know someone else well. We must be with them long enough, and attend to them carefully enough, to know not only who they are at the moment but also who they have been in the past and the vision toward which they are moving. We must ask them questions and tell them of our own life, but we must not do all the talking. We must listen to them unselfishly, cherishing their word even when it does not connect immediately to our own desires and interests. We must observe them in many different situations, learning about their values and commitments as we see them in action. We must discover the patterns, customs, and even the habits around which they organize their lives. If we look at them and see only our own reflection, we do not know them. If we look at them and see only an "other," an object of our scrutiny, we do not know them. Only when we know who they are *with us* can we claim really to know them.

An exegetical process "introduces" us to the text. It provides some crucial "biographical" information, and it even discloses some of the text's "secrets." It is up to the preacher, then, to bring the life of the congregation into the text's presence, to dwell there long and prayerfully, and to discern the reality of this text as it is "with us."

There is an eventful quality about this. Something happens between text and people: a claim is made, a voice is heard, a textual will is exerted, and the sermon will be a bearing witness to this event. As the final step in the exegetical process, the preacher throws the first cord across the gap between text and sermon by describing the text's claim upon the hearers, including the preacher. We are ready to move on to the creation of the sermon itself only when we can finish the following sentence: "In relation to those who will hear the sermon, what this text wants to say and do is—"

4

The Focus and Function
of the Sermon

Someone recently gave my son a compass. I see it almost everywhere around the house amid the rest of the clutter. Nothing in our house seems to stay in the same place, not even that compass. But the compass always seems to know where it is. Every time I see it, it is pointing in the same direction. This is the impressive thing about Christian witness.

— Carl Michalson,
"Communicating the Gospel" in *Theology Today*

The verb "to witness" has two main meanings: to behold and to attest. If I say, "I witnessed the third game of the World Series" or "I witnessed the efforts of the fire company as they battled to save the school," I mean that I was there at the event and saw and experienced for myself what happened. "To witness" means, in the first place, to behold, to be present and active as an observer, to "take something in."

The other meaning of "to witness," however, faces in the opposite direction. Rather than "taking something in," it means "giving something out." Rather than seeing something, it means saying something. Rather than becoming aware of some event, it means making others aware of that event. "Witness" in the first sense means to *perceive;* in the second sense it means to *testify.*

An unbreakable bond exists, of course, between these two meanings. One cannot witness in the second sense unless one has witnessed in the first sense. We can give testimony only to that which we have experienced. We can bear witness only when we have been an eyewitness. "I want to witness to the valiant and tireless efforts of the fire company at the school fire" is valid and reliable testimony only when said by one who experienced the firefighting firsthand.

At the point in the sermon development process when the preacher makes the turn from the exegesis of the biblical text toward the sermon itself, the preacher moves from being the first kind of witness to being the second kind. The one who has been sent to the scripture on behalf of the people and encountered firsthand the claims of the text now turns to tell the truth about what has been experienced. The move from text to sermon is a move from beholding to attesting, from seeing to saying, from listening to telling, from perceiving to testifying, from *being* a witness to *bearing* witness.

MOVING ACROSS THE BRIDGE

Virtually every homiletician recognizes that this move from text to sermon is a decisive moment. Although everything a preacher does can be viewed as sermon work in the broad sense, it is only at this point that the preacher begins to concentrate upon the sermon per se. The preacher now shifts from what the biblical text says to what the sermon will say, and since texts are larger than any single sermon, choices must be made. How do we move from text to sermon? Given the fact that biblical texts potentially yield many meanings and many possible sermons, how do we decide what to bring to the sermon from the text and what to leave behind? In other words, what sort of bridge should be constructed between text and sermon, and what kind of traffic shall it bear?

Some homileticians speak of this move from text to sermon as a trip across a bridge marked "from text to congregation," as if the scripture lay on one side of the span and the people on the other. Some of these books even advise that "exegeting the text" should now be followed by "exegeting the congregation." Such notions are ultimately misleading, since they imply that the congregation enters the picture only after the biblical exegesis has been done. As we have insisted, the hearers have already been present throughout the exegesis; the preacher goes to the biblical text *from* the congregation and, indeed, *with* the congregation. The congregation's struggle to be human and faithful to Christ in the contemporary world has been the context in which the interpretation of the text has taken place. Though the preacher bears responsibility for giving it voice, exegesis involves a conversation between the biblical text and the whole community of faith. Exegesis is a work of the church enacted through the preacher as its chosen representative.

So the move from text to sermon begins, not with a decision about how to inform the congregation about the results of the preacher's personal exegesis of the text but, rather, a decision about what aspect of the congregation-text encounter will be carried over into the sermon itself. The bridge the preacher must now cross is the one between the text-in-congregational-context and the sermon-in-congregational-context.

THE BRIDGE BUILDERS' DEBATE

The homiletical manuals of a generation ago tended to assume that what a preacher carried over the bridge between text and sermon was an idea. The Bible was understood to be a repository of theological ideas, or truths, and the purpose of exegesis was to reach into the textual vessel and extract its main thought. Once the preacher had grasped the text's central theme, the text itself could be left behind as the preacher carried this theme into the sermon. The main idea of the text became the main idea (sometimes called the "thesis") of the sermon, and this central thought could be subdivided into various parts, which would serve as the sermon's "points."

All in all, this notion of text-to-sermon movement served preaching surprisingly well. Done skillfully, it produced sermons that were long on a certain kind of biblical and theological content and strong on unity and clarity, since the resulting sermons were organized systematically around a single coherent concept.

Increasingly, though, homileticians (with the help of biblical scholars) became suspicious and critical of this "main idea" approach to biblical preaching. In the first place, they said, the Bible is not merely a box of ideas. No one who reads a rousing novel or sees a powerful play or views a provocative movie would be tempted to squeeze those rich experiences into only one "main idea." Engaging a biblical text is at least as multifaceted as any of those encounters, and while ideas are surely uncovered in biblical interpretation, there are also moods, movements, conflicts, epiphanies, and other experiences that cannot be pressed into a strictly ideational mold. Sermons should be faithful to the full range of a text's power, and those preachers who carry away only "main ideas," it was alleged, are traveling too light.

In the second place, homileticians complained that sermons organized around ideas and points tend toward plodding dullness. They march along according to the measured beat of linear logic, and while people *can* listen in linear fashion, they do not often find it very interesting to do so. Moreover, idea-centered sermons are prone to communicate, over time, that the Christian faith itself can be boiled down to a set of concepts to which people are supposed to give assent. The gospel thus gets presented as a list of propositions, and sermons become didactic devices for explaining these truths and how each of them logically connects to the others.

So, for the past several decades, homileticians have been aiming their cannons at the cognitive, propositional bridge between text and sermon. After a few warning shots in the 1950s and 1960s, a direct hit was scored by the publication, in 1971, of Fred Craddock's *As One Without Authority*. This little book, which represents an early phase in Craddock's homiletical thought, still stands as one of the most important modern books on preaching.

The problem that most caught Craddock's attention was the frustration that good and responsible preachers often feel when they try to squeeze the energy and creativity of their biblical study into an idea-centered propositional style of preaching. In Craddock's view, exegesis is, for the preacher, a potentially thrilling process of discovery. Facing the biblical text, the preacher follows hunches, explores possible avenues of meaning, and puts together clues on the way toward interpreting the text. Exegesis is, in short, an exciting adventure that darts first this way, then that way, resisting all reduction to a process of linear logic. It proceeds, rather, according to the logic of induction—moving from bits and pieces of information about the text to larger insights about textual meaning.

The problem with sermons, Craddock claimed, is that much of this excitement gets filtered out when the preacher turns from the exegesis to the sermon. An unfortunate shift in logic occurs, he said, between exegesis and preaching: The inductive anticipation of exegesis is replaced by the deductive exhortation of the sermon. On one side of the bridge the preacher has an exciting, freewheeling experience of discovering the text; but the preacher has been trained to leave the exegetical sleuthing in the study, to filter out the zest of that discovery, and to carry only processed propositions across to the other side. The joy of "Eureka!" becomes, in the sermon, the dull thud of "My thesis for this morning is . . ."

"The preacher," he wrote,

> cannot recapture his former enthusiasm as he breaks his theme into points, unless, of course, his image of himself is that of one who passes truth from the summit down to the people. The brief temptation to re-create in the pulpit his own process of discovering is warded off by the clear recollection of seminary warnings that the minister does not take his desk into the pulpit. What, then, is he to do? If he is a good preacher, he refuses to be dull. And so between the three or four "points" that mark the dull deductive trail he plants humor, anecdotes, illustrations, poetry, or perhaps even enlivening hints of heresy and threats of butchering sacred cows. But the perceptive preacher knows instinctively that something is wrong with his sermon: not its exegetical support, not its careful preparation, not its relevance; it is the movement that is wrong.[1]

Craddock's solution to this problem was for the sermon to regenerate, with the hearers, the inductive adventure experienced by the preacher in exegesis. The sermon itself, he maintained, should be patterned after the exegetical process, displaying the logic of induction, not deduction. In other words, in the sermon the preacher should invite the hearers to make a series of small discoveries about the biblical text building toward a larger "So that's what this passage is saying to us!" We will have more to say about this proposal in the next chapter, on sermon form, but at this point it is important to note the way Craddock redesigned the bridge between text and sermon. Instead of a cognitive bridge with main ideas from texts moving across to sermons, he proposed an experiential bridge carrying, as its traffic, the insights of exegesis powered by the energy of the discovery process. Craddock wanted the eventfulness of exegesis to become the eventfulness of the sermon. In the exegesis the preacher inductively arrives at the place of saying "Aha!" and the sermon is to re-create that process, allowing the hearers also to exclaim, "Aha!"

Craddock's proposal was immediately felt as a breath of fresh air, as a breakthrough in homiletical thinking, and he was joined by many other voices urging a general revolt against propositional preaching. Story preaching, image-rich preaching, sermons centered upon metaphors, sermons involving indirection, dialogue sermons, and other nondiscursive styles quickly became the homiletical fashion—in short, almost any sort of biblical preaching except "a thesis in three points." In many ways the climate was ripe for a protest against the deductive preaching of biblical "ideas," since the reigning biblical theology movement, which emphasized biblical concepts and the quasi-systematic theological unity of the Bible, was at that time rapidly giving way to the "new hermeneutic" and other event-centered approaches to biblical interpretation.

Craddock was widely praised for his innovative work, but in the heat of homiletical iconoclasm he was also criticized for not having gone far enough in his reforms. Some charged that what he had blocked at the front door—an idea-centered approach to preaching—he welcomed through the back door. True enough, in Craddock's scheme the preacher engages in an exciting inductive search through the text, but, when all is said and done, the goal of this adventure, the object of this quest, is an idea. The preacher romps through the text, looking under rocks and peering into hidden caves in a stimulating exegetical hide-and-go-seek, but what is finally discovered, albeit with energy and excitement, is a main idea from the text. Craddock said, in fact, that the goal of exegesis is to find *"the point* the author sought to make,"[2] and, as for the sermon, "There is a point, and the discipline of this one idea is creative in preparation, in delivery, and in reception of the message."[3] So, upon closer examination, it turned out after all that ideas from the text do come across Craddock's bridge between text and sermon. What made his approach innovative is that these ideas do not come alone but always clothed in the garments of the inductive sleuthing process by which those ideas were discovered in the first place.

Some homileticians rejected this "central idea" approach, no matter what kind of clothing it wore. What happens, Richard L. Eslinger asked Craddock, when the preacher encounters a biblical text that will not reduce to a single idea?

> Either the preacher must impose a thematic on the text from outside, or be threatened with a collapse of sermonic unity. . . . [T]he "weak link" in [Craddock's] approach remains the assumption that the interpretive payoff of every text is a proposition which then becomes the homiletic payoff of every sermonic form. Viewed from this perspective, the distance between a homiletics of induction and that of deduction closes considerably. Both seem to be bound to a rationalist hermeneutic.[4]

So the lines of the debate were set. Are preachers to bring a main idea across the bridge from the text to the sermon, or are they not? Do texts contain main themes and concepts that should serve as the unifying core of sermons, or is this merely the assumption of a "rationalist hermeneutic" that must finally give way to a more aesthetic approach to biblical interpretation?

A few teachers of preaching settled the dispute in their own minds out of sheer weariness. Tired of hearing their students and others deliver loosely constructed, vague, nonpropositional sermons with no clear message or guiding thought, they returned to the classic notion of moving from text to sermon on the basis of a unifying thesis, or proposition. Homiletician Ronald Sleeth was one who, having grown impatient with "private parables in the name of self-expression," argued forcefully for the traditional notion that texts do, in fact, yield "main ideas" and that sermons should be arranged to serve them:

> Surprisingly, there is a great deal of negative reaction to the idea that a sermon should have a clear, main idea that controls the sermon. Some suggest that we live in a frenetic, kaleidoscopic world where persons do not think logically, and we apprehend material holistically through an all-at-onceness. . . . To these persons, a thesis suggests a rationalistic discourse. . . .
>
> Yet, many sermons fail, simply because they are not clear. Preachers will raise several ideas in the beginning of a sermon and either develop one, or several, or none. People do not know what it is all about, and it becomes a mystery hour. What some take for creativity and expressive language may in reality be evidence of a fuzzy mind.[5]

Eugene Lowry, on the other hand, took the opposite position, claiming that the Bible itself is largely "nonpropositional" and warning that, at its worst, propositional thought "distorts and even reforms the experiential meaning" of the gospel.[6] He called for sermons to be essentially narrative in character, since the narrative form best conveys the "aesthetic communication" found in the Bible.

FROM EVENT TO CLAIM

This was all very confusing to preachers and students, of course, and formed something of a standoff among the homileticians themselves. Finally a shaft of light broke through the murkiness when homileticians (again aided by developments in biblical studies and hermeneutics) took a fresh look at the sort of biblical interpretation that preachers actually do. Put briefly, a preacher goes to a biblical text seeking to hear a word for the life of the church and, indeed, expecting to hear such a word. The preacher, then, views the text as a living resource for the community of faith and not merely as a historical object. A pure historian may examine a biblical text looking for data, but a preacher performs exegesis expecting something to happen, expecting some eventful word that makes a critical difference for the life of the church. To use David Kelsey's terms, the preacher approaches the Bible not as a set of texts, in the technical sense, but as scripture. "Part of what it means to call a text 'Christian scripture,' " he writes, "is that *it functions to shape persons' identities so decisively as to transform them . . . when it is used in the context of the common life of Christian community.*"[7]

So the goal of the preacher's exegesis is neither the plucking of an abstract idea from the text nor some nonconceptual aesthetic experience but, rather, the event of the text's actively shaping Christian identity. Every aspect of a biblical text—its concepts, its language, its literary form, its social and historical placement—works in concert to exert a claim upon each new set of faithful readers. Scripture, again to use Kelsey's words, "is taken as *doing* something that decisively shapes the community's identity."[8] Biblical texts *say* things that *do* things, and the sermon is to say and do those things too.

How do biblical texts shape Christian identity? That depends, of course, on the text in question. Some texts form Christian identity through the transmission of doctrine, others render biblical characters powerfully "present" through narration, some evoke wonder or provoke memory, and still others issue ethical demands. The list could go on, of course, since texts are multifaceted, and every text possesses its own unique and complex set of intentionalities.

Texts do all these things through words, of course, which means that they *do* things by *saying* things in certain ways. Here we find the key to building the bridge between text and sermon. The bridge must be able to bear the traffic of both word and event. The preacher should bring to the sermon both what the text says and what the text does; or, to put it another way, what the text does by its saying. The "main idea" crowd was half right about this—texts say something, and therefore express ideas—but they were only half right because they overlooked the fact that texts say what they say in order to cause something to happen. Content and intention are bound together, and no expression of textual impact is complete without them both.

The "aesthetic" crowd was half right as well—texts do create experiences—but they were also only half right because they downplayed the conceptual content by which texts create those experiences. In making his case for aesthetics, for example, Eugene Lowry said, "Perhaps you went to church and were overwhelmed in the singing of 'Amazing Grace'—and not at all because of the particularities of the propositional content of the third stanza."[9] If Lowry wants to say that the impact of singing "Amazing Grace" cannot be reduced to the content of the lyrics alone, he is certainly on the right track. When he says, however, that this experience is "not at all" related to the propositional content of the hymn text, he has allowed his argument to outrun the facts. Surely other lyrics— say, "Mary Had a Little Lamb"—even if they were sung to the same tune, would produce a quite different effect. What a text *says* clearly governs what it *does*.

This notion of biblical texts as eventful and intentional communication allows us to build a far more satisfactory bridge between text and sermon. As David Buttrick put it, "True 'biblical preaching' will want to be faithful not only to a message, but to an *intention*. The question, 'What is the passage trying to do?' may well mark the beginning of homiletical obedience."[10] O. C. Edwards, Jr., stated the same truth when he reminded preachers that a sermon "is not just about a thought, but about a thought that makes a difference."[11] Interpreting a biblical text is much like listening to one end of someone else's telephone conversation. We hear the text saying something to someone else for some purpose. As we discussed in the last chapter, the larger task of the contemporary interpreter is not simply to grasp that historical act of communication but rather to experience that communication as a claim upon us *now*. Once upon a time, everything about the biblical text made a claim upon its first readers, and now everything about that text makes a new claim upon us. What we bring across the bridge from text to sermon is not just an idea, or even an idea wrapped in our own inductive process of discovery, but rather this claim upon the hearers. A text's claim involves both a message *and* an intention bound up in the text's own manner of embodying that message, both what the text wishes to say *and* what the text wishes to do through its saying.

This is why the final step of the exegetical process presented in chapter 3 calls on the preacher to complete this sentence: "In relation

to those who will hear the sermon, what this text wants to say and
do is . . ." This is what the preacher should bring from text to sermon:
the claim of the text, the intention of the text to say and do something
to and with the hearers. The preacher has witnessed this in the
exegesis and now bears witness to it in the sermon.

FOCUS AND FUNCTION

What the biblical text intends to say and do now becomes what
the preacher hopes to say and do in the sermon. What the sermon
aims to say can be called its "focus," and what the sermon aims to
do can be called its "function." Since the whole sermon will be
gathered around these aims, the preacher needs to become clear
about the sermon's focus and function as a first step in the process
of developing a sermon. Most experienced preachers probably do this
sort of aiming of the sermon in their heads, but beginning students
are usually helped by writing out formal focus and function statements. Even experienced preachers need to do this from time to time
as an exercise in sharpening sermon intention.

A *focus statement* is a concise description of the central, controlling, and unifying theme of the sermon. In short, this is what the
whole sermon will be "about."

A *function statement* is a description of what the preacher hopes
the sermon will create or cause to happen for the hearers. Sermons
make demands upon the hearers, which is another way of saying that
they provoke change in the hearers (even if the change is a deepening
of something already present). The function statement names the
hoped-for change.

It would be silly and presumptuous, of course, to assume that the
preacher can predict and control all that is heard by the congregation
and all that happens to them in a sermon. Focus and function statements are merely compass settings for the sermon journey. They guide
the preacher in the creation of sermons that possess unity, clarity, and
a firm connection to the biblical text. Without them, the sermon runs
the danger of wandering aimlessly. But they obviously do not describe
everything that may happen to the hearers on the trip.

If the focus and function statements are to be genuinely useful to
the preacher in the development of the sermon, they should fulfill the
following three principles.

1. They should grow directly out of the exegesis of the biblical text

Suppose the text for the sermon is Romans 8:28–39, a passage that
ends with the affirmation that nothing "will be able to separate us

from the love of God in Christ Jesus our Lord." If the preacher comes to the text from a congregation wrestling with distress and trouble, issues of life and death, this text speaks an empowering word of reassurance and hope.

A congregation facing conflict in the church, the dissolution of families, poverty, cancer or other devastating illnesses, racial prejudice, death, persecution by the government, dwindling membership, hunger, or doubt will surely find its own cry in the text's key question, "Who shall separate us from the love of Christ? Shall tribulation, or distress, or persecution, or famine, or nakedness, or peril, or sword?" Then comes the response: "No, in all these things we are more than conquerors through him who loved us. . . . [Nothing] will be able to separate us from the love of God in Christ Jesus our Lord." The preacher who listens to this text on behalf of a troubled and perplexed congregation, then, may well describe the results of this exegetical encounter by saying something like, "What this text says is that the God we have come to know in Jesus Christ will not forsake us in distress, and what this text does is to reassure imperiled Christians of this loving care of God even in the face of experiences that seem to deny it."

Moving toward the sermon, this preacher may express this claim from the text in the following focus and function statements:

Focus: Because we have seen in Jesus Christ that God is *for* us, we can be confident that God loves and cares for us even when our experience seems to deny it

Function: To reassure and give hope to troubled hearers in the midst of, not apart from, their distress

What this preacher now has are two tasks for the sermon drawn directly from the exegesis of the text. The first task, embodied in the focus statement, is a message to say, and the second task, embodied in the function statement, is a deed to do. Note that these tasks are to be accomplished by the sermon as a whole. The preacher will design the total sermon around these tasks so that every aspect of the sermon will work toward their accomplishment. The entire sermon, therefore, will be an expression of, a witness to, this text's claim upon this congregation.

Is this the only set of focus and function statements that could come from this text? No, these statements express the claim that this preacher heard on this occasion for a congregation in these specific circumstances. Texts potentially make many claims, and a change in congregational situation would also alter the results of the exegesis and therefore the tasks of the sermon.

By way of example, suppose a preacher goes to the same text,

Romans 8:28–39, but this time from a congregation that has, among its members, a strong "sunshine and success" view of the Christian faith. Some in the congregation have a subtle but prevalent image of the gospel as "thinking positively" and turning problems quickly and easily into possibilities. The deep and enduring fissures in human experience cannot be faced honestly, since they fear that their faith may collapse under the heavy weight of the tragic. To an openly troubled church, Romans 8:28–39 speaks a word of encouragement and cheer. In the context of this congregation, though, a group trying desperately to remain at ease by carefully stepping over the threatening places in life and hewing to the smoothly cheerful path, the very same text speaks another word, initially of confrontation but finally of liberation from superficial faith. This new claim of the text may be expressed in the following focus and function statements:

Focus: Trying to hide from the tragic dimensions of life is a sign of lack of faith in God, whose love in Jesus Christ is experienced in the midst of peril and distress

Function: To enable the hearers to move from a superficial "sunshine and success" understanding of the faith toward a willingness to trust God in the fullness of their experience

These focus and function statements are quite different from the first set, but they are drawn just as firmly from the exegesis of the text. What makes them different, of course, is the changed congregational context, which evoked another claim from the text.

2. They should be related to each other

What a sermon *says* should be intrinsically related to what that sermon *does,* and the focus and function statements should reflect this connection. In other words, the focus and function statements should be a matched pair, one growing out of the other.

Suppose a preacher is developing a sermon from Luke 6:12–16, the text in which Jesus chooses the twelve apostles after a night of prayer. After interpreting the text, the preacher formulates the following focus and function statements:

Focus: Now, as in the very beginning, the leadership of the church and its mission grow out of the prayers of Christ

Function: To encourage a spirit of openness in the church by enabling the hearers to see that Christ calls many different kinds of people into service

These are useful statements, but the problem with them is that they are not matched. They belong to two different sermons, and each statement requires a different partner. For example:

Focus of Sermon 1: Now, as in the very beginning, the leadership of the church and its mission grow out of the prayers of Christ

Function: To strengthen the confidence of those who lead and those who serve that they are participating in the very mission of Christ

Focus of Sermon 2: Christ's call to service comes to many different kinds of people, just as Jesus' prayerful selection of the twelve embraced a surprising diversity of people, including a tax collector, a fisherman, a zealot, and even one who would betray him

Function: To encourage a spirit of openness in the church by enabling the hearers to see that Christ calls many different kinds of people into service

3. They should be clear, unified, and relatively simple

Whenever a preacher engages in responsible exegesis of a biblical text, the chances are good that many creative and engaging insights will occur. When a preacher dwells at length with a text, interrogating it with zest and open expectation, that text, which may have appeared at first to say little, or only one thing, often breaks open to reveal a richness of claims. The temptation facing the preacher is to attempt to bring everything heard and seen in the text into one sermon.

If this temptation is not resisted, the sermon will almost inevitably end up accomplishing little because the preacher has tried to accomplish it all. Sermons should say and do one thing: that is, they should be unified around a single claim from the text. One of the purposes of creating focus and function statements is to allow the light from the text to be refracted into a single clear beam illuminating these hearers through this one sermon on this given day.

The practical implication of this is that we should review our focus and function statements to assure that each embraces a single unified task. If the focus and function statements require that we accomplish several different tasks, the resulting sermon will probably lurch off in many directions at once. It is possible, of course, to overdo this piece of advice and produce sermons that are simplistic rather than simple, but the essential wisdom obtains nonetheless: The focus and function statements should attempt to express a single claim from the text.

A similar problem occurs when the focus and function statements lack crispness and specificity. Focus statements like "God is love," "the birth of Jesus," or "God calls us to justice," are too vague to be helpful to the preacher. Likewise, such function statements as "to help the hearers show forgiveness," "to create joy," or "to enable service" also lack specific bite.

Imagine that a preacher is studying, in preparation for a sermon, John 5:1–18, the story of Jesus' Sabbath healing of the lame man beside the pool at Bethzatha. The preacher finds this a fascinating text, one that moves simultaneously in several directions. In one sense the whole text seems to work in service of its final verse (v. 18), which explains why the Jewish authorities wanted to kill Jesus: He broke the Sabbath (by this act of healing, among others), and he equated himself with God. In another sense, the story of the healing itself has its own power apart from its connection to the Sabbath violation. The man had been sick for a long time, thirty-eight years, and Jesus' curious question, "Do you want to be healed?" implies the unstated "or do you now prefer your illness?" The man's cry, "Sir, I have no one to put me into the pool" (desperate need? whining?) is met by Jesus' firm command to action, "Rise, take up your pallet, and walk."

After wrestling with the claims of this text upon the hearers, the preacher makes a first attempt to compose focus and function statements:

Focus: Jesus was a controversial healer

Function: To help the hearers understand the importance of this for their lives

These statements are obviously too broad to be genuinely helpful to the preacher. To be sure, the text discloses that Jesus was a controversial healer, but how was he controversial, and what does this controversy have to do with contemporary hearers? Also, what specifically is important about this for the hearers' lives? So the preacher tries again:

Focus: Jesus unsettles our comfortable illnesses (blindness to injustice, paralysis of love, deafness to the cry of the needy) with the disturbing question, "Do you *really* want to be healed?" When people are healed, in the power of Christ, of such illnesses, opposition comes, not from evil people but ironically from good people who mistake their religious traditions for the will of God

Function: To enable hearers to become aware of Christ's continuing challenge to the sometimes comfortable complacency of our illnesses, and to enable hearers to perceive how our allegiance

> to religious traditions can sometimes stand in the way of the
> saving and healing work of God in our midst

These statements are an improvement over the first set because
they are far more specific. Because they are specific, however, they
reveal, through their length and complexity, that this preacher has
bitten off more than can be chewed in a single sermon. At least two
claims from the text are competing here for time and attention, and
while it is not impossible to imagine a sermon fulfilling all that is
embraced by these statements, the odds are that the sermon will end
up being either jumbled or a series of brief and independent "ser-
monettes" that happen coincidentally to share the same root text.

The efforts to compose adequate focus and function statements
have helped this preacher first to overcome vagueness and now to
make a decision that will bring unity to the sermon. The preacher,
recognizing that the sermon cannot express every claim of the text,
must now choose the word most urgently needed on this preaching
occasion. Perhaps it will be:

Focus: Jesus unsettles our comfortable illnesses (blindness to injus-
            tice, paralysis of love, deafness to the cry of the needy) with
            the disturbing question, "Do you *really* want to be healed?"

Function: To enable hearers to become aware of Christ's continuing
          challenge to the sometimes comfortable complacency of our
          illnesses

Or perhaps it will be:

Focus: When people are healed, in the power of Christ, of illnesses
            such as racism, lack of love, and unforgiving spirits, opposi-
            tion often comes not from evil people but ironically from good
            people who mistake their religious traditions for the will of
            God

Function: To enable hearers to perceive how our allegiance to religious
          traditions can sometimes stand in the way of the saving and
          healing work of God in our midst

There are other possibilities as well, of course, but the point is that
the preacher has arrived at crisp and concise descriptions of what
this sermon will say and do. Focus and function statements indicate
where a sermon is headed, and when they are formulated, the
preacher can begin to figure out how the sermon will get there. The
focus and function of a sermon seek an appropriate *form,* and this
is our concern in the next two chapters.

5

The Basic Form
of the Sermon

The very nature of the gospel . . . requires us to be concerned with form.

—H. Grady Davis,
Design for Preaching

Sermon form is a curious beast. In many ways, a sermon's form, or structure, is its least-noticed feature. Most hearers would be puzzled to be asked, "What was the form of the sermon you just heard?" Ask them about what the preacher said or about their own responses, and they can usually come up with an answer, but the form of a sermon slips by them as undetected as the meter of a hymn.

Despite the fact that it passes by relatively unnoticed, form is absolutely vital to the meaning and effect of a sermon. Like the silently shifting of gears in a car's automatic transmission, sermon form translates the potential energy of the sermon into productive movement, while remaining itself quietly out of view. "The power of a sermon," wrote Halford Luccock many years ago, "lies in its structure, not in its decoration."[1] Form is as important to the flow and direction of a sermon as are the banks of a river to the movement of its currents.

It is easy to get tripped up by our own language when we speak about this business of a sermon's form. We tend to talk about a sermon's content, on the one hand, and its form, on the other, as if form and content were two distinct realities. The picture we have in our heads is that of a preacher developing the content of a sermon and then hunting around for a suitable form, something like a shipping container, in which to box this content for delivery. In other words, content is the important stuff of the sermon; form is mere packaging, an afterthought.

Outside of the mail room, however, the notion of a form as a package does not work. In artistic creations (and sermons are artistic creations of a sort), form and content cannot be easily distinguished. Think of Michelangelo's *David*. What is "form" and what is "content" in that magnificent sculpture? Or recall the interplay of form and content in the shapes, patterns, and faces of Picasso's *Guernica*. Or again, see the blurring of form and content in the fluid grace of the youthful Willie Mays as he glided almost magically across center field tracking a hard-hit line drive (an aesthetic event as well as an athletic achievement).

Instead of thinking of sermon form and content as separate realities, it is far more accurate to speak of the form *of* the content. A sermon's form, although often largely unperceived by the hearers, provides shape and energy to the sermon and thus becomes itself a vital force in how a sermon makes meaning. Form is an essential part of a sermon's content and can itself support or undermine the communication of the gospel. If a sermon is structured in a manipulative, deceptive, or incoherent manner, then, regardless of what else is said in the sermon, manipulation, deception, or incoherence is spoken too. On the other hand, if the form of the sermon is clear, lively, and respectful of the listeners, then clarity, life, and dignity become a part of the sermon's word to the hearers.

In the simplest of terms, a sermon form is an organizational plan for deciding what kinds of things will be said and done in a sermon and in what sequence. If a preacher decides to open the sermon by posing a question that is on the minds of the hearers and then to spend the rest of the sermon responding to that question from the vantage point of the biblical text, this is essentially a decision about sermon form: The form will be Question/Response. If, on the other hand, the preacher decides to move back and forth between the text and the contemporary setting, first describing the historical situation out of which the biblical text arose, then showing how that situation is analogous to a contemporary situation, then going back to see what word was spoken by the text to its setting, then turning again to the contemporary circumstance to hear the text's word anew, this too is a choosing of sermon form: The form will be a weaving of old and new—Ancient Setting/Contemporary Setting, Ancient Word/New Word.

Since a sermon may assume many possible shapes and designs, the question for the preacher is how to create a form for a particular sermon that best embodies its message and aims.

OUTLINES: THE TRADITIONAL APPROACH

The classical way to plan the form of any message—sermon or other—is to create an outline, a schematic diagram of the parts and order of the message. Most homiletical textbooks of the past few generations enthusiastically endorsed the outlining process as the most efficient method for designing sermon structure. Developing an outline, it is said, forces the preacher to make choices, not only about what will be said when but also about the logical connections among the various pieces of the sermon. Once a good outline has been produced, the preacher can simply flesh out the parts to create the finished sermon.

How is a good outline created? Let us examine a representative sermon outline and explore the means by which it was fashioned. Here is one preacher's fairly typical sermon outline, this one for a sermon based on Psalm 19:1–14. The focus of this sermon (to use the language of this book) is "God speaks to people through the wonders of nature, the proclamation of scripture, and in everyday experience," and the function of this sermon (again to use our terminology) is "to enable the hearers to discover and name the variety of ways in which God is speaking to them."[2]

Title: How Does God Speak to Us?

I   God speaks through nature (19:1–6)
   A. In the silent processes of life
   B. In the cosmic wonder of the universe

II. God speaks through the divine word (19:7–11)
   A. In the Bible
   B. In the preaching and teaching of God's people

III. God speaks in our life experiences (19:12–14)
   A. In our sense of failure and sin
   B. In our hunger to be faithful

Now Psalm 19:1–14 can obviously yield this particular outline, but why did the preacher come up with this form and not some other? We do not yet know how the preacher managed to move from the biblical text to this design. The answer is that, once the overall focus and function had been established, the preacher broke these big aims into smaller ideas and tasks and arranged them into logical groupings. Though it is not always the case with sermon outlines, in this instance the structure of the text itself was a guide, since the preacher saw how the sections of the sermon could match divisions that can be made in the text. Even so, it should be observed that the outline was created by the preacher and not by the text. Psalm 19 can be analyzed from many angles; nothing dictates that it must be divided just this way. The preacher was aided by the flow of the text, but finally this sermon structure came—as all sermon forms do—through a creative act of the preacher's imagination.

But how can we know whether or not this outline is a good one? This outline looks fine on paper, but how do we know whether or not the sermon that will grow out of it will possess good sermon form? Homileticians have always been concerned about this question, of course, and over the years they have developed a catalog of virtues by which sermon outlines could be tested. Here is one fairly typical checklist:[3]

> *Unity:* Each major point should support the main proposition
> *Order:* The major divisions should be of equal importance
> *Movement:* Each major division should carry the thought forward by saying something distinguishable from what has gone before
> *Proportion:* The major divisions should be stated in parallel construction
> *Climax:* The major divisions should be arranged in an ascending scale of impact

If we apply these criteria to the foregoing sermon outline, the results are fairly encouraging. Our outline certainly has *unity*, since all divisions relate to the same theme. It also has *order*. Perhaps all divisions are not exactly equal, but there are no trivial molehills mixed in with the mountains. *Movement* is no problem, since each division covers its own territory; and the parallel phrases ("God speaks . . .") pass the *proportion* test. *Climax* may be a question (Does section II have more impact than section III? Should they be reversed?), but, all things considered, this outline appears to promise a sturdy sermon form.

QUESTIONING THE TRADITION

Lately, however, homileticians have developed some serious doubts about this business of creating sermon forms through outlines. The problem is not really with outlines themselves—they are innocent diagrams of structure—but rather with the kind of thinking people typically put into gear when they produce outlines.

To begin with, outlines often carry with them certain assumptions about the sort of logic that ought to hold them together. Whenever we see an outline, with its Roman numerals (I, II, III . . .), it is difficult to get away from the notion that these sections are major divisions of some overarching idea, and that the other parts of the outline (A, B, C . . . 1, 2, 3 . . . a, b, c, . . .) are subdivisions and subsubdivisions of various aspects of that overarching concept. In other words, like it or not, an outline conveys the inner logic of a main proposition broken down into its component parts.

Some sermons, of course, do aim to present the interconnections among the facets of a large concept, but this is not true, and should not be true, of all sermons. If every sermon were presented this way, the underlying message, presented over time, would be that the gospel is only a set of major concepts with rationally divisible parts. To be sure, every sermon should be logical, but there are many different kinds of logical structure—narrative, inductive, and metaphorical, just to name a few. Outlines—at least in the way we have been trained to construct them—reduce our logical options to a single choice.

Homileticians have also charged that, despite all the brave talk about "movement," the process of outlining actually tends to produce rather static and turgid sermons. For example, looking again at our sample outline, does this structure really have any movement from section I ("God speaks through nature") to section II ("God speaks through the divine word")? We can imagine the preacher of this sermon forcing some movement by saying something like, "And the second way God speaks to us" or "God speaks to us not only in nature but also in God's word," but these weak transitional statements merely reveal that the movement between these sections must be artificially constructed. Section I does not really lead into section II. The preacher simply swings on the trapeze from one to the other, hoping that the hearers will be game to follow along. Fred Craddock is surely correct when he observes that any experienced preacher with nerve enough to reexamine critically one's old, outline-style sermons will almost surely discover

> that some sermons were three sermonettes barely glued together. There may have been movement within each point, and there may have been some general kinship among the points, but there was not one movement from beginning to end. The points were as three pegs in a board, equal in height and distance from each other.[4]

The most telling criticism of the outlining process, however, focuses not upon logic or movement but rather upon what an outline aims to organize in the first place. Ever since we were taught how to outline term papers in high school, most of us have been schooled to think of an outline as a means for arranging the *material* of our paper, report, speech, or whatever. When we create a sermon form, though, we are not primarily asking "What is the most orderly way for this material to fit together?" We are, rather, asking, "How can people best *hear* the material in this sermon?" When we create sermon structure, we are forming communication, not merely shaping information. A sermon form is a plan for the experience of listening, not just an arrangement of data, and it is the listeners who are missing from the typical process of outlining.

EUREKA! ONE SIZE FITS ALL

Disenchanted with traditional outlining, many homileticians have begun searching for alternative means to create apt sermon forms. Quite a few recent works in the field of preaching have focused sharply upon the question of form;[5] these books are set apart from their immediate homiletical predecessors by their claim that sermon form must be controlled, not only by the material to be included in the sermon but also by the dynamics of the human listening process.

Actually this development in homiletics is not entirely new, since throughout most of its history homiletics has borrowed many of its ideas about form from "secular" rhetoric, a discipline that has always given serious attention to the inner processes of human listening. What has renewed the question of sermon form among contemporary homileticians is actually the rediscovery, aided by studies in the psychology of human listening, of an old truth: Sermon forms are not innocent or neutral. The shape of a sermon is not merely a convenient and logical way to arrange content; it is an invitation to—perhaps even a demand upon—the hearers to listen to the content according to a particular pattern. As such, form significantly influences what happens to the hearer in and through the sermon.

One of the charges against outlines, as we have seen, is that they tend to result in sermons shaped according to a single format, a 1-2-3 pattern of linear logic, thus reducing the formal options to one choice. Ironically, a few contemporary homileticians, in rejecting the outline scheme, have put in its place their own highly unified view of sermon form. When they thought deeply about how people actually listen to preaching, they came to the conclusion that the experience of creative insight on the part of the listener (as opposed to the process of rational thinking presupposed in the outline) was essential to the hearing of the gospel. Consequently, they argue that one and only one type of sermon form, one designed to engender this sense of discovery in listeners, is to be prized above all others.

Fred Craddock's landmark essay *As One Without Authority,* referred to in the last chapter, has often been read this way, even though Craddock warned that he was simply proposing one option among many for sermons and that the "forms of preaching should be as varied as the forms of rhetoric in the New Testament."[6] Craddock argued so persuasively for what he termed the "inductive" form in preaching, however, that it was difficult for readers not to be convinced that this was the method par excellence.

Put simply, Craddock proposed that sermons be shaped according to the same process of creative discovery employed by preachers in their exegetical work. When preachers study biblical texts, he said, they do not know in advance what those texts mean; they must search for meanings, putting clues together until meanings emerge at the end. Sermons, therefore, ought to re-create imaginatively this inductive quest so that the listeners can share the preacher's experience of illumination. The implication is that hearers best listen to and learn from sermons precisely the way preachers listen to and learn from biblical texts.

So instead of hearing in the introduction what the sermon is about, listeners ought to move through the sermon, putting together various bits and pieces of evidence, until they are able to discover the truth of the sermon in the conclusion. Indeed, by the time the hearers arrive at the end of an inductive sermon, they ideally have become so engaged in this discovery process that they, and not the preacher, complete the sermon by naming its resolution in their own minds and lives. Just as preachers at their exegetical desks finally claim for themselves the meaning of the text, so hearers in the pews should be empowered to claim for themselves the meanings of those texts through the gradual step-by-step process of the sermons.

Now what does this inductive sermon form look like in actual practice? Instead of being composed of points (I, II, III), a sermon would consist of a series of small segments, or movements, building cumulatively toward a climactic "Aha!" These smaller units are connected by "transitional expressions" that help the hearers put the pieces together, such as "It seems . . . , but still . . ."; "Of course . . . , and yet . . ."; or "Both this and this . . . , yet in a larger sense. . . ."[7] Taken as a whole, then, the sermon form proposed by Craddock is an attempt to organize the flow of the sermon so that it "corresponds to the way people ordinarily experience reality and to the way life's problem-solving activity goes on naturally and casually."[8]

Craddock's own label for his proposed form, "problem-solving activity," is the real key to understanding this approach to sermon structure. In Craddock's view, the preacher should imagine that the hearers are going to solve a specific problem, and then design the sermon to give them all the necessary information, and in the proper order, to resolve that problem for themselves. It is crucial to remember that in Craddock's scheme the problem being solved in the sermon is always the question, What does this biblical text mean for us today? That question hangs in the air at the beginning, and the sermon rolls along the pathway of discovery, gathering clues, until it finally arrives at the place where the listeners are prepared to make a decision for themselves about the claim of the text upon their lives.

A very different sort of problem-solving form has been suggested by Eugene Lowry in his book *The Homiletical Plot.* For Craddock, the one problem to be solved was the problem of the text's contemporary meaning, but for Lowry, any "felt need" on the part of the hearers—whether originating in the biblical text, a theological doctrine, or a situation in life—can serve as the organizing task. Lowry believes that sermons should begin by describing this problem, dilemma, or bind so clearly that the hearers feel "ambiguity" and desire its resolution. He writes that "there is one essential in form which I believe indispensable to the sermon event, and that one essential is ambiguity."[9]

Now sometimes, of course, the congregation is already aware of a problem and already feels its ambiguity. At a funeral, for instance, the circumstance of death poses its own deeply felt dilemma. The preacher does not need to raise the problem; it is already powerfully present. Most of the time, though, it is up to the preacher to generate this ambiguity by kicking over the apple cart in the opening section of the sermon. A preacher who begins a sermon by saying "Today I want to talk about love" is, in Lowry's view, "dull" because no suspense has been created at the sermon's beginning. Far better, he says, is the opening line: "Our problem is that so many times we extend our hand in love only to bring it back bruised and broken. To love is to risk rejection."[10] What makes that introduction better is that it creates imbalance: that is, it generates conflict by raising an experiential problem about love to the level of awareness. The listeners, he maintains, will want so much to see that conflict resolved they will listen to the rest of the sermon to discover how it all comes out.

The job of the remainder of the sermon, claims Lowry, is "the resolution of that particular central ambiguity,"[11] and he has a very specific notion of how the sermon should be shaped to get this task done. Sermons, he claims, should be designed around five basic movements, or "stages" (these five stages constitute, of course, a kind of "outline," but Lowry would be eager to claim that his outline is fueled by a different sort of logic than the traditional ones):

1. *Upsetting the equilibrium.* In this opening stage, which we have already described, the preacher poses the "problem" of the sermon in a way that can be felt by the hearers.

2. *Analyzing the discrepancy.* In this stage the preacher diagnoses the problem by exploring it in detail and articulating the reasons why it exists in human experience.

3. *Disclosing the clue to resolution.* Here is where the "Aha!" comes in Lowry's form. In this stage the preacher supplies the clue from the gospel that provides the resolution for the problem. Lowry is quick to point out, though, that since the resolution comes from the gospel and not from "worldly wisdom," this moment in the sermon has the air of surprise about it. There is a

"reversal" of the hearers' expectations, and this clue comes "by means of sudden illumination."[12]

4. *Experiencing the gospel.* In this stage, the clue disclosed in the previous stage is fleshed out in terms of its fuller meaning for the hearers.

5. *Anticipating the consequences.* In this final stage, the new discovery of the gospel is projected onto the future. "What—in the light of this intersection of human condition with the gospel—can be expected, should be done, or is now possible?"

Instead of a deductive structure fashioned with points growing out of a central idea, Lowry has thus given us a fluid, suspense-driven master form for sermons. He calls this form "narrative," since the five movements of the sermon work together like the episodes of a plot, but "narrative" is probably a misleading label. Lowry's five-fold form is shaped more according to the "creativity paradigm" familiar to researchers in the field of human problem solving than it is styled after actual narrative plots, which are quite varied. Many creativity studies have found that people who discover innovative solutions to old problems do so according to a similar pattern. They customarily report that they wrestled long and hard analyzing the problem, only to have the solution come to them in a sudden and surprising moment of illumination. Once this solution has been received, however, it becomes part of the person's problem-solving repertoire and can be applied to future puzzles. It is not much of a stretch, of course, to see that Lowry's master-sermon form is simply a renaming of the steps in this typical pattern of human creativity.

Homileticians like Craddock and Lowry have gone a long way toward restoring creativity and excitement in sermon form. Because they propose designing sermons around the process of discovery, they overcome many of the problems of the static outline and provide the means for enabling hearers to be active and responsible participants in the preaching event.

There are also problems, however, in their suggestions about sermon form. To begin with, any scheme that purports to be able to lead a group of people to the place where they exclaim, "Aha! I have discovered a surprising new truth!" must reckon with the fact that human creativity is fragile and unpredictable. It may be the case that people who have exciting discoveries can look back on those experiences and recount the steps they took to get to the moment of insight. It is not at all clear, though, that marching someone else through those steps will generate the same "Eureka!" This is particularly a concern for a scheme like Lowry's, with its sudden reversal and surprising shaft of light breaking through on cue in stage 3 of the sermon.

A deeper issue for the problem-solving form comes, however, not from the fact that these forms do not always work as advertised to create fresh insight, but rather from the fact that, skillfully done, they usually *do* work to create listener interest. Sermons that begin with an intriguing problem and then move themselves gradually toward a resolution have high listener appeal, and the preacher will be tempted to form every sermon according to a pattern so well received.

However, a sermon's form, as we have argued, is a part of its meaning, and if a congregation is treated week after week only to the problem-solving design, it is inevitably grasping that the purpose of the gospel is to resolve problems or that the best experience of hearing the gospel is a deeply felt "Aha!" Sometimes the gospel does not resolve ambiguity; it creates it. Sometimes the gospel does come to us as an unexpected word, surprising us or turning our world upside down, but other times it comes to us as a familiar and trusted word of confirmation, as the "old, old story." In short, the gospel is too rich, complex, and varied to be proclaimed through a single sermon form. Craddock himself, no doubt aware that some of his earlier readers had become practitioners of the inductive problem-solving form to the exclusion of others, firmly argued, in a later book, that the repetition of any one sermon form tends to constrict the fullness of proclamation:

> Form shapes the listener's faith. It is likely that few preachers are aware how influential sermon form is on the quality of the parishioners' faith. Ministers who, week after week, frame their sermons as arguments, syllogisms armed for debate, tend to give that form to the faith perspective of regular listeners. Being a Christian is proving you are right. Those who consistently use the "before/after" pattern impress upon hearers that conversion is the normative model for becoming a believer. Sermons which invariably place before the congregation the "either/or" format as the way to see the issues before them contribute to oversimplification, inflexibility, and the notion that faith is always an urgent decision. In contrast, "both/and" sermons tend to broaden horizons and sympathies but never confront the listener with a crisp decision. Form is so extremely important. Regardless of the subjects being treated, a preacher can thereby nourish rigidity or openness, legalism or graciousness, inclusiveness or exclusiveness, adversarial or conciliating mentality, willingness to discuss or demand immediate answers.[13]

MOTION PICTURES

The contemporary homiletician who has perhaps given the most sustained attention to the relationship between sermon form and the listening process is David Buttrick. Actually "the listening process" is too tame a phrase to describe Buttrick's main concern, which is the deeper issue of how sermons work to form faith in the consciousness of the hearers. "Sermon structures," he writes, "ought to travel through congregational consciousness as a series of immediate thoughts, sequentially designed and imaged with technical skill so as to assemble in forming faith."[14]

That rather complicated sentence receives a lengthy and elaborate exegesis in Buttrick's massive textbook *Homiletic,* much of which is devoted to the question of sermon form. Buttrick's ideas about good sermon form are based on a simple analogy: The human mind works something like a camera. Everything out there in the world is streaming through the lens of human consciousness, but, as every photographer knows, not everything can be captured on film. The photographer must pick something on which to focus, thereby creating both foreground and background. Just so, the mind selects some field on which to focus, either using a wide-angle lens, thus taking in a broad range of meaning, or narrowing its view to a single small area. It can employ "filters" to highlight certain structures of meaning and can even determine "composition" and choose "angles of vision."[15] When all is set, the shutter opens, the image is captured in memory, the shutter closes, and the film is advanced to the next frame.

This is all an analogy, of course, but Buttrick finds in it much guidance for the preacher. Preachers are something like photographers' assistants, setting up a series of interesting scenes and then urging the hearers to take pictures of them. When preachers interpret the scripture, they discover there "*fields of understanding* produced by symbols of revelation," and the task of preaching is to present those in such a way that the hearers can capture them on the mind's film. "Preaching," claims Buttrick, "mediates some structured understanding in consciousness to a congregation."[16]

What does this have to do with sermon form? Sermons involve a sequence of ideas. First the preacher speaks of this idea, then another idea, then the next idea, and so on. As the preacher presents one idea after another, the hearers are busily snapping away with their mental cameras. "Here is the first idea," the preacher says. *Click.* "Here is the second idea," and, again, *click.* Now, when the sermon is finished, what do the hearers have? If the sermon is poorly constructed, all they have is a cluttered box of random snapshots. If the sermon is well formed, though, they will have something like a filmstrip, a series of pictures that possess a lively sense of movement from one to the next and work together to produce coherent understanding.

Sermons, then, are "a movement of language from one idea to another," and because of this Buttrick likes to call the individual ideas, or units, of the sermon "moves." Because of his understanding of how human consciousness works, Buttrick insists that these moves must be built according to a single blueprint. Every move is required to possess three indispensable parts:[17]

1. *Opening statement.* The preacher must state, in one clear sentence, the main idea of this move, what this move is about (e.g., "We are all sinners"). This invites the hearers to "take a picture of *this.*" In addition, the opening must show how this move is connected to the one before, indicate the point of view of the move, and establish the move's emotional mood.

2. *Development.* In the middle section of the move, the main idea is elaborated, sometimes through clarification or illustration and sometimes through the raising of objections.

3. *Closure.* In a terse final sentence, the main idea of the move is restated, thereby signaling to the hearer that this move is complete. Thus, the shutter on the hearer's camera closes, and the film advances in readiness for the next move.

Buttrick is persuaded that, given the diminishing attention spans of contemporary people, about four minutes is the most people will devote to a single idea, so each move must complete its work within that limit. A well-designed twenty-minute sermon, then, consists of an ordered sequence of no more than five or six of these three-part, precision-designed moves.

So far, we have only viewed the rudiments of Buttrick's theory of sermon form (the whole scheme, presented at length in *Homiletic,* is quite complex), but we have seen enough both to admire Buttrick's scheme and to raise some critical questions about it.

On the positive side, Buttrick compels us to think long and hard about what is happening inside the heads of listeners as we preach. He has a high view of the power of language and form to make things happen, and he is convinced, correctly, that a sermon shaped one way forms faith quite differently from a sermon shaped another way. This makes sermon form a theological and ethical issue, and not merely a rhetorical one.

Moreover, Buttrick, like Craddock and Lowry, has shed additional light on the crucial matter of movement in sermon form. Buttrick's approach, unlike that of Lowry, does not really provide a single form but instead gives us a comprehensive way to think about sermon forms as processes of thought, which can yield many different structures. It is impossible to encounter Buttrick's method and not be attuned to the power of sermons to help, or to hurt, people as they move through the gradual and ordered process of coming to understand the gospel.

However, Buttrick's approach raises at least two troubling questions. First, do ideas really get formed in human consciousness in the way Buttrick claims they do? They *can,* I suppose, but surely not in every case. Buttrick wants every move to state the idea, to develop the idea, and then to restate the idea. Some of the best ideas I have, though (like the idea that God is gracious or the idea that my family loves me), simply did not "happen" in my consciousness that way. What Buttrick has done is to produce an abstract schematic description of *one way* of thinking and to declare that process as normative for each section of a sermon. Less direct, more poetic ways of coming to understanding get washed away.

The second question about Buttrick's understanding of form is whether it is adequate to conceive of a sermon as "a movement of language from one idea to another." Is a sermon only a string of ideas? Some moments in good sermons are like the congregational singing of "A Mighty Fortress" at a funeral. There are ideas involved to be sure, many of them, but these ideas are so woven into the fabric of memory and experience, grief and hope, that they cannot be sorted out and should not be reduced to a single concept. It would seriously miss the mark to ask, "What is the main idea in singing this hymn?" If a sermon contained no ideas, or a bewildering jumble of disconnected ideas, it would mean nothing at all. But surely sermons are more than a series of idea-laden boxcars moving down the track.

A VARIETY OF FAITHFUL FORMS

As the debate among homileticians about sermon form continues, it has become increasingly clear that a sermon's form should grow out of the shape of the gospel being proclaimed as well as out of the listening patterns of those who will hear the sermon. The dynamics of human listening, while certainly an important and often neglected ingredient in the creation of sermon form, must not serve as the only basis, and not even as the starting point, in considerations of sermon design.

If we begin to create forms for sermons by trying to discern how people listen in general to oral communication, we will inevitably produce abstract anthropological descriptions of the patterns of human listening into which preaching must then be fit. We are constantly tempted to say that people *always* listen (or at least *most deeply* listen) narratively, inductively, in order to resolve conflict and ambiguity, or something of the sort. The inescapable conclusion, then, is that sermons must be poured into narrative or inductive or problem-solving or move-system molds because that, after all, is how human listening is shaped. Homiletician Richard Lischer, objecting to this move from anthropology to homiletics, writes:

The implicit hope is that if only we could find the perfect glass slipper of form, not only would the sermon be transformed into a beautiful princess, but we ourselves would also be transformed. Some would understand rhetoric as a natural ally of homiletics. But when rhetoric is accompanied by an implicit anthropology, as it always is, it poses a danger to homiletics. Homiletics then finds itself in crisis to the extent that it takes its cues from principles not its own.[18]

Lischer's warning flag is a necessary one to wave. Form, as we have seen, is not neutral, and if we look to the culture to tell us what form our sermons must assume, then, like it or not, we will end up preaching the culture instead of the gospel. On the other hand, if we decide to avoid the culture altogether and search for a purified sermon form in heaven or in the Bible, we will look in vain. There is no such thing.

Indeed, the Bible itself demonstrates how quite diverse literary forms are borrowed from the culture to serve as vehicles for proclamation. One way to view the New Testament is as the record of the earliest attempts to express the gospel in comprehensible form, and when we examine its range of texts, we quickly discover that the gospel has found expression in a variety of forms. In this passage a logical argument is being developed; in that text a straightforward narrative is being told; over here an enigmatic parable is being unfolded; and over there a hymn is being sung. All these forms—story and syllogism, poem and pronouncement, epistle and apocalypse—are found in the culture, but in every case the borrowed form is employed to serve the proclamation of the gospel. No one form is adequate to display the fullness of the gospel. Many forms are used, each selected in turn to express some aspect of the gospel on a particular occasion.

The same dynamic has been present throughout the history of Christian preaching. "In the history of its preaching," writes Lischer, "the church has moved from form to form. . . . No form of sermon design has proven normative—only the rhetorical situation remains."[19] Whenever the gospel has been faithfully proclaimed, the intersection between the claims of the faith and the specific circumstances of the hearers has evoked suitable but ever-varying forms.

A good sermon form, then, grows out of the particularities of preaching this truthful word on this day to these people. Think of those occasions when a person must speak an important truth to another. Perhaps it is a joyful but risky word, like "I love you." Or perhaps it is a hard word, like "Your work is not satisfactory and must improve if you are to stay here." The one who speaks words like these must decide how to speak them. In some ways the nature of the message itself demands its own form. "I love you" must be said personally, directly, straightforwardly. In other ways, the form must be fitting for the one to whom the word is spoken. We say "I love you" differently to a person who already knows of our love and will hear this as confirmation than we do to a person who has reason to think that we do not care for them and who will receive this word as a shock. How we speak a word of truth is the result of an interplay between the word spoken and the ones to whom it is said.

The preacher is attempting to bear witness to the truth claims of the gospel that have been heard through a specific biblical text. The crucial question for form is, How can the preacher announce these claims in such a way that these people can hear them? The preacher, therefore, must be concerned about the truth being preached, but always in light of how this congregation will be able to hear it. Likewise, the preacher must be concerned about how this congregation will listen, but always in relation to the hearing of this truth. Many strategies and oral genres will be employed—story, logical presentation, historical account, rhetorical questioning, poetry, and so on—but always because they are adequate to accomplish the task of bearing witness to the gospel for these people in this setting. Every sermon form, then, must be custom tailored to match the particular preaching occasion.

FINDING A SATISFACTORY SERMON FORM

How does the preacher find, or create, a good form for a given sermon? Sometimes a good sermon form jumps out at the preacher, practically as if it were shouting, "This is the way to shape this sermon; no other form will do as well!" On other occasions the preacher simply begins to create the sermon, not knowing exactly how the sermon will arrive at its destination, letting the structure emerge as both preacher and sermon feel their way along toward the end.

Most of the time, however, good sermon form results from careful thinking and planning in advance. Good sermon form is an artistic achievement, and no universally accepted and always reliable process exists for creating a satisfactory sermon form. What follows, however, are three suggested steps designed to raise the central questions that form must address.

1. Start with the focus and function

The place to begin in creating a sermon form is with the focus and the function—what the sermon aims to say and to do. If we keep our eye firmly on these, the sermon form will have unity, since the whole sermon will be shaped to accomplish these aims. Everything the sermon needs to accomplish the focus and function should be included in the structure, and anything that does not help us to achieve these aims is extraneous and should be weeded out. As an example from the last chapter, recall focus and function statements for a sermon on Romans 8:28–39:

Focus: Because we have seen in Jesus Christ that God is *for* us, we can be confident that God loves and cares for us even when our experience seems to deny it

Function: To reassure and give hope to troubled hearers in the midst of, not apart from, their distress

Together, this focus and this function constitute the claim of this sermon on Romans 8. If all goes well, when the sermon is completed the focus will have been said and the function will have been done. Now the preacher asks, What is the best form for saying and doing these things? How can the claim be presented in such a way that the listeners can hear it?

2. Divide these larger tasks into smaller components

Focus and function statements express the overall tasks of the sermon, and these tasks cannot be accomplished all at once. They will be done bit by bit, over time, through the sermon. Thus the preacher should try to break them down into a set of smaller undertakings.

Our example focus statement indicates that the sermon will say that, "because we have seen in Jesus Christ that God is *for* us, we can be confident that God loves and cares for us even when our experience seems to deny it." If the sermon as a whole does in fact say this, along the way the following tasks are necessary:

a. Say where and how we have seen in Jesus Christ that God is for us

b. Name and describe experiences that seem to deny God's love and care

c. Describe clearly how what we have seen in Jesus Christ is able to create present confidence in God's love and care

Our example function statement indicates that the sermon intends "to reassure and give hope to troubled hearers in the midst of, not apart from, their distress." If the sermon as a whole is to accomplish this, then along the way it must:

d. Provide reassurance, based upon God's continuing love and care, to troubled hearers

e. Evoke a sense of hope for people who struggle with situations that seem to have no future

and, perhaps:

f. Call into question all shallow reassurances that do not deal honestly with suffering.

3. Decide the sequence in which these tasks should be done

Up to this point we have named the various tasks the sermon must accomplish if the focus and function are to be achieved. Now we must decide the order in which they can best be done. If we are building a house, decisions about sequence are usually fairly obvious and a matter of necessity. We must draw the plans before we order the materials, pour the foundation before placing floor joists, erect the wall frames before constructing the roof, and so on. In sermons, though, the choices are not nearly so clear. Should we begin with this task or that one? Sermons are not buildings made of wood and brick; they are oral events that take place in the imaginations of the hearers. In a sermon, we can even construct the roof first and then, allowing the hearers mentally to suspend it in midair, imagine the sort of framework necessary to hold up that roof.

Decisions about sermon sequence are made almost exclusively on the basis of the needs and capacities of the listeners. "Should I begin by describing the biblical text," the preacher may ask, "and then show how that text speaks to our experience? Or will they hear the text's word better if I begin with a description of human need and then show how the text speaks to it? But if I begin with human need, will they only hear the text as an 'answer' to what is already present rather than a new way of seeing life altogether?" This is the sort of thinking that goes into decisions about the ordering of sermon tasks.

Returning to our example sermon, one preacher may decide that the best sequence is as follows:

1: Start with the experience of the hearers
   b. Name and describe experiences that seem to deny God's love and care
2: Give the "typical" religious responses to these experiences and describe how these are insufficient
   f. Call into question all shallow reassurances that do not deal honestly with the kind of experiences described in (b)
3: Say how the text gives a deeper response to suffering
   c. Describe clearly how what we have seen in Jesus Christ is able to create present confidence in God's love and care and is different from the shallow reassurances of (f)

      a. Say where and how we have seen in Jesus Christ that God is for
      us
  4: Move to what this deeper response means for our living
      e. Say how (c) and (a) evoke a sense of hope for people who
      struggle with situations that seem to have no future
      d. Say how the hope, described in (e), provides reassurance, based
      upon God's continuing love and care, to troubled hearers

What this preacher has done is to take the set of six tasks and
organize them into a sequence that will allow each one, at least in
this preacher's view, to be done at just the right moment in the
sermon. This preacher has clearly decided that the place to begin is
with the felt need of human crisis, and that the remainder of the
sermon should be a careful working through of the gospel response
to that crisis.

This is not the only way, though, to order these tasks. Here is
another's preacher's design:

  1: Start with the ways the Christian community has responded to suffer-
    ing
      f. Call into question all shallow reassurances that do not deal
      honestly with suffering
      a. Say where and how we have seen in Jesus Christ that God is for
      us, indicating how this points toward a deeper response to
      suffering than we have seen in (f)
      c^1. Describe clearly how what we have seen in Jesus Christ (a) is
      able to create present confidence in God's love and care
  2: Ask whether even this deeper response can face up to our immediate
    experience of suffering
      b. Name and describe experiences that seem to deny God's love
      and care
      c^2. Return to the description of the relation between what we have
      seen in Jesus Christ and our present confidence in God's love
      and care, this time relating what is said directly to the
      experiences named in (b)
  3: Reflect upon what this deeper response now means for our living
      d. Provide reassurance, based upon God's continuing love and
      care, to troubled hearers
      e. Evoke a sense of hope for people who struggle with situations
      that seem to have no future

What we have in this form is quite a different sermon. The focus and
function are the same; the same tasks get accomplished; and yet the
new sequence creates a different process of listening. The first sermon

form presented the human dilemma and allowed the claim of the text to emerge as a response. The second sermon set forth the text's claim early and then tested it against human experience. This second strategy caused the preacher to divide one of the tasks into two parts. The first part (c^1) presented the theological affirmation of the text over against less profound religious ideas about suffering, and the second part (c^2) related that affirmation to particular experiences of suffering.

Both of these forms for the sermon are good ones, and there are others as well. One can imagine a structure in which the preacher would raise the question of human suffering (b), move to descriptions of how Christian people have learned to live in the face of such events (d) and (e), and then ask, "What gives faithful people hope and trust in the midst of all that seems to deny God's care?" (a) and (c). In this form, the full claim of the text would not come until the very end of the sermon.

Another example of sermon form can be seen in Edmund Steimle's superb Christmas eve sermon on Luke 2:1–20, "The Eye of the Storm."[20] The focus of this sermon is that the beautiful story of Jesus' birth in a manger, its "all is calm, all is bright" character, should not lull us into a romantic view of the Christ child disconnected from the conflict, pain, suffering, and violence of Jesus' life—or ours. The function of the sermon is to replace the sentimental and nostalgic "I'm Dreaming of a White Christmas" understanding of Jesus' birth with the deeper truth of the nativity as God's response to a world of conflict and confusion.

Steimle had, then, a difficult task. He was to face a sanctuary full of people on Christmas eve, including many families with children, and challenge, on the basis of the biblical text, a warm, homey, and cherished view of Christmas. He decided to form his sermon as follows:

1. An image: Hurricane Hazel and the eye of the storm

In this step, Steimle described his experience of Hurricane Hazel in the 1950s. The storm hit with fearsome force. There were drenching rains, screaming winds, uprooted trees, and broken power lines crackling on the pavement. Then, suddenly, there was breathless calm—the eye of the storm—followed by the renewed fury of the storm.

2. Apply the "eye of the storm" image to the biblical story

In this step, Steimle compared the story of Jesus' birth in Luke to his experience of the hurricane, a moment of calm in the midst of raging winds before (the anger of God at Israel, the biblical flood, the exile, the Roman occupation) and violent storms to follow (the massacre of the innocents, the rejection of Jesus by his own people, the crucifixion).

3. Describe how the early Christians themselves saw the stories of Jesus' birth as the "eye of the storm"

In this step, Steimle explained that the stories of Jesus' birth were never intended to be gentle departures from the world of pain and conflict but rather were told and cherished precisely by early Christians well acquainted with conflict.

4. Draw out the implications for the present hearers

In this step Steimle named some of the contemporary storms swirling around the hearers—poverty, violence in the Middle East, families breaking up—and claimed that if the Christmas story is merely a nostalgic means for forgetting these storms, then it is not worth the effort of listening. But the Christmas story, he went on to say, is not a sentimental peace but like a peace in the eye of a storm, a peace that passes all understanding.

We can see that Steimle carefully constructed the form of this sermon. He was concerned not simply with saying something, but with saying it in such a way that his hearers could visualize it, be compelled by it, and perhaps let go of an inadequate view of Christmas and grasp the text's view of Jesus' birth as their own.

Deciding which form to employ is a matter of discernment on the part of the preacher. If the sermon is to be an act of Christian proclamation, the hearers must not be passive. They should participate with the preacher in the creation of the event of proclamation, and the preacher should choose the sermon form that best allows the hearers to exercise their ministry of active and creative listening.

ENERGIZING THE FORM

These steps help us to make some initial decisions about the basic form of the sermon. All we have at this point, though, is the barest of structures. We know the overall aims of the sermon (the focus and the function), the smaller tasks that must be accomplished along the way, and the sequence in which the sermon will take them up. A full sermon form, however, is more than a sequential listing of tasks. Now we need to put some energy and life into the form by thinking through how these tasks are dynamically linked together and what it will actually take to get these tasks done. These will be our concerns in the next chapter.

6

Refining the Form

Poets and preachers are moved whenever they remember that forms of words are expressions of the ceaseless creative activity of God without whom no words can be made and used in meaningful conjunction.

—Robert E. C. Browne,
The Ministry of the Word

In the last chapter we discovered how a preacher can think through the creation of a basic sermon form. When we viewed sermon form through a magnifying glass we saw that form presents a picture, a plan—a map, really—of a sermon's itinerary, showing each step to be taken along the journey. From the point of view of the preacher who is developing the sermon, each step represents a task to be done. When these tasks are added together, they equal the larger aims of the sermon: the focus and the function. A basic sermon form simply names these tasks in order, showing how they move and develop from beginning to end.

Some preachers will need no more than the basic form to complete the sermon. They can get right about the business of creating the full sermon, using only the simple form to chart their way on the journey. Fleshing out a basic sermon form, like adding fractions, can sometimes be done in one's head.

Even so, it is important not to pass unreflectively over this moment in sermon creation. A sermon form does describe a sequence of tasks to be done; that is true enough, as far as it goes. If that is all the sermon form is, though, it is a rather graceless creature. Preachers are not machines stamping out tasks, and sermons are not assembly lines. If we are not careful, a task-defined sermon form can lead to a mechanical and task-oriented view of preaching, one that overlooks the fact that all that is done in a sermon is done with and for the people who hear.

Suppose the personnel director of a company has been given the responsibility of informing a certain employee that the company would like to promote her to a new position but that the promotion will entail relocation to another city. Furthermore, the personnel director is instructed to tell this employee that she is free to accept or reject this promotion without penalty, but that realistically another opportunity like this may not develop for a long time.

Only the clumsiest personnel director, given this task, would push open the woman's office door and announce, "We'd like to promote you to regional sales manager and move you to Detroit. You don't have to take it, of course, but this may be your last chance for a long time. What d'ya say?" That would get the task done, to be sure, but not the mission. The employee would no doubt be overwhelmed, experiencing this news as a bombshell rather than as a promising option. A more skillful and sensitive personnel director would think through how to break the news in a way that both the company's hopes and the woman's true choices would be understood and thoughtfully considered.

In a similar but much more profound manner, bearing witness to the claim of the gospel upon the lives of the congregation requires discernment about the way that claim will be heard and received. Refining the form of a sermon is the process of thinking through *how* to present that claim in such a way that people can truly hear it and respond to it. This is a question of clarity, of course, but it is also a question of freedom. A sermon should present the gospel so that people can understand it, and it should also present the gospel so that people are liberated to respond to it. Sermon forms can be, if we choose, strategies for manipulation, deception, and coercion. But when they are shaped in obedience to the gospel, they become arenas for free and human decision making.

MEASURING THE DISTANCE

In order to see what sort of discernment a preacher must exercise to refine and flesh out a part of the basic form, let us take a closer look at the initial step in one of our example sermon forms from the previous chapter. One of our hypothetical preachers decided to begin the sermon on Romans 8:28–39 with this step:

Step 1: Start with the experience of the hearers
        Task b: Name and describe the human experiences that seem
             to deny God's love and care.

It is clear what this preacher hopes to accomplish in the opening section of the sermon. This preacher has decided that the good news in the text can best be heard in response to the cry, "Where is God in our suffering?" and the initial step of this sermon is aimed at disclosing the places where the hearers, at least implicitly, are already uttering this cry in their own experience. It is also clear, when we remember the focus and function of this particular sermon, that this step is a necessary one to take in the overall logic of the sermon's claim.

Hidden from view, though, is a fuller recognition of what taking this step will mean for the hearers. Every sermon step implies some sort of change on the part of the hearers. Perhaps they will learn something new, deepen their understanding of something familiar, see something in a fresh way, feel something, or be motivated to do something. The preacher needs to assess where the hearers are in relation to this step and should measure the distance the hearers will be invited to travel in this section of the sermon. To put it another way, the preacher should ask, "What sort of change is the sermon asking for here, and what will it mean for the hearers to make this change?"

So what change does our sample step demand? This particular step invites the hearers to recall certain experiences from their own lives and both to understand and to feel these experiences as moments of doubt about the providence of God. If the hearers already have a keen and urgent awareness of "the human experiences that seem to deny God's love and care," then obviously no change is called for, this step is unnecessary, and the task is superfluous because the hearers are already there. The presence of this step in the basic form assumes, though, that the hearers are not yet there, and the step must provide the resources for movement from one place to another.

What will it mean, then, for the hearers to make this change? What is it in the hearers' circumstances that calls for this step in this sermon? Where *are* the hearers in relationship to our example step? One possibility is that the hearers simply are not aware that people have "experiences that seem to deny God's love and care." In other words, they don't know about such experiences and need to be informed about them. That is possible, but, given the fact that most people, by the time they reach adulthood anyway, have had an ample measure of loss, pain, inexplicable suffering, and other doubt-provoking experiences, it hardly seems likely.

Perhaps, then, the hearers do know about such experiences and have had them in their own lives, but they are probably not actively thinking about them at the beginning of the sermon. That is a much stronger likelihood, and, if so, this step in the sermon becomes a means for bringing to the surface the hearers' memories of these experiences.

Pressing the question a bit deeper, it is probable that the hearers possess quite different attitudes toward these experiences. Some of the hearers will be more than ready to claim their experiences of suffering and loss as God-denying moments. A child died, a marriage dissolved, a business collapsed, a sense of personal worth was crushed, an accident left paralysis and pain in its wake. For some, experiences like these stand as raw and active threats to their faith, and they are prepared to have them named as such. They will immediately recognize themselves in this step of the sermon and will welcome the preacher's raising of the issue. Just mentioning doubt-provoking experiences will bring them quickly to the surface.

Other hearers, however, have surely had such experiences, but they may be reluctant, even fearful, to let these open wounds touch their understanding of God. They sense the potential destruction that unresolved suffering can do to the structures of faith, so they keep their creed and this dimension of their experience at arm's length. They cannot, must not, admit to doubt, not because they are stubborn but because they are afraid that doubt, once loose, would consume them. If the preacher charges through this section of the sermon, heedlessly naming painful experiences as times of doubting God's care and love, these listeners will respond with fear, anger, or, more probably, by closing their ears. If the sermon is to be for these people a place of freely hearing the gospel, the preacher must take their fear into account.

Still others have also had experiences of suffering in their lives but have worked through them to some sort of resolution. Perhaps it is a healthy resolution, perhaps not, but some of the hearers will have discovered ways to remain faithful in the teeth of suffering. The preacher, then, cannot open the sermon presuming that suffering provokes an unanswered theological question for everyone.

Now, obviously we have been thinking this through with a "typical" group of hearers in mind. The more deeply we know the hearers, the sharper our thinking will be. As we have said before, the one who bears witness to the gospel in preaching comes from the community of faith and is a part of that believing community. The more intimately one is involved in the struggles of a particular community of people to be faithful to the mission of Christ, the more fully one can know how to shape sermons so that the gospel can be heard by these people.

It should also be said that we are not really adding at this point a new ingredient, the hearer, to the process of sermon development. As we maintained earlier, the hearers are already present in the interpretation of scripture. The preacher is sent by them to the text on their behalf, and their needs, fears, questions, commitments, theological views, relationships, struggles—all that makes up their lives—actively shape the preacher's interrogation of the text. The preacher has already heard the claim of the text specifically in relation to those who will hear the sermon. So we are not bringing the hearers in only now as an afterthought. Instead, we are trying to discover how the sermon, as it moves step by step from beginning to end, may faithfully express the interaction between text and hearer already present in the exegesis.

Even in our rather general portrait of a "typical" group of hearers, we can see that fleshing out this first step in the example form is quite a complex matter. The preacher knows that the hearers begin this sermon journey at several different places. Some hearers will welcome the change demanded in this first step, others will resist it, and still others see themselves as already having moved past it. Is there a way to develop this step so that all the hearers can make this part of the journey?

Sometimes the answer to that question, frankly, is no. Not every sermon can or should attempt to speak with equal power and pertinence to every hearer. Most of us, as hearers, have had the experience of being deeply addressed by one sermon and not so directly spoken to by the next one, knowing that others in the congregation were having the opposite experience. Part of the ethic of Christian worship is giving up the idea that every sermon, every prayer, every hymn must be focused upon me and my needs. Sometimes hearing the gospel actually means "overhearing" the gospel being spoken directly to others whose circumstances are unlike our own. From the vantage point of the preacher, the encounter with the biblical text often yields a word that speaks more immediately to some in the congregation than to others, and trying to speak to everyone all the time can drive us into bland generalities. If, on the other hand, the preacher always addresses the same group—the strong or the adults or the families or the men or the women or the resourceful or the lonely or those who do not believe—then the fullness of the gospel is not being proclaimed.

NAMING THE RESOURCES

Let us suppose, though, for illustrative purposes, that the preacher of our example sermon believes that this sermon can speak directly to the whole congregation and desires to bring along on the steps of the journey all the hearers we have named. How can this initial step be developed?

At this point, the preacher is perhaps not ready to compose this portion of the sermon but is prepared to name the kinds of materials, the sorts of resources, that will be necessary.

1. This step demands material that will evoke in the hearers' minds their own experiences of loss, suffering, and separation, experiences

that cause crises in their faith. What sort of material can do that? What kind of communication evokes memories? There are several possibilities. The preacher thinks first of all of *narrative* resources. A story can release the spring of memory, and the preacher takes stock of the stories that may be appropriate here.

Perhaps a well-known example from history would be useful, something like the story of poet John Milton becoming blind at age forty-three, including the well-known plea from his poem about this experience, "Doth God exact day-labour, light denied?" Here is a person's experience in which the theological question of providence was explicitly raised, and the recounting of it could well spur the hearers to recall similar events in their own lives.

Upon reflection, however, our preacher decides that this is not the best resource to use. Historical examples such as the one from the life of Milton raise the crucial issue, all right, but they seem too remote for this sermon and this congregation. They may come across more as examples from cultural and literary history than as pieces of real life. The task of this part of the sermon is to evoke the hearers' own experiences, and so the preacher decides that something closer to home is needed.

One experience closer to home, the preacher knows, involves the recent and tragic death by cancer of a young woman who was a strong and devoted leader in the congregation. This event will surely be on the minds of many during this sermon, but the preacher knows, on second thought, that it would be unwise to mention it directly. It is, in a way, too close to home because the unfinished grief about this woman's death would make it impossible for the sermon to be anything but a response to this one incident.

Finally the preacher decides that what is needed is not a narrative at all, not a story about this or that experience, but rather a series of vignettes, each one briefly picturing the sort of human circumstance that could prompt a crisis of faith. These vignettes, drawn from the lives of everyday people, would be punctuated by pauses in the sermon, inviting the hearers to fill in the silences with their own experiences. So the preacher sketches a preliminary list of these vignettes.

> For some, a marriage that began with rice and romance ended with anger and alienation. "What God hath joined together" came apart at the seams, and they wonder where God was in the coming apart.
> For some, a cruel disease is at work in their bodies, stealing strength and hope, and they wonder in the pain about the loving care of God.
> For some, there is an empty place at the table where once one

they loved shared bread and life, and they wonder about a God whose world holds such loss.

For some, there are deep wounds inflicted by parents who cared too little or who gave violence instead of love, and they wonder if God is also this kind of parent.

The list could be longer, and perhaps will be longer in the actual sermon, but the preacher now knows the sort of material to include.

2. We have seen that, in addition to material that will evoke in the hearers' minds their own doubt-provoking experiences, this step also demands material that will reassure those who are fearful that an honest claiming of doubt is a part of growing in faith. The preacher considers simply *saying* this. In other words, the preacher's own authority and conviction could be resources for giving the hearers permission to admit that there are circumstances in life that cause even the most faithful among us to question the care of God.

The preacher decides, though, that the Bible itself is a more effective resource, and the sermon, after presenting the vignettes, could say, "The people in the Bible were themselves no strangers to doubt." This would be followed by scenes from the scripture, and the preacher jots down some biblical stories in which faithful people were provoked to doubt:

Elijah in the cave (1 Kings 19)
Job
Lamenting psalmists (e.g., Psalms 77, 88)
Jeremiah's accusation of God (Jeremiah 20)
The father who cried, "I believe; help my unbelief!" (Mark 9)

When the sermon is actually composed, the preacher will probably not find room for all these examples, but at this point the necessary biblical resources have been identified.

3. But what about those hearers who have experienced doubt-provoking crises in their lives but who have moved, to their own satisfaction, beyond them to some kind of resolution? The preacher knows that subsequent steps in the sermon will explore (and challenge) the often-given religious responses to moments of doubt and then move to the deeper and richer promise found in the text. Since this is coming later in the sermon, the preacher decides that no additional material is needed in this step.

Now, obviously, different preachers in different settings would make different decisions about all of this. What is important to see is the process by which a preacher thinks through each step of the sermon, each portion of the basic form. Each step of the form names a task, and the preacher asks what it will mean for the sermon to perform this task with *these* people. In the light of this, the preacher makes decisions about what kinds of materials are needed: stories, descriptions, definitions, teaching sections, hymns, prose quotations, dialogue, images, practical examples, rhetorical questions, personal confession, persuasive argument, poems, verses of scripture, exegetical information, or whatever.

What is happening here is that we are beginning to understand a sermon as a "system of communication" and the form of a sermon as a description of that system. "System of communication" is an ugly phrase, to be sure, but it is a helpful one nonetheless, since it makes clear that every portion of a sermon works in concert with the others toward a unified effect. Each step of the sermon picks up a piece of the total sermonic task, and we must decide what resources are necessary for each piece of the larger job to get done. This steers us away from general and misguided advice about sermon form (found in some homiletical manuals) based upon arbitrary and mechanical concerns (for example, "every sermon 'point' should have an illustration") or pseudopsychological considerations (for example, "the congregation always needs a 'break' between points").[1] Abstract rules like these miss the mark. All choices about form are ad hoc decisions, since each step of a sermon calls for the preacher and the hearers to perform a labor specific to this sermon and this sermon only.

MORE EXAMPLES

Here are some examples, based on actual sermons, demonstrating how several preachers went about the process of refining and elaborating basic sermon form.

1. William Willimon, in a sermon on the story where Jesus tells the rich man, "You lack one thing; go, sell what you have, and give to the poor" (Mark 10:17–22), wanted to include a step in the sermon form in which the hearers could become critical of all attempts—their own and others'—to tone down this word into something more comfortable, less demanding. The problem was, if Willimon had directly attacked this tendency to reduce the demand of Jesus, some of the hearers may well have considered Willimon, as preacher, to be an uninvited, unwelcomed adversary and retreated to safer ground. So Willimon decided that what was needed here was not direction but indirection. Rather than criticizing the hearers, he instead gave voice to *his own* resistance to the word of Jesus, letting the congregation "overhear" his ironic and amusing attempt to wiggle free of the text's demand. Here is that portion of his sermon:

"Jesus loved him and said, 'Go, sell all you have and give it to the poor!" He lacked "one thing needful," something beyond the bounds of conventional morality and realistic, practical ethics.

Of course, if I had been Jesus that day, that's not what I would have said. I might have asked the well-heeled young man for an endowed fund for student scholarships, a bigger pledge for the church budget, not everything. This I call pastoral care, compassion. Unlike Jesus, if I had looked upon the young man, I would have been sensitive to his personal limitations, his need for some earthly security, his desire for something practical, workable. I've had courses in pastoral counseling. I know that even though the man is well off financially, he is still a poor, struggling beggar—spiritually speaking, psychologically speaking. He, like all the rest of us, is doing the best he can.

And that's good enough for me. So my flock, when it comes to me for counseling or guidance, doesn't expect to be told something "irrational" like, "Go, sell all you have and give it to the poor." It expects to be assured that they are doing the best they can, that whatever they have already decided in their hearts is right, is fine with me.

. . . "What must I do to inherit eternal life?"

"Well," Jesus should have said (if Jesus had the benefit of a seminary education), "What do you think is practical—considering your socioeconomic circumstances? What feels right to you?"

. . . And yet Mark says that Jesus spoke an unpleasant word to the Rich Young Man because he loved him. I fear that I (and most of my church), in the name of "love," have decided to make people's lives a little less miserable rather than a lot more redeemed.[2]

2. Henry Mitchell once developed a sermon on Philippians 4:8, KJV ("Whatsoever things are true, whatsoever things are honest, whatsoever things are just . . . think on these things"). In one of the sections, or steps, of the sermon, he wanted to enable the hearers to understand what he viewed to be the central concept of the text: namely, that Christians, when they follow Paul's counsel and think about true, honest, just, and pure things, are using their faithful memories to participate in the creation of the world in which they live. The task of this step, then, was to teach this concept clearly, and Mitchell decided that what he needed were some teaching examples that would render plain this Pauline idea. He chose two: an analogy from the world of television and an example from the history of

Mitchell's own slave ancestors. The result in the sermon was as follows:

> To put it another way, Paul's word is advising us to make wise choice of our re-runs. Whatever previously aired programs you may see this summer, you may be sure they are the best and not the worst of any series. It occurs to me that my ancestors had just such a selective process at work. They were instinctively seeking things to praise God for, largely as a result of their African religious roots. That made them live it over and over again. One small blessing lived through a hundred times could make a huge difference in the quality of their lives, if not the variety. The joy of a visit from a relative on another plantation, or the health of an infant once hardly expected to live were very big on their always-summer schedule. Without being aware of why it was so, they were driven to build secret "praise houses," and to praise and shout. . . . They survived because of it. It's still good for survival: Think on these things.[3]

3. Barbara K. Lundblad, when she interpreted the story of young Samuel and old Eli in the temple (1 Sam. 3:1–18), saw in this text an expression of the interplay between old and young in the faith, especially in terms of the blessing of wisdom that those who are old can give to those who are young. In order to express this claim, she needed to include in the sermon form two sections: (1) a step in which the hearers were enabled to see Eli, not as a "cardboard" biblical figure but as a real man, encountering the struggles of aging, and (2) a step in which the hearers saw Eli use his maturity to bless the much younger Samuel. She decided that what was needed in these two steps was a weaving together of the biblical information about Eli with very contemporary descriptions of aging, so that the hearers would simultaneously participate in the biblical narrative and experience its present relevance. Here are those two steps in her sermon.

> Then, there is Eli. An old man whose eyesight was so dim he could no longer see. His old age was not filled with the joy of family, for his own sons had done evil in the sight of the Lord, evil which he was either unwilling or unable to stop. Time itself is measured out for him . . . no longer are there plans, plans for career, or college, or raising children. But even more painful, as [Joseph] Sittler says, "the inter-personal filaments snap loose one by one." The people who have been friends, colleagues, partners over a life-time are gone. One by one the filaments snap. No one remains alive who knew me when I was a child

. . . no one who was a classmate in college or a colleague in the earliest days of my work. An older woman told me not long ago of the agony she felt over tossing out bundles of old letters. She simply had to get rid of the boxes in her apartment . . . there was no room. "But," she added, "sometimes I think to myself, if I don't have something in writing, I won't be sure I was really around thirty years ago. Who is left who remembers I was there?"

The filaments had snapped in Eli's life. His ministry, his life work, his faithfulness—all were in question. He had passed on nothing good to his sons. (The congregation he had served for thirty years was now down to a handful of members . . . the books he had written were now sold on the bargain table for $2.98 or given away to the Salvation Army.) There was only past tense, and it was not worth remembering.

But there was one nagging phrase which begs Eli to stay a while longer. It is not even about Eli, but about the young boy Samuel . . . the boy who came to Eli in the night at the sound of a voice in the darkness. "Now Samuel did not know the Lord, and the word of the Lord had not yet been revealed to him." How could the boy ever imagine that it was God's voice calling to him in his sleep?

It was the aged man of dim eyesight who alone was there to speak the word of the Lord . . . to tell young Samuel that there *was* such a thing as the "Word of the Lord." It was Eli, the melancholy priest whose life seemed over who alone was the link between the ancient stories and the squint-eyed, sleepy boy standing beside his bed.

. . . And so it was that Eli spoke from a place deeper than his own broken spirit, deeper than the despair over children gone bad, deeper than his own doubts . . . from that very deep place of the spirit which perhaps only the very old really know. For they have seen life in its fulness and its emptiness; they know life's possibilities but also life's limitations. Such things the sleepy boy could not yet know. "It is the Lord," said Eli, "go, lie down."[4]

4. As he developed a sermon on Revelation 3:14–22, Edmund Steimle decided that a teaching step was needed in the sermon. A key line in this text reads, "Behold, I stand at the door and knock; if any one hears my voice and opens the door, I will come in to him and eat with him, and he with me." Steimle knew from his exegesis of the passage that this image presents to the church an urgent and demanding call to repentance. Steimle also knew that the popular understanding of this verse is as a sentimental picture of a gentle and

inviting Christ. The task of this teaching step in Steimle's sermon, then, was to replace this popular misunderstanding with the text's own intention.

How does one enable people to give up a familiar understanding of a Bible verse in favor of a harsher, more challenging word? Steimle decided that he first needed materials that would bring the popular view to mind but that he also needed some solid evidence from the text itself to counter that view. Here is the step as he ultimately composed it:

> For generations of Christians the image of Christ standing at the door and knocking has been influenced by Holman Hunt's painting of a gentle-faced Christ, lantern in his hand, knocking quietly on the door of an old house; and also by William W. How's familiar hymn:
>
> > O Jesus, Thou art standing
> > Outside the fast closed door,
> > In lowly patience waiting
> > To pass the threshold o'er . . .
> > O Jesus, Thou art pleading
> > In accents meek and low.

Now, whatever comfort that hymn and that painting may have brought to generations of Christians and no matter what lofty sentiments may have been stirred up in us, they both distort almost beyond recognition the actual situation in which that familiar line occurs, "Behold I stand at the door and knock."

To begin with, the face is not gentle. Here is how John of Patmos pictures the face of the Lord Christ as he speaks to the churches in the opening chapters of the Book of Revelation: "Then I turned to see the voice that was speaking to me, and on turning I saw seven golden lampstands, and in the midst of the lampstands one like a son of man, clothed with a long robe and with a golden girdle round his breast; his head and his hair were white as white wool, white as snow; his eyes were like a flame of fire, his feet were like burnished bronze, refined as in a furnace, and his voice was like the sound of many waters . . . from his mouth issued a sharp two-edged sword, and his face was like the sun shining in full strength."

And the voice, like the sound of many waters is speaking hardly in "accents meek and low." It is an impatient voice, and angry voice, addressing the Church at Laodicea: "I know your works: you are neither cold nor hot. Would that you were cold or hot! So, because you are lukewarm, and neither cold nor hot,

I will spew you out of my mouth. For you say, I am rich, I have prospered, and I need nothing; not knowing that you are wretched, pitiable, poor, blind and naked. . . . Those whom I love, I reprove and chasten, so be zealous and repent." Then—precisely then—comes the familiar line, "Behold I stand at the door and knock." It is an urgent last call to a self-satisfied and lukewarm church rather than a privatized picture of a gentle Christ, "in lowly patience waiting to pass the threshold o'er" of our hearts.[5]

5. One of the more difficult tasks of sermons is translating a theological claim into everyday experience. It is one thing to say that the gospel calls us to love, forgive, trust, believe, or whatever; it is quite another thing to help people see what this could look like in their lives. In a sermon on the unusual story of Jesus' cursing of the fig tree (Mark 11:11–25), I was attempting to communicate the claim that I had heard in that text: Living in the kingdom's power means praying for, working for, and expecting fruitfulness in places where the world sees only barrenness and expects nothing. As I developed the basic form of this sermon, I knew that one of the necessary steps would be to enable the hearers to see and to experience what this claim looks like when it is lived out in everyday circumstances. I decided that a story in which a person actually did what the text described was the best resource for this task (for a more complete discussion of the use of stories and exeriences in sermons, see chapter 8). Here is that portion of the sermon:

Sometime ago I found myself in a conversation with a man seated next to me on an airplane, a conversation that took a rather serious turn. He told me that he and his wife were the parents of a son, now in his thirties, who was confined to a nursing-care condition for a number of years because of an injury to his brain. "We had stopped loving him," said my companion. "It's a hard thing to admit, but we had stopped loving him. It's hard to love someone who never responds. We visited him often, but our feeling for him as a son had begun to die. Until one day we happened to visit our son and discovered a visitor, a stranger, in his room. He turned out to be the pastor of a nearby church whose custom it was to visit all the patients in the nursing home. When we arrived we found him talking to our son—*as if* our son could understand. Then he read Scripture to our son—*as if* our son could hear it. Finally he had prayer with our son—*as if* our son could know that he was praying. My first impulse was to say, 'You fool, don't you know about our son?' But then it dawned on me that, of course, he *did* know. He knew all along. He cared for our son *as if* our son were whole, because he saw him through the eyes of faith, and he saw him already healed. That pastor renewed in us the capacity to love our son."

Rejoice! Rejoice that in the power of the kingdom come in Jesus even those broken in disease are never out of season in God's love.[6]

6. Sometimes a sermon step seeks to enable the hearers to feel something as well as to understand something. Evoking feelings usually requires special language: stories, images, songs, poems, or perhaps the language of silence gradually filling with meaning. In a sermon about the meeting of the risen Christ with the two followers on the Emmaus road (Luke 24:13–35), John Vannorsdall described how the followers, unaware that they were speaking to the risen Christ, told the stranger on the road of their dashed hopes. "We had hoped," they said, "that he was the one to redeem Israel." Vannorsdall saw himself and his hearers in the role of the followers, and he wanted the hearers not only to understand the disappointed hopes of the disciples on the Emmaus road but also to feel their own broken visions and crushed hopes. He knew that to do this he would need language that would touch the hearers' imaginations. This is what he composed:

There was a time when we thought that the world could be a better place. We were capable of visions, you see. We could imagine a world of green lawns rather than a street full of junk, a world where neighbors greeted one another rather than pass silent with hidden faces, a world in which the aged were wise and cherished, where bullies were defeated, where games were for fun rather than profit, and dancing was the purest pleasure. We had a vision of a world of clean, white snow, smelling of Spring, carpeted with Autumn's color. There was a time when we thought the world could be a better place.

There was a time when we thought that we could be better persons. We could imagine our families proud of us rather than ashamed. Imagine a crucial time when we would dare to tell the truth and everyone would be amazed and say, "Thank God the truth's been told at last." We could imagine a time when we would be the champion for some kid beaten on the street, or be the lawyer fighting for the innocent and oppressed. We would be the scientist discovering a way to feed the hungry, an engineer making heavy work light. There was a time when we thought we could be better persons.

There was a time when we believed that God had a plan for his people. His plan was to bless marriage with joy and children, to free us of our sins and guilt, fill our lives with peace, to remake the world without war, a world in which the woods were cool on a summer's day and the animals played with one another. There was a time when we believed that God had a plan for his people.

"We had hoped," said the two on the road to Emmaus, "that he was the one to redeem Israel."[7]

OUT OF THE STOCKROOM

In the last chapter, and in all of this one to this point, we have presented the question of sermon form as a creative activity, a thinking through the interaction between the claim of a specific sermon and the listening process of particular hearers. Every sermon event possesses its own set of variables and peculiar circumstances, and therefore we have insisted that every sermon form must be freshly minted and custom made.

Surely, though, there must be some outer edge to the possibilities for sermon forms. The idea of running a never-before-seen, never-before-tried form out onto the test track every Sunday strains our creative energies and boggles the mind. Is there not a limited set of tried-and-true sermon forms that can prove serviceable for most occasions? There may have been severe problems with the notion that *all* sermons should have three points, each with an illustration mounted on it like a bulb inserted into a chandelier, but at least that form worked as a sturdy, time-honored template.

Indeed, many older homiletical manuals provided handy lists of sermon form "types."[8] These lists characteristically included a half dozen or so frequently used patterns of sermon form. The problem with them was that they were presented apart from any discussion of how an apt sermon form emerges through the interplay between the claim of the biblical text and the receptivity of the hearers. In other words, there was no theory, no theological or communicational grounding, for how sermons should be formed; there was only a list of "stockroom" forms. The implication was that preachers were to rummage through the stockroom until they found an attractively shaped form and then fit the sermon into it.

This is not to say that these lists were not of value. In fact, such lists continue to be very worthwhile when we get away from the notion that they are boxes in the stockroom and view them instead as answers to the kind of dynamic questions about sermon form we have been asking. In other words, when we think through, for each and every sermon, all the issues about sermon form, the end result of our thinking will often be not some utterly new and wildly innovative form but, rather, a form that has been employed by many preachers many times before, and quite effectively.

Here, then, are some of these frequently appearing sermon forms,[9] along with some commentary about the kind of sermon each is likely to "fit."

1. If this . . . then this . . . and thus this

In this form, each step of the sermon builds logically on the previous step. The full claim of the sermon comes at the end, as the final link in a chain of smaller claims. This is a fairly heady form, best suited to sermons in which the function is a teaching one.

2. This is true . . . in this way . . . and also in this way . . . and in this other way too

Luccock called this form the "jewel sermon," and Sangster called it the "facet sermon" because the preacher presents the central claim of the sermon and then turns it in the light so that its various facets can be seen. This form is particularly apt for those sermons with claims of some internal complexity or for sermons in which the central claim affects various hearers in different ways.

3. This is the problem . . . this is the response of the gospel . . . these are the implications

Sometimes called a "law-gospel" or "problem-solution" form, this form begins by exploring the human dilemma and announces the claim of the sermon in response to that. It is most effective when the hearers have some shared sense of need or crisis.

4. This is the promise of the gospel . . . here is how we may live out that promise

Rather than beginning with a particular human dilemma, this form starts by announcing the claim of the text and then explores the convictional and ethical demands of that claim. Some call this the "indicative-imperative" form, and it is most appropriate when the function of the sermon contains ethical implications.

5. This is the historical situation in the text . . . these are the meanings for us now

In this form, the circumstances of the text are given (e.g., Amos's word to the socioeconomic situation of Israel in the eighth century B.C.E.) followed by the word of the text for today (e.g., Amos's word to our socioeconomic situation). This may be done in two large steps (then/today) or as a series of interweavings (then/today/then/to-day/then/today). Another variation is to employ a "flashback" (today/then/back to today). This form is best suited to those texts in which the preacher has identified what James Sanders has called a "dynamic analogy" between the text and the contemporary situation. No historical situation is repeated exactly, but a dynamic analogy results when we identify in some ways with characters or circumstances in the text and thus participate in the tensions and resolutions of the text.[10]

6. Not this . . . or this . . . or this . . .
or this . . . but this

This sermon form usually begins with some kind of question or quest, such as, "What could Jesus possibly have meant when he said, 'Blessed are you when people hate you'?" The sermon then proceeds by suggesting possible erroneous or incomplete answers, gradually eliminating them until the full claim of the text can be heard. This form is most effective when the original question is an enigmatic one or when the function of the sermon is to provide new insight on a familiar issue. Variations on this form are *This . . . and this too* and *Either this . . . or this.*

7. Here is a prevailing view . . .
but here is the claim of the gospel

This is sometimes called the "rebuttal" form, but that name unfortunately carries a debating connotation. At its best, this form describes, as fully and as sympathetically as possible, a prevalent cultural attitude toward something and then allows the claim of the gospel to enrich, correct, challenge, replace, or renew that view. It is an apt form when the function of the sermon calls upon the hearers to see something in a new way.

8. This . . . but what about this? . . . well, then this . . .
yes, but what about this? . . . and so on

This form represents a dialogue in a monological format. Each step of the sermon is followed by a questioning or probing of that step, modeled on the style of inquiring conversation. The form is most effective when the claim of the sermon is complex, nuanced, or controversial.

9. Here is a story

The story form of preaching actually represents a cluster of related forms:

A single story. Although it is rare, sometimes the entire sermon is simply the telling of a story, either a retelling of a biblical story or the recounting of a contemporary story. The story itself carries its own insight.

Story/reflection. In this form, a story is told and then reflected upon for insight and guidance.

Part of a story/reflection/rest of the story. Sometimes a preacher will recount the first part of a story and then stop before the story is finished. The tension of the unresolved story is then explored in some manner before the story is finished. A variation on this is to break the story into several narrative/reflection episodes.

Issue/story. This is a version of the "problem-response" form listed above. In this case, a story serves as the response to some issue or question presented in the opening step of the sermon.

10. Here is a letter

In this form, the sermon is composed as a letter, addressed either to the congregation or to someone else. The sermon follows normal epistolary form. This form is especially effective in evoking the sense of personal address and in disclosing the affective dimensions of the gospel.

11. This? . . . or that? . . . both this and that

This form presents a sermon claim that is either paradoxical or two-sided, such as "Jesus was a servant; Jesus is Lord; Jesus is Servant-Lord," or "Disciples are wise as serpents; disciples are innocent as doves; disciples are both wise as serpents and innocent as doves."

This list could be extended, of course, but there is no need to do so. Already variations, combinations, and other possibilities are probably coming to mind. The important thing to remember is that we do not begin with one of these abstract forms and then try to force the sermon to fit it. We begin with the focus and function of the sermon and try to create the right form. These standard patterns are for the preacher like chord patterns for a musician. We study them, and they are there in our repertoire, but the sermonic song itself seeks its own best form.

THE IMPORTANCE OF VARIETY

The diversity of rhetorical forms among biblical texts, combined with the flexibility of the process we have described for creating sermons, will inevitably produce a wide variety of sermon forms. As a matter of practical experience, preachers must guard against gravitating toward a narrow range of sermon patterns. As preachers, we tend to create sermon forms that match our own ways of listening and learning, and therefore we must self-consciously move beyond our own preferred patterns.

Although the reasons for this are not entirely clear, it is widely known that hearers possess many different styles of listening. A sermon that includes many personal references and pastoral experiences will be for one listener a powerful and touching word, while another hearer will find it intellectually thin. A free-flowing, artistic, image-rich sermon will stimulate some hearers to see the faith in new ways, while others will find the same sermon opaque and confusing. A carefully ordered, tightly argued sermon will be received by some as a model of clarity and the occasion for deep insight, while others will find such a form dull and confining.

I once spoke with a minister who was puzzled because some members of his congregation had complained that he was "not preaching the Bible" in his sermons, despite the fact that he spent hours each week on exegesis and richly supplied his sermons with the results of his labor. The problem, as it turned out, was not that his sermons lacked a biblical dimension but that the form of his sermons did not match the listening styles of many of those in his congregation. They were listening for "biblical principles"; he was supplying them with biblical images. They were listening for information from the passage; he was attempting to re-create the experience found in the passage. They were listening for direction; he was supplying indirection. The biblical text was governing his sermons, but not in ways that many of his hearers could listen for it or recognize it.

Preaching was once thought of as an activity much like putting eggs into baskets. The "eggs" were the key ideas, or points, of the sermon; the "baskets" were the minds of the hearers. Preachers did the placing; hearers did the receiving. Thus, preachers were active; hearers were passive. If the preacher worked skillfully and carefully, a fairly substantial number of eggs could be placed, without breakage, into everybody's basket during the course of a sermon. If a preacher wanted an indication of how effective a given sermon was, the hearers could be asked, after the sermon, how many of the main points they remembered. In other words, "How many eggs do you have?"

Studies in human communication have confirmed, however, what insightful preachers knew all along: The hearer is not at all passive in the listening process. The space between pulpit and pew bristles with energy and activity. As the preacher speaks, the hearer races ahead in anticipation of what might be said next, ranges back over what has already been said, debates with the preacher, rearranges the material, adds to the message, wanders away and returns (sometimes!). In short, the hearer is a co-creator of the sermon. Preachers may be passing out eggs, but hearers are making omelets, and a sermon preached to seventy-five people is actually transformed by them into seventy-five more-or-less-related sermons.

Now the wonderful and frustrating truth about the cooperative artistry that goes on between preacher and hearer is that it demands both dissonance and consonance. If there is not at least some measure of dissonance between preacher and hearer, some degree of surprise and even conflict in their interaction, there will not be enough energy to maintain lively communication. Too much consonance produces dull predictability. On the other hand, there must be enough common ground for the task to be mutual, for too wide a variance between preaching and listening styles results in a breakdown in communication. This is what happened to the minister just mentioned whose congregation could not hear the biblical influence in his preaching. Dissonance overwhelmed consonance.

What impact does all this have on the task of forming sermons? In light of the fact that any given group of hearers, no matter how compatible and homogeneous they may seem, can be expected to contain a complex and diverse set of listening styles, we are tempted to factor out the whole issue as hopelessly confusing, design our sermons the best we know how, and let the hearers fend for themselves. If they cannot hear our style, let them go down the street to another church and find a match.

The realities of the situation, however, do not warrant such an overreaction. Listeners *do* have diverse listening styles, and these *are* complex and not-fully-understood processes, but these styles are to be seen more as band spreads than as single frequencies. In other words, while it is true that certain hearers may prefer to listen to sermons that are shaped in a particular way, may say they get more out of a certain style of preaching, and may in fact find such sermons clearer and more compelling precisely because they are designed in a way that more or less matches their listening style, it does not follow that this is the only style of sermon they can "hear." If they are exposed to a sermon in an alien form, they may resist it somewhat, not like it as much, or even reformulate it so that it fits more comfortably into their listening equation, but the fact of the matter is that they *can* hear it if it is not completely outside their range. Not only that, but the chances are good that they will begin to develop a deeper capacity for listening to sermons shaped that way. The preacher who speaks week in, week out, to a congregation is learning how to preach effectively to them, but they are learning also, discovering how to listen to this preacher. Over time, and under the surface, preacher and listeners are gradually adjusting to achieve the best communication fit.

Even so, differences will remain. There will always be in any given congregation those who prefer straightforward, one-two-three sermons and those who do not. There will be those who need the sermon to remain open-ended and those who need full closure. When we recognize these differences among people, we begin to see that forming sermons is an act of pastoral care. It is important for those preachers who tend to design the sermon journey in a free-flowing, loosely connected way, with many side trips and scenic excursions into symbolic imagery, to depart from that form on occasion and to create a more tightly structured form for the sake of those in the congregation who travel better that way. Likewise, the preacher who tends toward the firmly guided sermon journey, with conceptual mileposts clearly marked, needs on occasion to supplement that sort of form with other, more fluid designs.

The gospel comes to us in a wide variety of forms, and the preacher who faithfully bears witness to the gospel will allow the fullness of the gospel to summon forth a rich diversity of sermon forms, as well.

7

Beginnings, Connections, and Endings

Sometimes when I was starting a new story and I could not get it going, I would sit in front of the fire and squeeze the peel of the little oranges into the edge of the flame and watch the sputter of blue that they made. I would stand and look out over the roofs of Paris and think, "Do not worry. You have always written before and you will write now. All you have to do is write one true sentence. Write the truest sentence that you know." So finally I would write one true sentence, and then go from there.

—Ernest Hemingway,
A Moveable Feast

A great deal of ink has been spilled in the pages of homiletical literature over the matter of how to begin a sermon. This degree of attention paid to sermon beginnings, or "introductions," as they are traditionally called, is somewhat curious, since much of what needs to be said about them applies equally to every other part of a sermon. A sermon introduction has a job to do, but so does every other part. An introduction requires certain kinds of materials to get its job accomplished, but, then again, the same is true of every other sermon step. From one perspective, a sermon introduction is not at all a special case. A sermon's journey involves several steps, and the introduction simply happens to be the first one.

THE SERMON INTRODUCTION

From another perspective, however, sermon introductions merit special attention, since it is widely held by homileticians that the opening move in a sermon's development is an extremely important one. Every step of the sermon embodies a task, true, but the task of the introduction is unique and crucial to the outcome of the sermon. A sermon must begin well, it is said, and the introduction must get

133

its special job done in good order, or the whole sermon will be impoverished.

The problem is that the same homileticians who argue the urgency of the introduction have never been able to agree about *what* precisely is the distinctive task of an introduction. Almost everybody seems to be convinced that sermon introductions do something extraordinarily important, but what, exactly, do they do? When we read about sermon beginnings in the homiletical manuals, two "commonsense" notions about the task of introductions surface repeatedly, and since they are so frequently cited they deserve critical examination.

1. Often the notion is advanced that sermon introductions ought to be attention-getting. Introductions, in other words, have the task of pricking the ears of the hearers. They serve the same purpose as a drumroll or a trumpet fanfare; they provoke curious interest in what may come next. "We are simply trying," Gerald Kennedy says of the introduction, "to get our people to want to hear what we have to say."[1] George Sweazey is even more direct and graphic:

> The congregation may be settling down after the sermon hymn, staring around the room. If a Scripture reading just before the sermon was not interesting, minds may have wandered. People may expect to enjoy the sound of the minister's voice as mood music for daydreaming. The audience is hanging in the balance, poised to be lost. The minister's opening words have to mean, "Wait a minute! Don't touch that dial; this is something you want to hear!"[2]

This notion that a sermon introduction is to arouse the listener's interest seems so obvious that we almost overlook the fact that it is based upon the rather pessimistic assumption that hearers, at the outset of a sermon, are uninterested or distracted and need to be whistled to attention. The truth, though, is that most hearers, unless they have been knocked into semiconsciousness by an unbearably tedious liturgy, come to the moment of the sermon with an air of expectancy and a genuine readiness to listen. One of the graces of preaching is that hearers, though they have perhaps often been disappointed by the sermons they have heard, still approach each new sermon prepared to believe that this day they will hear an urgent and important word. Randall Nichols is surely correct when he observes:

> Time after time, we have all heard that the purpose of an introduction is to "get people's attention." Now really, when was the last time anyone saw a preacher step into the pulpit at sermon time and *not* have everyone's attention? The rather more painful fact is that we already have their attention and their willingness as a free gift—for a while.

What we have is *their offer* to participate in the preaching that is about to happen.... There will hardly ever be a time when the preacher does not start with the people's attention; there may be many times indeed when it is completely gone five minutes later.[3]

It is deceptive, then, to think that the purpose of a sermon introduction is to snap the listeners to attention. The listeners, for the most part, freely choose to give their attention, and this gift, eagerly granted, must not be squandered by the preacher. Sermon introductions do not grab the hearers' attention; we already have that. It would be more accurate to say that sermon introductions must not lose the listeners' attention, but that wisdom applies to every other part of the sermon as well.

2. Others have claimed that the task of the sermon introduction is to do what its name implies: to *introduce* the whole sermon, to be a preview of coming attractions. This means both providing a taste of what the whole sermon will say and disclosing something of the plan the sermon will follow in saying it. As Ilion T. Jones described it:

> The introduction to a sermon may be compared to the chart which the ranger draws on the blackboard before he takes a group of tourists over a trail through a national park. This chart is not merely to help them decide whether or not they wish to take the trip, but to give a prospectus of what is ahead.[4]

Thinking about this from the vantage point of the hearer, the introduction becomes an announcement of the agenda that the sermon will follow and that the listener can expect. Since the hearers are told what the whole sermon will be about and how, in broad terms, the sermon will develop, they can anticipate what will be required of them as listeners and set the dials on their receptivity accordingly.

In this light, Randall Nichols has proposed replacing the customary term "introduction" with a concept borrowed from the world of psychotherapy: "contract." He states:

> An introduction's purpose is to establish between preacher and hearers a "contract for communication," a shared agreement that in the message to follow we will be talking about certain things in certain ways, trying to get to certain points of understanding or action and each contributing this or that to the unfolding process. The idea of a "contract" is familiar enough in pastoral care and counseling, where it refers to the agreement to work toward certain goals and in certain ways between care giver and care receiver. It operates the same way in preaching; both are incidents of the same communication phenomenon.[5]

In this view the preacher leans across the pulpit during the introduction and says, in effect, "Today I plan to talk about thus and so in such and such a way. Would you like to listen?" This appears to be a clear advance over the idea that introductions are supposed to grab people's attention because it presents a more positive image of the listeners. Instead of picturing them as distracted and lethargic, we now see them as people who are attentive, prudent, perhaps cautious, and who deserve to be told ahead of time what is in store for them. They can then choose either to listen actively and intelligently or to let their minds roam to other thoughts.

But do hearers really need—or want—to be told in advance what is to follow in a sermon? Or, to put it another way, does a sermon get heard better when the listeners know ahead of time what to expect? David Buttrick does not think so, and he is sharply critical of the "tell them what you're going to do" approach to sermon introductions on the grounds that such an approach destroys the spirit of discovery and the suspense so vital to rich human communication.

> Introductions should *not* give away the structure of a sermon ahead of time in a pedantic fashion. If playbills in the theater were to print a synopsis of plot which we could read before the curtain rises, suspense would be destroyed; we would know what is going to happen ahead of time. Human thought is intriguing precisely because human beings think and speak differently, so that we are continually surprised by turns of mind or sudden shifts in imagination. Destruction of suspense (the possibility of the unexpected) is positively unkind.[6]

Proponents of the preview concept of sermon introductions would no doubt freely admit that such a strategy is destructive to suspense but would claim this as a virtue rather than a failing. Suspense may be crucial to Broadway plays and detective novels, they would say, but sermons, after all, aim at clarity and forthrightness, not intrigue and suspense.

As a matter of fact, though, good sermons, as we have noted in our discussion of form, vary widely right on this point. Some good sermons pull back the veil on their claims early and then spend the remainder of their time elaborating upon those claims, while other equally effective sermons develop slowly and gradually toward the moment when their claims can be disclosed as the result of a process of discovery. No Christian sermon should be coy, artificially building suspense by withholding required information or playing with the hearers by keeping them guessing unnecessarily. Every sermon, though, requires decisions about timing: When should certain things be said so that they can best be heard?

The problem, then, with the preview notion of sermon introductions is that it imposes on all sermons a decision about timing that is suitable for some sermons but not for others. Suppose I want to tell you about an argument I had with a colleague, a dispute that was angry and bitter but that led finally to reconciliation and a deepened friendship. How do I tell you about it? I can imagine some circumstances in which I might begin this way: "I want to tell you about a disagreement that developed between me and Matthew. It was tough for a while, but now that it's over I count Matthew as one of my closest friends. What happened was . . ." I can also imagine, in other circumstances, simply beginning, "Three months ago I got a telephone call from Matthew, and he seemed upset." In the first instance, I am giving you a thumbnail sketch of the whole incident and then filling in the details. You know in advance how the incident will turn out; you listen to the rest of the story not in order to discover *what* happened but *how* it happened. In the second instance, you know neither what happened nor even what my story is about. You listen, though, confident—for the moment, anyway—that this tale is about *something* and that whatever it is will emerge in due course.

In the first instance I have deliberately chosen not to be suspenseful, to lay my cards on the table at the beginning. I have decided to do this because I have some goal in mind in telling you this incident that does not need, or would be harmed by, suspense. Perhaps you too are involved in a dispute, and I wish to give you an encouraging example of a similar tangle that developed for the best. So I inform you right at the outset, "This one turned out all right." In the second instance, however, I have another kind of aim in mind. Perhaps I want your empathy and desire that you feel the pain of Matthew's anger as I did. I want the dispute to surprise and disturb you in the same way that it surprised and disturbed me. So I let it unfold, preserving the shock and drama of the narrative. I do this not to be deceptive or coy but rather because suspense is essential to the emotional effect of the incident.

The point here is that I have described two quite different ways to introduce the same narrative, and your experience of hearing my story will vary accordingly, but both beginnings are effective in their own ways. Choosing which of the two is the "better" way to get my story going involves assessments about the circumstances of our conversation and the use I hope to make of the incident. The same is true of sermon introductions. Sometimes it is better to tip the sermon's hand at the beginning; sometimes it is better to wait and let the shape of the sermon's claim emerge as the sermon unfolds. It will not do, then, to think of the purpose of a sermon introduction as always previewing the form and content of the sermon to follow.

So sermon introductions do not have the responsibility of arousing the hearers' interest, and they are not necessarily charged with the task of disclosing in advance the agenda of the sermon. What, then, *are* the special responsibilities of the introduction? We can identify four.[7]

1. A sermon introduction should make, implicitly or explicitly, a promise to the hearers. When people listen to another person speaking, they are taking in what is being said, but they are also running ahead of the speaker, anticipating where the speaker's words are leading. The phone rings, and we answer it. "This is Amanda Smith calling," says the voice on the line, and already our minds are racing off on a search process, guessing who Amanda Smith is and what she may say next. "I'm with the Civic Improvement Council, and we are conducting our annual spring fundraising campaign," she continues, and we are way ahead of her. In her next sentence—we just know it—she will ask us for a contribution.

We listen faster than people speak, and our minds are constantly scampering ahead of the speaker, positioning ourselves in that spot where we have reason to believe the conversation is going. Indeed, when impatient listeners get paired up with sluggish speakers, the listeners, continually guessing where the speakers' words are heading and often growing weary of waiting on them, may even be tempted to finish the speakers' sentences for them.

When we begin a sermon, the listeners are also running ahead, anticipating where this sermon may lead. Whether we know it or not—and even whether we like it or not—the listeners are using the opening statements of the sermon to form a guess about what the rest of the sermon holds in store. The hearers, then, are not only listening *to* the sermon; they are also listening *for* the sermon they have been led to expect.

So, our first rule for sermon introductions is more a description of what actually happens than it is a law to be obeyed. Whether they want to do so or not, preachers are giving hints and are therefore making promises to their congregations in the opening sentences of their sermons about where the remainder of the sermon will be heading. The fact that this happens in the expectations of hearers regardless of our intent does not mean, however, that the preacher has no control over what promises are made and what expectations get formed.

As we discussed, some homileticians are persuaded that preachers best exercise their responsibility here by eliminating any mystery surrounding this moment and setting forth a synopsis of the rest of the sermon. As we have argued, though, that overstates the case. Full disclosure is not essential, nor is it always desirable. What listeners need at the beginning of a sermon is not necessarily a thumbnail prospectus of the whole sermon but rather an *orientation*, a reliable direction for listening. In some sermons, this orientation may be quite full and complete; in other sermons it may be only a hint of what is to come. Listeners need to know only that they are traveling on the right path, not necessarily the contours of the path itself. That is why we have chosen the word "promise" as a descriptive term for the introduction. To make a promise is to point toward a certain kind of future without necessarily specifying precisely how that promise will be fulfilled.

So, in simple terms, a preacher should begin a sermon in such a way that the hearers can accurately anticipate *something* of what the whole sermon will be about. Depending on the particular sermon and its circumstances, this promising can range from a subtle but reliable hint to a rather full disclosure of the sermon plan.

How does the preacher decide what promise to make in the introduction? Actually, that decision has already been made when the preacher formulates what we have called the focus and function statements. These statements articulate what the whole sermon will say and do, and the task of the introduction is to point toward those aims.

In order to see, in practical terms, how introductions make promises, let us examine a few sample sermon beginnings. We can start with an example in which the promise made by the preacher is quite obvious. This introduction comes from a sermon based on selected verses from Galatians 5 and 6:

> When I was invited to preach in this series on the overall theme of "Freedom, as expounded in Paul's letter to the Galatians," it was suggested that I emphasize the theme of freedom and political responsibility. While I am very much aware that freedom for the Christian has to do with such things as freedom of the individual conscience, freedom from internal fears, freedom from guilt, and other personal matters, these are not the subject matter this morning. All freedoms, as Christians conceive of them, are interrelated, but from time to time we hold certain kinds of freedom up for more detailed scrutiny, and that is what we are doing this morning with freedom and political responsibility.
>
> Question: Can one draw insights about political freedom out of Paul's letter to the Galatians—without cheating? Answer: It's not easy. I wasn't sure at first that it could be done. Politics is not the stoutest arrow in Paul's quiver, and he says things elsewhere, notably in Romans 13, that are often cited by Christians as reasons to side with the *status quo*. But as I have worked with this letter, it has seemed clearer and clearer to me that,

while Paul is obviously not writing with our own political situation in mind, he says some things that are applicable to it.[8]

This is a fairly full and straightforward introduction. What does this preacher promise? Anyone hearing this beginning can reasonably expect the rest of the sermon to explore the implications of the theological concept of freedom in Galatians, not in the usual sense of individual concerns but in relation to political circumstances. Indeed, the preacher makes this promise quite explicitly, and if the rest of the sermon did not do this (it does, as a matter of fact), the hearers will have been misled.

Now let us turn to an introduction in which the promise is less explicit. This introduction comes from a sermon based on the story of the healing of the blind man named Bartimaeus (Mark 10:46–52):

> Please ask no up-to-date questions of the great account of the deliverance of Bartimaeus from his blindness, which is not an up-to-date account. Do not say, "Was it a disease of the eye? Did Jesus do the first corneal transplant? Was Bartimaeus psychosomatically blind, perchance, his physical blindness caused by emotional illness?" These are smart questions, all right, but the wrong questions, and questions the Mark account provides no answers for. Instead, try to stand down nineteen centuries to another world view held by another people in another land. Listen to the story the way the story was told.[9]

In this case, the preacher does not tell us how the sermon will unfold. Indeed, we are not yet even sure about the theme of the sermon. We are told more about what the sermon will *not* do (answer our modern questions about Bartimaeus's blindness) than we are about what it *will* do. Nonetheless, this preacher has made an implicit promise: In this sermon, inappropriate modern questions will be ignored and the Bartimaeus story will be explored for insight on its own cultural and historical ground. The listeners do not have an inkling about what these insights may be, but they have every reason to believe they will hear something new and unexpected from the story in the remainder of the sermon. They will have their previous understandings of this story challenged by this new angle of vision.

Here is yet another example introduction, this time from a sermon on prayer:

> Why do we pray? Why is it we say into this vast space or cry out into the darkness that which is deepest upon our hearts? Why did David fast and weep as his son lay dying? Why did Jesus go to Gethsemane? Why do any of us bow our heads or raise our hands or fall to our knees and call upon such silence as surrounds us in hopes of hearing a word for us? The reasons

are both too many to fit into the space of a Sunday morning sermon and at the same time too inaudible to find their way into words. Why do we pray?[10]

What is the promise contained in this introduction? The preacher is making a qualified promise to answer the question "Why do we pray?" I say "qualified" because the rhetorical question that closes the introduction ("Why do we pray?") is prefaced by the disclaimers that the reasons are both "too many" for a single sermon and "too inaudible" to be expressed in words. The hearers, then, have every reason to expect the question to be addressed, but they are not promised more than the sermon can deliver since they are notified that the answers will be partial and open-ended.

This understanding of the promise-making dimension of sermon beginnings exposes one of the typical flaws of many introductions. Often preachers, usually in well-intentioned attempts to begin sermons in an exciting fashion, generate sparkling, ear-catching, arresting, even glitzy, introductions. Such introductions undoubtedly intrigue the hearers, but they also make promises to the hearers that go unfulfilled, and, as John Killinger maintains, they are "like the story of the boy who cried 'Wolf! Wolf!' when there was no wolf. The preacher says, 'Listen! Listen! You are going to hear a great sermon.' But after a few deceptive beginnings, when there was nothing of substance to follow, the crowd learns not to pay any attention."[11]

2. A sermon introduction should make a promise that the hearers are likely to want kept. Since sermon introductions are heard by listeners as promises about what is to come in the sermon, it is important for the promise to be one that the hearers find valuable. We do not need to arouse the hearers' interest at the beginning of a sermon, but we do need to maintain it by promising a sermon that bears meaning for their lives. Consider the following introduction for a sermon on John 20:11–18, the story of the encounter between Mary Magdalene and the risen Christ on Easter morning:

> The story of the meeting between Mary Magdalene and the risen Christ on that first Easter is a very strange one indeed. Mary is weeping, not only because her Lord is dead, but also because she has found his tomb to be empty. Turning toward one whom she assumed was the gardener, she said through her tears, "Sir, if you have carried him away, tell me where you have laid him, and I will take him away."
>
> His reply was but a single word: "Mary." In the hearing of her name, she moved from sadness to amazement, from the assumption that she was speaking to a caretaker to the awareness that she was in the presence of her living Lord.

But then, just as her tears were giving way to an embrace, Jesus said a disturbing and curious word. As Mary reached out to Jesus, crying, "Teacher!" Jesus drew back from her. "Do not hold me," he said, "for I have not yet ascended to the Father. . . ."

"Do not hold me." What an odd statement from the risen Christ. What could he possibly have meant? Throughout the centuries students of the scripture have been puzzled by these words and have offered many suggestions about their meaning. Are any of these suggestions correct? What *did* Jesus mean?

This preacher, through the introduction, is promising a sermon that will explore the history of interpretation of John 20 in quest of an accurate rendering of Jesus' statement, "Do not hold me." Is this a promise that the hearers are likely to want to see kept? That depends, of course, on who happens to be listening to this particular sermon. Some congregations, no doubt, would be eager to sift through Johannine exegesis in search of the best interpretation of Jesus' words, but most hearers probably would not find this prospect very appealing. They may feel they *ought* to be intrigued by this quest. After all, these *are* Jesus' words, and we should want to know what they meant. What nags at them, though, and what is unheeded in this introduction, is the question, "Suppose we do find out exactly what Jesus meant? So what?"

Presumably this preacher believes that determining what Jesus meant potentially makes some kind of difference to people today. If so, at least some hint about this should be a part of the promise of the introduction. Here is another preacher's introduction to a sermon on the same biblical text:

As I was mulling over this sermon on the meeting between Mary Magdalene and the risen Lord outside the empty tomb, I happened to be flying from Chicago to New York on a fantastically brilliant, clear night. Even at 33,000 feet, the thousands of sparkling lights on the ground below seemed so close you could almost sense the people living in and around them: people watching TV in the early evening, friends visiting, children doing homework, people at their basement workshops, cars darting here and there. And I thought suddenly, how utterly absurd to imagine that any of them could care one bit about the scene outside an empty tomb, or about what Mary said to Jesus, or what Jesus said in reply, as compared with their interest in their favorite television program, the rising cost of food in the supermarket, the latest bit of town gossip, or the fortunes of the local high school basketball team.

And yet virtually all of them would be concerned about the

tension between the old and the new, the good old days and the perplexing present, the tension between old life-styles and new ones, between old moral standards and new ones, between a fairly stable and simple past and an almost terrifying present with its rapidly changing customs, morals, standards.

And most of them would want to cling to the old and resist the everchanging new. When radical change comes along and hits us almost every day, it's understandable that we seek reassurance and stability by clinging to the past. And that does bring us directly to the story of Mary Magdalene and Jesus outside a tomb on Easter morning.[12]

The sermon that follows this beginning also explores the meaning of Jesus' enigmatic statement "Do not hold me," but notice that the introduction promises something other than an abstract examination of interpretive options for the meaning of that phrase. This introduction promises that the sermon will wrestle with the biblical text in order to throw some light on an issue of direct importance to the hearers: namely, the tension we all experience between the old and the new. This is a promise that most hearers will desire to see kept.

Now there is an obvious objection to this idea that sermon introductions ought to make promises that hearers want to see kept. Does this not lead to a comfortable, demand-free, tell-them-only-what-they-want-to-hear approach to the gospel? What about those occasions when the sermon, if it is faithful to the biblical text, must bring a hard word, a painful word, a demanding word? What about those aspects of the gospel people *need* to hear but do not necessarily *want* to hear?

We can explore this problem by thinking about ourselves and our own listening tendencies. It is surely true that all of us prefer to hear things that bring us pleasure over things that cause us discomfort. We prefer praise to criticism, encouragement over demand, endorsement rather than judgment. If this is *all* that we truly want, the advice to make promises in sermon introductions that people want to see kept is bad advice, since it simply panders to the self-serving preferences in human listening.

As a matter of fact, though, our wanting is more complex than this. A part of ourselves wants to hear only comfort, but another part of us wants to hear the truth whatever the cost. The first part struggles against the second, sometimes winning the battle but never entirely eradicating the hunger for the truth. If someone comes to us and says, "I have some concerns about you that I would like to discuss," we wince, anticipating a critical word. At one level we do not want to hear what is coming next, but at another level we do want to hear. If we do not trust this other person, or if we believe this word will damage us beyond repair, we close our ears. But if we do trust the other, and if we have reason to believe that this critical word, though painful, will finally prove to be beneficial, we brace ourselves and listen.

When we place this reality about human listening into the context of the Christian community, it becomes deeper and richer. The story of the church is one of closed ears and resistance, to be sure, but it is also a story of hearing and repentance. It is unrealistic to suppose that congregations (or preachers) are always ready to hear the demanding side of the gospel, but it is cynical to assume that people want to hear in sermons only those things which reinforce their ease and buttress the status quo. Congregations do not hear sermons in the abstract, but rather in the midst of the larger experience of their faith. We confess our faith in terms of a story that values God's judgment as a part of God's love; without being naïve about the obstacles involved, we can nonetheless affirm that congregations *want* to hear sermons that promise challenge and demand.

So when we say that sermon introductions should make promises that the hearers want to see kept, we are not making a distinction between "pleasant" sermons and demanding ones but rather a distinction between relevant sermons and irrelevant ones. Some sermon introductions promise only that the rest of the sermon will move chess pieces around on the board of some self-enclosed religious language game. Something deep inside the hearers cries out, "So what?" and the listening process halts. Other introductions, however, say, implicitly or explicitly, that if we listen to this sermon, it will intersect some crucial issue in our life together. It may bring joy or it may bring judgment; it may call us to express our love or to confess our sin; it may reinforce our beliefs or undermine our illusions; but it will make a difference in our real lives.

There is also another lesson to be learned here. Given the choice, people are simply unwilling—perhaps even unable—to hear a thoroughly destructive message. The demands of the gospel are not given to destroy but to give life. The preacher who opens a sermon by swinging a scythe of punishment will only find that the hearers learn quickly how to step out of the way. A church member reported that her preacher began a sermon by saying, "I'm going to have to step on some toes this morning." Note the arrogance of that beginning: Not the gospel, not the claim of the biblical text, but *I* am going to step on some toes. The response of this church member was, "He says something like that in almost every sermon, and what he doesn't know is that our toes are hardened by now." The point is that hearers pick up immediately whether the preacher, and the sermon, intend to do good or ill. Again, the distinction we are making about sermon introductions is not between a beginning that promises an "easy" word versus a "hard" one but between the promise of a destructive word versus the promise of a redemptive one.

3. A sermon introduction should make a promise at the same communicational level as the rest of the sermon. The promises we make in sermon introductions carry with them certain tonal qualities. If the sermon begins by raising some issue in thoughtful and precise language, the hearers have every reason to expect that the rest of the sermon will also be thoughtful and precise. If the introduction arouses an emotional response, the rest of the sermon must not suddenly switch to a highly cognitive treatment of the issue.

Consider the following introduction for a sermon on Mark 5:21–43:

> In the middle of today's Gospel there is an uncommonly moving scene (Mark 5:25–34). A woman whose life has been bleeding away for twelve years pushes through a tremendous crowd, comes up behind Jesus, touches his garment. Instantly the bleeding ceases; she feels in her body that she has been healed. Jesus is aware that power has gone forth from him; he quickly asks: "Who touched my garments?" The disciples are amazed, almost amused: "You see the crowd pressing around you, and yet you say, 'Who touched me?' " But he keeps looking around, keeps looking until the woman comes in fear and trembling and tells him the whole truth. And Jesus explains to her what has happened: "Daughter, your faith has made you well; go in peace. . . ."
>
> "Who touched me?" Three years ago, for the first time, that question laid hold of me, made me shiver. I cannot get it out of my mind. Increasingly it has told me something: something about Jesus, something about myself, something about Christian living. A word about each.[13]

What is the promise in this introduction? From one perspective we can see that this preacher has promised to open up Jesus' question "Who touched me?" in three ways: what it says about Jesus, what it says about a person, and what it says about Christian living. When we consider the tone of this introduction, however, it becomes clear that there is more to the promise than this. Note the emotion-laden language: "uncommonly moving," "bleeding away," "feels in her body," "fear and trembling," "laid hold of me," "made me shiver," and so on. Language like this signals to the hearers that this introduction is proceeding at the affective level as well as the cognitive level, and the implied promise is that the sermon will do the same. In short, some sermons promise an intellectual and analytical thinking through of some issue, but not this one. This sermon aims to let

Jesus' question "Who touched me?" "lay hold" of the hearers too, perhaps even make the hearers "shiver."

The introduction to the sermon, then, should match the communicational level of the rest of the sermon. As David Buttrick claims, "Introductions . . . orient a congregation's hermeneutical understanding. After an introduction, people should be ready to hear a sermon, and to hear in a certain *way*."[14]

4. A sermon introduction should anticipate the whole sermon, but it should also connect directly to the next step of the sermon. "A good introduction," claims John Killinger, "is conductive. It leads people into the sermon."[15] In the larger sense, this means that introductions lead people into the *whole* sermon. A sermon beginning, as we have seen, makes a promise, and it is the task of the rest of the sermon to fulfill that promise. In addition to leading the hearers into the whole sermon, though, there is a smaller sense in which the introduction simply leads people into the next part of the sermon. When the introduction is done, the hearers should have an idea about where the total sermon is going, and they should also be ready to take the next step.

David Buttrick imagines a sermon on 1 Corinthians 11:17–32, a text that discusses the meaning of the Lord's Supper in the context of a bitter dispute among the Corinthian Christians. The whole sermon is aimed at dealing with the issue of peace and conflict in the church, so the introduction should anticipate that. In the second part of this sermon, though, the part directly after the introduction, the preacher intends to discuss the Lord's Supper in particular. The introduction should also anticipate that. Buttrick composed three possible introductions:[16]

> The little church in Corinth was such a problem. As with many churches today, it was sadly divided. Factions! There were rich and poor, slave and free, bluenose and libertine—all bunched together in a bundle of conflict. Corinth was the kind of church ministers avoid, unless they've taken courses in "conflict management." For every faction got together, chose leaders, and snarled at every other faction. Corinth was a church divided.

This introduction gets rather nicely at the general issue of the whole sermon: conflict in the church. It does not, however, prepare the hearer for the next step: a discussion of the Lord's Supper. "As the introduction stands," Buttrick observes, "a sudden . . . shift to the Lord's Supper will seem an abrupt non-sequitur." So Buttrick tries another beginning:

The Lord's Supper is a sacred moment for most congregations. We gather at the Lord's table with solemnity. "This is my body," the minister announces, and we break bread together. For centuries, the table has been set as Christians gather to share one cup and receive the bread of life. So, the Lord's Supper is special, a special sacred moment in the life of the congregation.

This introduction has a problem opposite to the first try. It anticipates the next step of the sermon, but there is no hint here of the concern of the whole sermon. This introduction promises *only* a discussion of the Lord's Supper. "As a result," claims Buttrick, "when the sermon does turn toward a discussion of conflict and unity, the introduction will seem trivial or even misleading." Buttrick then formulates a third introduction:

Some years ago, there was a movie about a family reunion. The family was a contentious bunch. They scrapped and split and never got along. Yet, every year, they scheduled a party, a family reunion. At a long table, they'd all sit down together. But, you couldn't help noticing the sidelong glances, the cold shoulders, the obvious slurs. Perhaps that's the way it was in Corinth. Though they gathered at one table and shared one cup together, they were at odds. Corinth was a divided church.

This introduction manages both to anticipate the theme of the rest of the sermon, conflict in the church, and to lead the hearers fluidly into the next step of the sermon, a discussion of the Lord's Supper. It is, therefore, a better sermon beginning than the first two examples because it introduces both the sermon as a whole and the very next segment of the sermon.

MAKING CONNECTIONS

Many names are used to describe the component parts of a sermon: points, moves, steps (our term), episodes, units, and so on. Regardless of the label applied to these parts, the underlying idea is that a sermon consists of a series of segments arranged in a logical sequence. We might even picture a sermon as a long corridor with a set of doors leading to separate rooms, much like a school hallway. The "rooms" are the points, steps, chunks, or whatever we choose to call them, and the "corridor" is the logical thread that holds them together and provides movement from one to the next. We start down the hallway and enter the first room, where perhaps a story is told, a history lesson is given, an image is developed, or a concept is explained. Then we reenter the corridor to move to the next room, where something else is said, seen, learned, and experienced.

We need now to think through what happens "out in the hallway," to consider the material that appears between the major segments of the sermon. Traditionally these small pieces of the sermon have been called "transitions," since they mark the points of transfer from one section to the next. Many preachers mistakenly do not consider them to be very important, and it is common for "transitions" to be dull and mechanical insertions into the sermon flow ("in the second place," "the next thing I want to say," "in conclusion").

When we view this transitional material from a communicational point of view, however, it becomes clear that these "connectors" (as we will call them) between the segments of the sermon are absolutely vital to the sermon's clarity and movement. Although they are usually brief, connectors accomplish three crucial communication tasks:

1. Connectors provide closure for the preceding segment of the sermon, thus reassuring the hearers that they are on the right track. Each step of the sermon contributes something to the sermon's overall development, and if a hearer is to move successfully to the end of the sermon, the listening task of each step must be accomplished effectively. A connector, first of all, concludes a sermon step, often by naming whatever it is that is most important about that step.

Here, for example, is a typical connector:

> The early church, then, lived its life on tiptoe, expecting that the kingdom would come any minute, ringing down the curtain on history and sweeping all of creation up into the victorious hand of God. No wonder Paul could say, "Rejoice . . . the Lord is at hand!" But, for us today the time has grown long, and we have become weary scanning the horizon, searching for the coming triumph of God.

This connector obviously follows a portion of the sermon in which the expectations of the early church regarding the imminent end of time were explored. The first thing this connector does, then, is to repeat the essence of that section: "The early church, then, lived its life on tiptoe, expecting that the kingdom would come any minute."

What does this do for the hearers? For those who have been following this section of the sermon well, it provides reassurance that they have, indeed, gotten the message. It is like the experience of following a set of handwritten directions to a friend's party. "Go six miles down Bogan Road," they say, "and take the third left after the bridge. When you make this turn, you will see a blue house on the hill." So we travel six miles down Bogan Road, we count the streets past the bridge, and we make the left turn at the third one. We *think* we are going correctly, but when we see the blue house, we *know* that we are on the right road. Just so, when we hear, in a sermon connector, a reinforcement of what we think we have just heard, we *know* we have listened well.

For those hearers who have become confused, however, or whose minds have wandered, the connector provides an opportunity for them to reenter the sermon flow, to get back on track.

2. Connectors indicate how the upcoming section of the sermon is logically related to the previous section. Look again at our example connector, especially at the phrase, "But for us today." That little word "but" signals to the hearers that the next section of the sermon will be a logical contrast to the section before. The hearers thus anticipate a tension being established between these two sections of the sermon.

Many types of logical connections may exist between sermon segments.[17] Some of the more common ones are:

The "and" connection. This type of connector joins sections that build cumulatively. It says, in effect, "this is true, and this is also true." Such terms as "in addition," "moreover," "again," "not only ... but also," "besides," and "another" are characteristic of this kind of connector.

The "but/yet" connection. This type of connector creates logical contrast and typically employs such terms as "but," "yet," "however," "upon second thought," "despite this," "still," or "on the other hand."

The "if ... then" connection. This type of connector indicates that the validity of the next section of the sermon depends in some way on the previous segment. Characteristic terms include "so," "because," "since," "thus," "therefore," and "if ... then."

The "reconsider" connection. This type of connector signals that a segment of the sermon will go back over the same ground as the previous section, but this time with another point of view. Typical terms are "look again," "in a deeper sense," and "perhaps" and rhetorical questions such as "Why is this so?"

The "new departure" connection. This relatively rare type of connector actually breaks the logical chain of the sermon by announcing a discontinuity between sections. Typical terms include, "leaving this behind," "the real question, though, is," and "what if?"

3. Connectors anticipate the content of the next section of the sermon. A good connector not only names the essence of the previous section, it also hints, at least, about what is to follow. This enables the hearers both to listen *to* the next segment and to listen *for* its message. Note again our example connector. The sentence "But for us today the time has grown long" gives the hearers advance notice that the next section of the sermon will discuss the difficulty of maintaining, in our own time, the early church's sense of kingdom expectancy.

So connectors provide closure for a sermon segment, indicate the kind of logical "glue" that bonds that section to the next one, and guide the listeners in their expectations about what is coming next. Our example connector accomplished these tasks in complete fashion. The first two sentences provided the closure, the word "but" named the logical bond, and the final sentence anticipated the content of the next section of the sermon. All three tasks belonging to connectors were accomplished overtly.

If all of the connectors in a sermon were as fully expressed as our example, though, it would mean communicational overkill. Sometimes a single word ("but," "nevertheless," "hogwash!"), a simple gesture (a raised eyebrow, a shrug of the shoulders, a shake of the head), or just plain silence will be all that is necessary. What we are trying to accomplish in the connective moments of a sermon is to provide enough guidance to the hearers to ensure that they are following the movement of the sermon. If we provide no help, or insufficient help, the listeners are likely to hear the sermon as a series of confusing and disconnected episodes. We know why one thing follows another, but they do not, and we must allow the logical movement of the sermon to become plain. On the other hand, if we provide too much help, the hearers can become bored or feel that we are being too simple or condescending.

Deciding how complete to make the sermon connections is a matter of judgment. If, for example, we are considering the sort of connector needed after a sermon section in which the material is completely clear and the message is transparent, we are probably better off to omit any closure statement. The listeners already have the point and do not need any restatement. If, however, the material is complex or ambiguous, a solid closure statement is important. On the whole, erring on the side of fullness and clarity in connectors is to be preferred to less complete sermon connections that leave the movement of the sermon in doubt.

THE FINAL WORD

There are two urgent questions about sermon endings: *when* to conclude and *how* to conclude.[18] Regarding the first, Luther is reported to have advised, "When you see your hearers most attentive, then conclude." That is hyperbole, of course, but there is wisdom in his exaggeration nonetheless. The fact is that hearers intuitively know when a sermon is finished. In the same way that people know when a story is done, a joke is complete, a conversation is over, they also have the "sense of an ending" about sermons. When a listener says something like "There were two or three places in that sermon where the preacher could have stopped but didn't," this is not necessarily a complaint about dullness or length. Hearers have an intuitive grasp of a message's symmetry and wholeness, and when the listeners' need for completion has been resolved, they unconsciously close the book on their hearing. If the sermon continues after that point, it will surprise and often irritate the hearers. Sermon conclusions that come *after* the hearers have finished listening can only serve as pallbearers.

Highly skilled preachers can adjust their sermons on their feet. They can almost palpably discern the hearers' sense of closure and round out the sermon with dispatch if need be. Most of us, however, do not possess this skill. Once we have begun the sermon, we are like tightrope walkers whose only choice is to continue all the way to the other side, even if the crowds have departed and the safety net has been taken down.

For most of us, then, the decision about timing the sermon's conclusion must be made during preparation and not in the pulpit. Our best friend in this regard is a crisp, clear, coherent, and economical sermon form. A sermon with a sharp focus and function will aim to say one thing well and to do one thing well, and the form should be the vehicle for efficiently accomplishing those aims. If we look critically at the form of our sermons and discover that we are actually trying to say more than one thing or do more than one thing, we probably have two or more sermons competing for the same space. One of them will inevitably win the hearers' attention, leaving the others to tug desperately at the listeners' ears crying, like Esau, "Have you but one blessing? Bless me, even me, too." Someone in the congregation will surely say, "There were two or three places in that sermon where the preacher could have stopped, but didn't."

In regard to *how* to conclude sermons, the key factor is what the sermon aims to *do,* what we have been calling the function statement. Sermons obviously, and joyfully, always do more than preachers intend for them, as the hearers make their own uses of what is proclaimed, but this is not the same thing as saying that sermons should have no aims, or only vague goals. As preachers we do intend for each sermon to accomplish something, and that intention is gathered up in the function statement.

Generally speaking, sermons aim to teach, to evoke a feeling, to call for action, or some combination. These are obviously intertwined objectives. To teach a new idea, for example, also evokes feelings and motivates action, so we should not think of these as discrete categories but as places of emphasis.

Let us examine four actual sermon conclusions to see how each ending matches the basic function of the larger sermon.

1. This conclusion appears in a Palm Sunday sermon in which the preacher began the sermon by asking whether Palm Sunday was a happy and optimistic parade, an occasion of despair, or a tragedy. The preacher spent time in the sermon giving rich interpretations of those three terms—optimism, despair, and tragedy—because he wanted the hearers to know what is at stake in these terms and to realize that Palm Sunday could only be understood theologically if it were viewed as a tragedy. The sermon, while not lacking in feeling and ethical implication, was primarily a *teaching* sermon in the best sense. Here is the conclusion:

> Optimism is all right, I suppose. We should walk on the sunny side of the street, away from the dark side of life. And despair is understandable, and all of us despair sometimes, but it's an easy way out. Neither optimism nor despair are large enough, profound enough, to trace the outline of what any of us would recognize as an image of what our lives can be.
>
> Tragedy, on the other hand, is clean. It tells the truth. It clears our heads. Tragedy strengthens our backs. Palm Sunday is a tragedy. It's the day that Jesus the Christ, knowing the facts of life, does what he is called to do, and does it without rancor; does it simply; without apology. A tragedy. Strong and clean. Worth celebrating. "Blessed is he who comes in the name of the Lord."[19]

In this conclusion no new information is given. Every statement in the conclusion is a reiteration of something already said in the sermon. The conclusion is, in essence, a summary of what has been taught in the sermon. It gathers together in two concise paragraphs all that has been learned, and it serves well the teaching function of the whole sermon.

2. The following conclusion is a part of a sermon on Ezekiel's vision in the Valley of Dry Bones (Ezek. 37:1–14). In this sermon, the preacher did some teaching about the biblical text, relating it to the blowing of the Spirit at Pentecost and also to current political and ethical realities. She cited the racial crisis in South Africa, recounting in particular the experience of blacks in the small town of Mogopa who were ordered by the government to leave their town to be resettled in a "homeland." The government sent bulldozers and destroyed Mogopa, turning it into a modern Valley of Dry Bones.

This preacher wanted the hearers not only to understand the text and to perceive the "dry bones" places in the contemporary world, she also, and primarily, wanted the hearers to *feel* the presence of

God's Spirit blowing now through all hopeless and hungering places, bringing new life. Here is the conclusion:

> God breathes into the clay and into the dry bones and into the people of Mogopa and into the disciples . . . and into your life, too, where you are sitting today. For it is the same breath, the same spirit. A protesting and a comforting presence. This breath of God connects us with the people of Mogopa, with the disciples in Jerusalem. This breath means that faith is *more* than memory or wishful thinking. This breath is tied to the stories passed down—yet it is the Spirit alone which breathes into the bones of history to call the stories to life.
>
> Send your breath, O God, to our sisters and brothers driven from Mogopa. Send your breath that they may live. Blow within them a protesting and comforting presence. Send your will, O God, to shake our churches that they may be more than buildings, more than bones of history. Blow within us so that we will dare to speak the truth against the lies. Send your spirit, O God, into the parched, hopeless valleys of our own lives—the same spirit promised by Jesus. Blow within us so that we mean what we pray: "Thy Kingdom come, thy will be done on earth as it is in heaven." Amen.[20]

Note that this conclusion is a dramatic and passionate one. The preacher uses rousing language, powerful language, prayer language. This is not a strategy, not a device, but a cry. The preacher has heard this text speaking to the deepest places in human life. The sermon speaks to those places, and the conclusion is an appeal both to and from the heart.

3. Here is another conclusion for a sermon that speaks at the affective level. The biblical text is Isaiah 40:31, KJV ("But they that wait upon the Lord shall renew their strength; they shall mount up with wings as eagles; they shall run, and not be weary; and they shall walk, and not faint"). In the sermon the preacher interpreted the phrase "wait upon the Lord" to mean trusting God to do what we cannot, in our own strength, do. This preacher, however, wanted to do more than explain the meaning of the text; he wanted to encourage the hearers to feel and to experience this trust of God. So he closed the sermon by telling a story about his own struggle with heart disease. His physician prescribed swimming exercises, and as he engaged in this activity he learned a lesson about trust. "The most important thing I learned," he said, "was the fact that all the while I was swimming . . . I was assuming that the water would hold me up. . . . Forty years ago, as a teenager, I wasn't able to swim a mile nearly so easily as now, having learned this lesson. Likewise the

deadly tension and tightness of subtly striving and worrying without waiting has gone." Carrying this image of the trusting swimmer into the conclusion, he said:

> They that lie back on the water of life and wait on the Lord between strokes shall renew their strength. They that lie trustingly in the bosom of providence, knowing that God will care for them while they recuperate—these are they that shall renew their strength in every way, physically, mentally, and spiritually. They shall even mount up with wings as eagles and soar through life in joy and victory. They shall both run and swim marathon distances, and not get weary. They shall walk and walk and walk and not faint.[21]

In this conclusion we do not so much learn something as we feel something. The language is poetic, biblical, and image-rich, matching the affective aim of the sermon as a whole.

4. This conclusion is a part of an Advent sermon that has as its aim behavioral change. Wishing to call the congregation to Christian service and action, the preacher ends the sermon this way:

> A new birth is required if we are to see the signs of his presence. We need new eyes that perceive what is hidden, new hearts of courage to risk all in order to gain what the world deems lost. This new birth is the good work that Paul says God has begun within us. What does it mean for everyday life? The list of specifics is long and filled with risk. It means caring about human problems that most people would rather ignore. It means speaking up for the the poor who are not present to speak for themselves. It means calling for forgiveness when others call for blood. It means insisting upon justice when others are prepared to settle for order. It means giving money and time without asking, "What's in it for me?" It means turning our backs upon the idols of pleasure, convenience, and class. It means being satisfied with nothing less than the coming of the kingdom of God.
>
> Keep the Advent faith, and you will sometimes feel terribly alone. But you are not alone, for we read, "God is leading Israel in joy by the light of his glory, with his mercy and justice for company" (Bar. 5:9,NAB). Jesus is the light of his glory. Jesus is the sign and seal of his mercy and justice. He has been here before. In stark and bitter loneliness, he cried the victim's cry, "My God, my God, why have you forsaken me?" In the triumph of Easter, God raised him from the dead and made him the new man for all men. He is God's pledge that your work is not in vain. He is God's pledge that you need not fear the future,

that you can welcome change, for it is by change that the kingdom comes. Prepare the way, then—not for an unknown power, not for a stranger, but for the Lord who has been, and will be, your companion on the way.[22]

There are clearly affective and cognitive aspects to this conclusion, but the main feature is a listing of specific actions that the hearers may take: caring about human problems, speaking up for the poor, calling for forgiveness, insisting upon justice, unselfishly giving money and time, and so on. An alternative way to have concluded this sermon would have been for the preacher, instead of providing a list of possible actions, to have told a story about one person putting the claim of the sermon into practice.

Good sermons do not really end, of course, with the preacher's concluding words. They continue to work in the minds of the hearers (and the preacher too) and in the life of the community of faith. "I count a sermon a success," said one member of a congregation, "if I think about it again during the week." That is a modest standard, perhaps, but not a bad one. Sermons that are too neatly finished, that have a "well, that's that" feel about them, that have no loose ends for the hearers to struggle over, communicate a tidiness that the gospel itself does not possess. "If I could understand religion," commented Baron von Hugel, "as I understand that two and two makes four, it would not be worth understanding."[23]

8

Images and Experiences
in Sermons

The Christian faith **always** *has to do with flesh and blood, time and space, more specifically with your flesh and blood and mine, with the time and space that day by day we are all of us involved with, stub our toes on, flounder around in trying to look as if we have good sense.*
— **Frederick Buechner,**
Whistling in the Dark

The kingdom of heaven, Jesus said, may be compared to a farmer who sowed good seed in a field or to a ruler who wished to settle accounts with his servants. Jesus also said that the kingdom of God is like leaven which a woman took . . . a grain of mustard seed . . . treasure hidden in a field . . . a merchant in search of fine pearls . . . a net thrown into the sea . . . a woman searching for a lost coin . . . a man going on a journey who called his servants and entrusted his property to them. Jesus came preaching in stories and parables, and when he spoke of the reign of God he often did so in familiar images drawn from ordinary experience. Christian preachers ever since have followed Jesus' example and have continued to communicate the gospel through narratives, images, metaphors, and similes drawn from everyday life.

There is nothing surprising about this, of course. The gospel makes claims upon life as people actually live it, and Christian witness naturally gathers in experiences and examples from the common round of human existence. Indeed, any sermon that remained entirely in the realm of abstract thought, never touching the real world of fields and crops, parents and children, employers and workers, feasts and banquets, toil and play, would hardly qualify as Christian preaching at all.

But what sort of experiences and images should we bring into sermons? How should we incorporate them? What are the effects we hope to achieve? Beneath the seemingly simple and spontaneous use

156

of ordinary experience in preaching lie rhetorical and theological issues of great complexity. Stories, images, analogies, and experiences are not mere decorations in sermons; they are active ingredients of communication. They cause certain things to happen in the minds of the hearers and are thus powerful, but also potentially disruptive, poetic elements. An image can clarify, and it can also mislead. An example can ground the truth of the gospel in actual experience, but it can also make the gospel seem merely mundane. A story can be richly evocative or insipid and cloying. A well-chosen experience can enable people to envision new possibilities for discipleship, but a contrived one can manipulate them and be a form of verbal entrapment.

Moreover, whenever we include a "slice of life" in a sermon, we are making implicit theological claims whether we know it or not. By the kinds of experiences and images we choose to employ in sermons, we are forming, implicitly or explicitly, specific connections between the nature of contemporary life and the character of the gospel. A sentimental sermon story, for example, implies that the gospel itself is sentimental. A sermon full of experiences involving only clergy telegraphs the message that *real* faith is reserved for the ordained. Or suppose that a preacher decides to relate in a sermon several stories of people who learned to trust God in the midst of difficult and painful circumstances. If this preacher is honest about these experiences, the accounts will include some of the ambiguity and unresolved questions surely present whenever people struggle from suffering toward faith. A truthful relating of the experiences, in other words, carries with it the theological claim that the "yes" of the gospel does not instantly make the "no" of human doubt and struggle disappear. If, on the other hand, the preacher files the rough edges off these experiences and transforms them into stories with simple, happy, and purely victorious endings, an unrealistic triumphant picture of the gospel is conveyed, with little room for unfinished suffering and continuing struggle.

So if we are to be wise in using stories, examples, experiences, and images in preaching, there are many factors we must take into account. What we need is an understanding of how these elements function in sermons, the range of effects they potentially evoke in hearers, and what implicit messages about the character of the gospel they may communicate. We need to ask, in other words, What are these elements supposed to *do* in sermons?

The answer we give to that question depends, of course, on our prior understanding of the overall purpose of preaching. Early homileticians, schooled in classical rhetoric, generally assumed that the ultimate purpose of preaching was persuasion. Since preachers were supposed to be persuasive, these homileticians thought of sto-

ries and examples mainly as rhetorical devices employed to make the
sermon more convincing.[1] They borrowed, from the ancient rhetori-
cians, technical names (e.g., example, parable, sign) for the various
types of stories, metaphors, legends, figures, and analogies that a
preacher might employ, and they provided elaborate descriptions of
the uses, functions, and probable effects of each. Preachers were
viewed as carpenters, working with words instead of wood, whose
job was to build solidly convincing sermons. Stories, examples,
analogies, and so on were seen as very specialized tools to accomplish
that task of persuasion.

BREAKING THE WINDOWS

A quite different understanding of the role of images, examples,
and stories in preaching emerged, however, in the homiletical textbooks of the nineteenth and early twentieth centuries. The assortment of technical names and categories was largely abandoned in
favor of the single encompassing term "illustration." Every imagin-
able sort of contemporary element in a sermon was called a "sermon
illustration"—stories, historical anecdotes, examples, word pictures,
analogies from nature, and even persons presented as role models.
The ancient homileticians at least gave their carpenter-preachers tool
chests filled with many specifically named and specially designed
rhetorical tools. Now, however, the hammers, saws, and awls were
replaced with a single all-purpose device: the illustration. This remains true today in the popular vocabulary of preaching. Published
anthologies of sermon stories and examples are called collections of
illustrations, and preachers typically speak of every means of bringing everyday life into their preaching as illustrating their sermons.

The rise to prominence of the word "illustration" was neither
neutral nor innocent. Beneath this change in terminology lay a
deeper shift in the overall understanding of the purpose of preaching.
To illustrate means "to bring light," and homiletics, as it moved from
the Enlightenment toward the twentieth century, was gradually dis-
placing the earlier concept of preaching as persuasive rhetoric with
an understanding of preaching as the clear, logical, and rational
presentation of ideas derived from the gospel. The "persuader" was,
little by little, being pushed out of the pulpit in favor of the "ex-
plainer." If the main job of the preacher was to make the truth of
the gospel lucid and understandable, then a good, light-bearing illustration was an obvious aid for this task.

Ironically, even those homileticians who would have been horrified theologically by the idea that preaching the gospel was simply
the logical presentation of a systematic set of concepts tended, nevertheless, to reinforce that very view in the practical sections of their

textbooks.[2] Every sermon was supposed to develop a "thesis," and illustrations were seen as devices designed to illumine and clarify that thesis. Intriguingly, the older language of persuasion did not disappear all at once; it was simply relegated to a far less important role. Nineteenth- and early twentieth-century homiletical manuals typically provided lists of the purposes of illustrations, and such phrases as "they help to persuade people,"[3] they "can break down resistance,"[4] and "illustrations are used to make the truth persuasive"[5] still occurred. These persuasive purposes, however, were now placed far down on the lists,[6] and top priority was given to the matter of creating understanding. The number one purpose of illustrations, these textbooks maintained, was to "make the truth concrete,"[7] to "make the message clear,"[8] and to "help the congregation understand"[9] the main ideas of the sermon.

Now and then, when homileticians of this period were searching for a way to explain this clarifying function of illustrations, they employed a very revealing image (sort of an illustration about illustrations). Illustrations, they said, are "windows on the word." The sermon, they argued, is a house built with timbers of reason and logic, and illustrations are the windows bringing in the clear sunshine of comprehension. The nineteenth-century preacher and homiletician Charles Haddon Spurgeon employed this image when he advised his preaching students, "The chief reason for the construction of windows in a house is . . . to let in light. Parables, similes and metaphors have that effect; and hence we use them to illustrate our subject."[10] The idea here is fairly obvious: A sermon moves along, logically developing this or that concept, but at some point along the way the concept becomes too obscure or conceptually difficult for the hearers to handle it without assistance. So the preacher opens a window by supplying an illustration, thereby throwing some light on an otherwise shadowy topic.

It is fairly easy to see now that this whole business of calling all experiential elements in sermons "illustrations" and thinking of them as "windows on the word" rested upon a didactic, rationalistic, and conceptually oriented understanding of preaching. As a matter of fact, though, preaching as an event in the Christian community is not, and never has been, exclusively such an activity. Even on those occasions when preachers tried their best to construct and preach rationalistic sermons, the church happily managed to hear in those sermons, over time, something more and something other than didactic messages. One evidence of this is that the rationalistic theory of illustrations, which made such logical sense in the homiletical textbooks, never would quite work between pulpit and pew. There were telltale cracks in these "windows on the word."

Preachers who preached sermons week after week intuitively knew there was something misguided about the theory all along. This view of illustrations looked good on the drawing board, but there were problems in actual practice. When preachers tried to use stories, examples, and images as clarifying devices, opening illustrative windows here and there in the logical progression of the sermon (some homiletical manuals methodically prescribed "one illustration for each point"), they quickly encountered a troubling side effect: the illustrations often overpowered the rest of the sermon. Hearers were frequently more engaged by the illustrative material than they were by the main thread of the sermon. In other words, people cherished and remembered the "windows" and promptly forgot whatever it was that the windows were supposed to be illuminating.

At first, homileticians suspected that the trouble was not with their theory but with the preachers and their practice. Preachers, they said, were using too many illustrations and the wrong kind of illustrations. They were filling sermons with strings of cute, ornamental stories that distracted from the central business at hand. Sermons were becoming "glass houses" with too many windows, attractive from the outside but structurally unsound. Dire warnings were issued about the "overuse" of illustrations, and preachers were constantly advised to avoid padding their sermons with trivial "sermon anecdotes" and even to use solid illustrative material "sparingly," "judiciously," and with "caution" lest the illustrations thrust "themselves into the light instead of casting light."[11]

Frankly, some preachers *were* using indulgent, disconnected, and merely decorative anecdotes in sermons (and some preachers still do), but the main reason congregations were more engaged by the illustrative material than by the conceptual parts of sermons was that there is more communicative power and energy in stories, images, and examples than the terms "illustration" or "windows on the word" would allow.[12] Hearers are engaged by illustrations because illustrative material, when it is well chosen, communicates the faith in subtle and complex ways. Illustrations can be "windows on the word," to be sure, but they can also be arenas for encountering, discerning, discovering, and experiencing the word as well. As Fred Craddock maintains:

> In good preaching what is referred to as illustrations are, in fact, stories or anecdotes which do not illustrate the point; rather they *are* the point. In other words, a story may carry in its bosom the whole message rather than the illumination of a message which had already been related in another but less clear way.[13]

Craddock's statement represents a strong trend in recent homiletics to rethink the entire matter of the role of illustrative material in sermons. We may, as a matter of convenience, want to keep the word "illustration," but we can no longer think of it as a single, unified category. There are many types of illustrative material, each of which has a specific and different potential function in a sermon. Some illustrations clarify concepts, but not all of them do. Some assist persuasion, but others produce quite different effects. Preachers must know how each type of illustration functions in order to be able to select the best material for a given sermon.

Homileticians have always recognized that well-crafted sermons possess unity, each element of the sermon working in concert to create the whole, but contemporary homileticians have sought to refine this insight by understanding precisely how each part of a sermon, including the various types of illustrative material, works together with all the other elements to achieve an integrated act of communication. When a slice of contemporary experience, a story, a metaphor, or an image is brought into a sermon, it is in order to accomplish some particular task that contributes to the larger sermon objective. The major flaw in the "windows on the word" view of sermon illustrations was that it harnessed all illustrative material to one and only one communicational task: the clarification of concepts. Illustrative material possesses a much larger communication repertoire than that. What we are searching for, then, is an understanding of illustrations large enough to help us perceive their true communicational range.

RESTOCKING THE TOOL CHEST

In chapter 6 we saw that creating a sermon involves dividing the overall objectives of the sermon (the focus and the function) into a series of smaller tasks and then deciding what kinds of materials are needed to accomplish one. For some tasks, what is needed are quotations from scripture, sections describing theological concepts, analyses of issues, or the like. For other tasks, however, illustrative material of some sort is required. In order to see when this is so and what kinds of illustrative material may be called for, we need to explore the potential functions of the several types of illustrations. We need, in other words, to take out of the preacher's tool chest that one, clumsy, multipurpose tool called "illustration" and replace it with the very specialized illustrative tools available to us.

Essentially, an illustration operates in a sermon as a figure of speech works in a sentence. More specifically, most sermon illustrations function as one of three different kinds of speech figures: simile, synecdoche, or metaphor. The three basic kinds of illustrations, then, are the simile type, the synecdoche type, and the metaphor type.

The Simile Type

Here is a simile: "George is as slow as molasses." Now "George" and "molasses" are obviously two quite different realities, and normally we would not think to mention both of them in the same breath. Thus the first observation we can make about a simile is that two very unlike entities are unexpectedly brought together for the sake of comparison. Now even though "George" and "molasses" are very different, there is this one area of similarity: their common lack of speed. A simile, then, specifies a particular area of overlap, and it uses the words "like" or "as" to make this connection. "George" and "molasses" are like each other in one, and presumably only one, way.

A simile is a very disciplined figure of speech. It has surgical precision. If we try to press a simile beyond the bounds of its intended comparison, things go quickly awry. If someone says, "When she finally comes to a decision, she is like a bulldog," the obvious intention is to communicate that this person is tenaciously determined when she makes up her mind. If a listener somehow got the idea that she is like a bulldog in other ways as well—prone to bury bones in the backyard, say—this would be a fatal diffusion of the simile's intended communicational intent.

This points us toward the basic purpose of a simile: to create clear and emphatic understanding. When we say to someone, "George is as slow as molasses," we are trying both to help that person understand something about George and to understand it in a vivid and memorable way. We could have said, "George is very slow," and that would have gotten the idea across, but not nearly so graphically.

Some sermon illustrations, then, operate like similes and possess the same communicational purpose. If we are presenting an idea or concept in a sermon, and we want to help the hearers to understand it, we can bring in some example from the world of nature or human experience and say or imply, "It's like this. . . ." We may not actually use the words "like" or "as," but we establish that sort of relationship between the idea and the illustration. Here is a simile-style illustration:

> As a boy, I loved to go puddle gazing, wandering from one puddle to the next, wondering how so much of the sky could be reflected in such small bodies of water. Today I often marvel at how so much of the story of heaven and earth is captured in small biblical tales such as the story of Jesus and the paralytic.[14]

Now the experience of seeing the vastness of the sky in a tiny puddle and the wonder of seeing the story of heaven and earth in a small biblical passage are *not* the same thing. The preacher suggests that they are *like* each other. They operate on parallel tracks and are analogically related to each other because, in both of them, the vision of something large is captured in a small space. That is, for the moment at least, the one and only connection we are supposed to make between this feature of the Bible and the preacher's childhood puddle gazing.

The effect of this type of illustration is to provide vivid understanding. Its chief function is to give clarity, but it does so with a bit of a wallop. The simile-style illustration, with its graphic clarifying function, is the sort of illustration the homiletical manuals of several generations ago had most in mind when they emphasized the word "illustration" and claimed that its primary purpose is to make a concept plain.

Here is another simile-style illustration, this one from a sermon by James S. Stewart. At the point in the sermon where the illustration appears, Stewart has introduced the idea that an active memory of God's loving presence in the past can sustain a person in those times when God seems to be absent.

> I remember once near Interlaken waiting for days to see the Jungfrau which was hidden in mists. People told me it was there, and I should have been a fool to doubt their word, for those who told me lived there and they knew. Then one day the mists were gone, and the whole mountain stood revealed. Next day the mists were back, but now I had seen, and knew myself that it was true. . . . [L]et us trust our own moments of vision: what matter if there are days when the mists come down and the face of God is hidden? We have seen, and we know for ever that this is real, so real that by it we can live and die.[15]

Although this experience is vivid and the language Stewart uses has obvious emotional power, the primary purpose of the illustration is to create understanding. It is a simile-style illustration because the dynamic of the theological idea is *like* the dynamic in the experience, but they are not the same reality.

Simile-style illustrations are perhaps the most common type of illustrative material in sermons. Sometimes they are complete stories; more often they are simply vignettes of experience or single images ("Like a rural tent-revival preacher, John the Baptist thundered from his desert pulpit" or "Jesus was at a fancy dinner party in the home of Simon the Pharisee, a party much like those covered on the 'Fashion' page of the *Tribune*"). Here is a simile-style illustration from a sermon on Zechariah 8:1–8, in which the preacher takes one contemporary image and develops it at length:

What is the Kingdom of God, according to the prophet Zechariah? It is a public park! It is a park where old people are no longer cold and lonely and ill and senile, but participants in a community. It is a public park where the elderly can sit together and bask in the sun, and talk and laugh over the good old days in full vigor and clear mind and satisfaction of life.

The Kingdom of God is a public park where little children can run and play in its squares, in safety and fun and delight. . . . It is a place where no child is abused or unwanted or malnourished, and where there is not even a bully among the group, shoving and taunting the littler ones until they break into tears. The Kingdom of God, says Zechariah, is a public park where the streets are safe for children.[16]

In every simile-style illustration—regardless of whether it is a complete narrative, a fragment of experience, or simply an image—something familiar is held alongside something less familiar, and a comparison is made: This is like that.

The danger in using a simile-style illustration, as we have seen, is that it will spill over the boundaries of its single point of comparison and thus overflow its narrow educational purpose. For example, countless preachers, trying to communicate the character of faith, have told stories about their children trustingly leaping off tables and refrigerator tops into their open arms. What they intended to say, of course, was that this sort of unwavering trust in a parent is something *like* faith in God, but the illustration tends to slosh over the walls of the intended analogy and to communicate that leaping heedlessly into danger *is* faith or that the relationship between a parent and a child is in every way the same reality as the relationship between God and people. Again, the often-employed comparison of the resurrection to the emergence of a butterfly from a cocoon tends to perform all sorts of unintended mischief, including trivializing the resurrection and implying that it was merely the outcome of a natural process.

If we decide that we need a simile-style illustration in a sermon, how do we ensure that we select one that is suitable, that accomplishes its intended purpose? David Buttrick has suggested that such illustrations ought to be able to pass three simple tests:

1. There must be a clear analogy between an idea in sermon content and some aspect of the illustration [I would add to this the caution that what is clear to the preacher may not always be as clear to the hearers, so preachers should ensure that, in the telling of simile-style illustrations, the point of comparison is not left in doubt]

2. There ought to be a parallel between the structure of content and the shape of an illustration

3. The illustration should be "appropriate" to the content [meaning that serious and important concepts should not be paired with small, trivial, or mawkish illustrations][17]

Buttrick applies his three tests to the following stock illustration, intended to clarify the idea that God-in-Christ chose to come to us as one who was poor and lowly rather than in power and with status:

> In an art gallery, side by side, are two paintings. One is by the famous artist Rembrandt; it is the portrait of a great man, an important world leader. But the other painting, by an unknown artist, is of a peasant kitchen—a rough board table, and a bunch of asparagus waiting to be cooked. Which painting do people stand and stare at? Not the portrait of the great man; no, they stand transfixed before the picture of the peasant kitchen and the picked asparagus. So God might have come to us in power, in the flesh of a famous man, but instead God came as . . .[18]

On the basis of his three tests, Buttrick judges this to be a failed illustration. Why? There is a clear analogy between the illustration and the theological concept—a peasant kitchen is lined up with Jesus' birth—so the first test is passed. The second test is also successful because the illustration and the concept share a similar two-part structure; the contrast between high and low, between nobility and peasantry, operates in both. It is the third test that, in Buttrick's view, causes the stumble. The illustration is not appropriately matched to the theological idea it is supposed to illustrate, claims Buttrick, because, "unfortunately, without realizing it, the preacher has turned Jesus into a bunch of asparagus!"[19]

That assessment may be slightly overdrawn, but Buttrick's basic point is well-taken, and his three tests are on target. A simile-style illustration seeks to teach an idea with vividness, to provoke deeper understanding of a concept. Buttrick rightly wants to caution preachers about the potential for confusion created when an illustration leaks stray messages through its seams.

The Synecdoche Type

Synecdoche is a figure of speech in which a part of something is used to stand for the whole. When we say, "My ship set out across the waves," we really mean that our ship set out across the *sea*. We name one part of the sea—the waves—to poetically evoke the whole. Notice one of the important differences between synecdoche and simile. Similes make comparisons; synecdoche does not. To use our example, we are not saying that the sea is *like* the waves. We are not comparing the sea to the waves; the waves are a part of the sea itself. A simile says, in effect, "Let me make this clearer; it's like. . . ." Synecdoche, however, aims not at comparing two things but at naming the essence of one thing.

To say "My ship set out across the waves" implies that the essence of the ocean is motion, action, perhaps even restless energy. In other words, instead of naming the whole thing—"the sea"—we name instead that part of it that most fully represents its basic character— "the waves." If we had chosen another example of synecdoche and said, "My ship set out across the deep," we would have named another part of the whole and thus evoked something else about the sea's nature: its vastness, maybe even its danger and terror. Synecdoche says, in effect, "This is the heart of the thing itself."

Sometimes in sermons, when we are presenting a concept or an idea, we use an illustration not to say, "This is what it's *like,*" but rather to say, "This is what it *is;* this is the heart of the thing itself in human life." No experience, no story, no example ever embodies, of course, all there is to know and experience about a concept like grace or hope or sin or love or repentance or forgiveness or faith. But we can point to places in human life where grace or hope or sin or love has been experienced and allow those experiences to stand as signs of the larger truth toward which they point.

Synecdoche-style illustrations are crucial in preaching because they put flesh on theological concepts. Like similes, synecdoche-style illustrations make concepts clearer, but that is not their main purpose. They provide for the hearers a taste, a vicarious experience, of the reality being presented. It is one thing to explain a doctrinal idea—sanctification, for example—in a sermon; it is quite another thing to be able to say, "Here is sanctification as it is experienced in human life." A good way for a preacher to discover the potential of synecdoche-style illustrations is to take the manuscript of a sermon and mark all those places where theological concepts, challenges, and claims appear. The preacher should ask, "If the hearers took these statements seriously, what would the results be in their real lives?" If we cannot say what a sermon idea would look like in human life, the chances are good that we are pushing a mere abstraction in our listeners' direction. If we call upon them to take a theological idea seriously, to believe it and to live it, then we have the responsibility to help them envision specifically what that would mean for them.

Here are some theological statements that could typically be found in sermons, and some questions the preacher could ask:

"God has given us the opportunity to be responsible and loving partners in the redemption of creation."

Suppose the Jones family, sitting in the third pew, decided to join with God in the redemption of creation. What exactly would they do?

"All around us we see signs of God's care."

Where are they? Can you name some?

"Still today Jesus calls to each of us, 'Follow me!' "

Specifically, how does this call of Jesus come to the people out there in the congregation? To the single parent? To the school-teacher? To the woman who has cancer? To the elderly man whose eyesight is dimming and whose memory is failing? To the child beginning school this year? To others? What might it mean for these people if they decided, in some new way, to follow?

"In our time, too, it is sad to say, people are prone to worship idols, false gods who are nothing more than projections of their own selfish desires."

Which idols? How do we know they are "gods"? What evidence do we have that they are being "worshiped"? What are the telltale rituals, ceremonies, and solemn vows? What allows us to say that they are "nothing more than projections of their own selfish desires"?

"As disciples of the crucified Christ, we are called to stand with all who suffer because of hatred, with all who are victims of the world's cruelty."

Are there some ways in which these hearers are already doing this? If so, how? Beyond the powerful examples of people whose lives deeply embody this claim—the Mother Teresas and the Martin Luther Kings—are there less dramatic but nonetheless significant ways in which Christian people can "stand with those who suffer"?

These questions are, of course, difficult ones. It is far easier to find simile-style illustrations to explain these theological ideas than it is to find synecdoche-style illustrations that actually embody them in human experience. This difficulty, however, does not release us from the responsibility to articulate the theology of our sermons in the terms of specific contemporary experience. The task of preachers, Robert E. C. Browne once observed, is to know doctrine in such a way that they know life in terms of doctrine and doctrine in terms of life. "It is not," he claimed, "that doctrine is supremely important and that life proves its importance; it is that life is supremely important and doctrine illuminates it."[20]

Suppose we are developing a sermon around the theological theme of Jesus' call to bear a cross. In the sermon we say that "bearing a cross" does not mean heroically enduring some misfortune that unexpectedly comes our way but rather *choosing* to take suffering upon ourselves in the service of others. There is the concept, but what does it look like in real human life? An illustration is needed, perhaps one like this:

In the newspaper last week there was a story about the process families go through in adopting children. The account related the usual details: the huge number of couples wanting to adopt, the much smaller number of "desirable" children, the extremely long waiting lists, the high legal fees, the red tape, the resulting increase of interest in "surrogate parents," and so on.

The story also told of the experience of the Williams family. The Williams, a deeply religious couple, have adopted four children so far, and they hope to adopt at least one more child in the future. For the Williams there have been no delays and no waiting lists. The reason is that all of the children the Williams have adopted are disabled. One, a son, is severely retarded, and the other three, two daughters and another son, had major birth defects. All of the Williams' children are, in the euphemism employed by the adoption agencies, "difficult to place." In a world where virtually every prospective parent dreams of a bright, beautiful, and perfect child, the Williams have chosen to offer the embrace of their parental love to children almost no one else wanted. "Our children are our greatest joy," Mrs. Williams was quoted as saying. "Caring for them is what we're on this earth for."

Of course this illustration does not say everything that can and should be said about cross bearing. It leaves unstated, for example, the explicitly theological connection between this family's faith and their action. But if cross bearing is indeed choosing to embrace suffering in the selfless service of others, this episode gives us one incident in human experience of the thing itself, a part that evokes the whole.

Again, imagine that we are creating a sermon that will present the theological claim expressed in Paul's statement, "I consider that the sufferings of this present time are not worth comparing with the glory that is to be revealed to us. For the creation waits with eager longing for the revealing of the children of God" (Rom. 8:18–19). Our hope is that the hearers will not only understand this theological affirmation but also grow in their capacity for discerning it in the lives of others and for living it themselves. If so, we must do more than explain it; we must show what living this theological truth looks like in human experience—something like this:

In the early 1970s Margie McCoy wrote a book about dying. On a winter Saturday in 1985, Margie McCoy faced her own death.

Margie was an effective seminary teacher and a popular author. In addition to her book about death, she had written a book about Mary, the mother of Jesus, and co-authored a book about the cross. At the time of her death she was almost finished with the manuscript of yet another book, but, before she could complete it, she began to develop strange and troubling physical symptoms. She had, it was soon discovered, a malignant brain tumor of the most aggressive kind. Surgery, then radiation therapy, and finally chemotherapy were required, but none of these treatments did more than delay the inevitable.

As her condition rapidly deteriorated, she continued to work on her book. Students, family, and friends helped out by doing those labors her weakening body was unable to perform. When she could no longer hold a pen in her hand, she would discuss her thoughts with Charles, her husband, and he would write them down. Near the end, when she could no longer speak, Charles would say what he thought she would want to say, and she would respond with a squeeze of his hand.

Most people in Margie's situation would probably have been thoroughly defeated by the pain and the relentless malice of the disease. Margie looked instead to her faith and to the people around her, telling them that they had helped change "difficult days into times of wonder and joy."

Something she said in her book, now published, perhaps best reveals the shape of her faithful and final struggle:

" 'What does it all mean?' we ask in puzzlement . . . ? How can all this struggle and turmoil and suffering and caring too much or too little not have some significance beyond being 'a tale told by an idiot, full of sound and fury, signifying nothing'?

" 'No one *knows*,' we must respond to these questions that well up out of our wayward longing. We are called to *trust*, not to *know*. And trusting is difficult for us. . . . [A]ll our 'knowing,' if we know anything at all and if it can really be called knowing, is knowing by faith. . . . Suppose . . . that we could step into faith wholly, cast off from the anxiety of the tension, and dwell fully in the mystery. Suppose that we could learn really to *trust*. Is this not what the Gospel calls us to . . . ?

"And why not? I am here and might as well, through trust in God, make the most of it—being on my own particular journey, wrestling with and sometimes overcoming my own anxieties, in the midst of mystery. Perhaps I can even learn to say . . . , 'All's lost. All's found. Farewell.' "

The tumor gradually expanded, stealing her ability to write, to speak, and finally to move, but never defeating her strong will and loving spirit. On Saturday, February 16, 1985, at 5:15 in the afternoon, Margie died.

After Margie's death, Charles discovered a piece of paper with some words in her own handwriting. They were probably the last words she ever wrote. "I am discovering," she had written, "that, when all is lost, all will be found, because the end of all our journeys is in God, with the dancing of stars and angels down the steeps at the heart of the world. SO SAVE A DANCE FOR ME!"[21]

Once more we recognize, of course, that this experience, as powerful as it is, does not approach the full depth or breadth of the passage from Romans. Instead it gives us a glimpse of the text's promise as it finds halting expression in a real person's life. It is a fragment, a part, which allows us to feel that portion of the gospel's power which is ours to touch and then to find our faithful imaginations guided in pilgrimage toward the whole truth which lies ahead.

Because the synecdoche-style illustration points to a slice of life and claims, "This is a piece of the very thing we are talking about," its use raises a thorny theological problem. Can we ever present an episode of honest human experience, lived out in the brokenness of the world, and say, "This is the gospel in action. Here, in this incident, we can see the very kingdom we proclaim"? The answer, of course, is no, not fully. As the theologian Jürgen Moltmann maintains, "Christian proclamation cannot be supported by analogies in the cosmos or historical events. A damaged world and the history of guilt and death do not in themselves reflect any messianic light."[22] The promises of the gospel—forgiveness of sin, freedom from bondage, the triumph over evil and death, oneness with God— are just that: promises. Promises are made in the present, and, if they are believed and trusted, they make a difference in how we live now. But promises refer to the future, and their full realization lies ahead. Just so, the promises of the gospel speak of God's future, of the God who promises to renew the whole creation and of the faith of those who wait, watch, and work in hope.

It is crucial that preachers be clear that the proclamation of the gospel is, again citing Moltmann, "the Word that opens up the future,"[23] lest we replace the promises of the gospel with only the sad announcements of the possibilities available for life self-contained in the present circumstances of the world. We see this happening among those preachers who substitute "positive thinking," psychological adjustment, and "creative values for living" for the radical promises of the gospel. We also see this in the sort of preaching that implies that the kingdom of God can be muscled into reality through right thinking, correct behavior, or social reorganization.

More subtly, we see this as well in sermons that employ in a thoughtless manner just the sort of synecdoche-style illustrations we have been discussing. Our sermons will and should include experiences of forgiveness, reconciliation, liberation, victory, and answered prayer, but we must not do so in ways that imply to the hearers, "And if you could only think more clearly, work more diligently, believe more deeply, trust more fully, these realities would be completely in *your* grasp as well." We may tell, for example, of the experience of a person who recovered from a life-threatening illness, giving thanks to God for this gracious sign of healing. We must also remember, though, the many faithful people who will not experience such a healing but who cling nevertheless to the gospel promise that the disease destroying their bodies does not have the power to speak the final word. We live in a Good Friday world, where Christians must pray for reconciliation as yet unrealized, hope for liberation even as people lie captive, water the seeds of forgiveness where there is still enmity, apply the oil of healing while pain and death yet rage, and pray with all our might, "Come, Lord Jesus."

What right do we have, then, to point to any moment in human experience and say, "This discloses the truth I am speaking about"? We may do so only if we recognize that such moments are but foretastes and anticipations of the new creation. They are, to use the language of the New Testament, "signs and wonders" of the coming kingdom.

The resurrection of Christ—and the proclamation of that resurrection in the power of the Holy Spirit—is the clearest and deepest of these signs. The church, also, the gathered community of faith to which we preach, is a sign in the present of that future kingdom. As Moltmann states:

> [The Church as messianic community] is the fellowship which narrates the story of Christ, and its own story with that story, because its own existence, fellowship, and activity spring from that story of liberation. It is a "story-telling fellowship," which continually wins its own freedom from the stories and myths of the society in which it lives, from the present realization of this story of Christ. It is a fellowship of hope, which finds freedom from the perspectives of its society through the perspectives of the kingdom of God. Finally, it is a fellowship which, by virtue of its remembrance of the story of Christ and its hope for the kingdom of man, liberates men and women from the compulsive actions of existing society and from the inner attitudes that correspond to them, freeing them for a life that takes on a

messianic character. In Christianized societies this does not merely lead to the critical freedom of faith towards the respective social systems; it leads to the critical freedom towards the church which is tied up with the social system, and towards Christianity in general. . . . The messianic community belongs to the Messiah and the messianic word; and this community, with the powers that it has, already realizes the possibilities of the messianic era, which brings the gospel of the kingdom to the poor, which proclaims the lifting up of the downtrodden to the lowly, and begins the glorification of God through actions of hope.[24]

And finally, our life together in the community of Christ allows us to look with realistic and yet hopeful eyes toward the world as the arena where God's Spirit is even now working, making the impossible possible, creating faith where there is nothing else to believe in, creating love where there is nothing lovable, creating hope where there is nothing to hope for.[25] Trusting the promise of God to redeem the whole cosmos, we see in every place where misery is alleviated, hostility is lifted, and chains of bondage are broken, signs of the coming triumph of God.

3. The Metaphor Type

In a simple metaphor we call something familiar by an unfamiliar name. We speak of locomotives as "iron horses," of sunset as "the dying of the light," or of much talking as "a blizzard of words." In a simile, one thing is compared to another thing. In a metaphor, something is unexpectedly summoned to stand for something else. A simile seeks to help us to understand. A metaphor seeks to create new meaning, to help us experience the reality of something in a new way. A simile is the tool of good teachers; a metaphor is the instrument of poets.

In one of his poems, Wendell Berry describes how the frosts and rains of winter have pushed the stepping stones on a hillside out of line. He pictures himself walking over these stones, stepping short, then long, to the right, then to the left. The poem closes with these words: "At the winter's end, I dance the history of its weather."[26] Now, what does that mean? If he had given us a simile, say "trying to step along these random stones is like dancing," we would know the intended point of comparison. But instead he speaks metaphorically. "At the winter's end, I dance the history of its weather." Does this mean that he moves in the way dancers move? Or that his steps follow a rhythm and a pattern shaped elsewhere and not of his own making? Or that he celebrates, by his stepping, the power of winter?

Or that his stepping is a kind of unconscious remembering? All of these things? Something else? There is mystery at the heart of a metaphor. It continues to tease our minds into active thought, urging us to discover more and more ways to re-vision what we thought we already saw well.

Many of the parables of Jesus are metaphors in story form. In telling these parables Jesus did not say, "Let me explain some feature of the kingdom with this little story," but rather, "Listen to this story. Live in its world. Find yourself among its characters and situations. Feel its claims upon your life. And when you have allowed its world to become your world, then, and only then, speak the phrase 'the kingdom of God.' " Because a parable grows out of a metaphor, observed C. H. Dodd, it leaves "the mind in sufficient doubt about its precise application to tease it into active thought."[27]

Sometimes sermons employ human experience in a metaphorical way. This is the rarest type of illustration, and in some ways the riskiest, because it sacrifices precision and clarity for the sake of imagination and multiple meanings. In simile-style illustrations, we present a "slice of life" as in some ways *like* the concept we are talking about. In synecdoche-style illustrations, we present a "slice of life" which is itself a partial expression of the larger concept. In metaphor-style illustrations we place experience and concept side by side and invite the hearers to make imaginative connections.

For example, in a sermon titled "From the Sixteenth Floor," Charles Rice invites the hearers to view a city from a sixteenth-floor window, high above the streets. From this vantage point we can see the busyness below, the people moving about like dots in motion. We pick out a person in a hospital jacket, another walking along the street wearing a purple shirt. We see "faces . . . lost in endlessly fascinating canyons, heartache obscured by well-furnished windows." Because we view this from above, though, we ironically become less aware of individual motion and more attuned to the rhythms of the whole, to the larger motivations and moral impulses. We see not just people moving about but joy and pain, malice and fate, ugliness and beauty. We begin, as Rice guides us, to have compassion, for the cunning as well as for the dying, and even to pray for this city and its people.

After holding our gaze on the city for a long time, Rice pauses and then concludes the sermon this way:

> The gospel tells the story of Jesus' coming to Jerusalem riding upon a lowly donkey.
>
> "And when he drew near and saw the city he wept over it, saying, 'Would that even today you knew the things that make for peace' " (Luke 19:41–42).

Not long after that, he carried a cross to the hilltop outside Jerusalem.

Nailed up there, he had a good view of the city.[28]

"Nailed up there, he had a good view of the city." That is the last line of Rice's sermon, but that is not where the sermon ends for the hearers. Our minds go back to the time spent on the sixteenth floor. We remember the sadness we felt, and then we remember Jesus' tears. We recall our own good view of the city and its pain, and we then think about Jesus' pain and his "good view" of the city. We recite again our prayer for the city's redemption, and then see the cross as the answer to our cry. Most of all we wonder. We do not yet know all that this sermon means. We feel its redemptive power long before we can name its many truths.

Here is another metaphor-style illustration, this time from a sermon by Patrick J. Willson:

When I was six years old I played on the most marvelous playground. As I remember it now, it was all mine, though certainly other children must have been around to play on it. I still see it through my six-year-old eyes, and it stretches out forever behind our two-story house in Frankfurt, Germany, but I suppose, in truth it was only as big as several city blocks.

I remember it as a place filled with wonderful things. I climbed up and over broken brick walls, and I was a cowboy standing on a mountain. I scaled enormous slabs of concrete that slanted up out of the ground and found a dozen secret places that only I knew about. Raspberries grew on my playground, and gooseberries, and red currants: I picked them right off the vine and ate them and stained my shirt with them. In a shoe box I collected little scraps of melted glass that littered the earth. You could find all sorts of things on my playground.

One day I was digging in my playground and uncovered a little blue rubber motorcycle. I scraped the dirt away. The wheels still rolled. The little blue motorcycle could have been mine. I knew it wasn't. It belonged to someone else, to another little boy. It belonged to whoever had played on my playground before me.

I wondered what had happened to that little boy, and as I wondered, a fact I had known, assumed, and taken for granted slipped from the surface of my knowing into the very depths of my awareness. What I had dug up that day was not only a little blue motorcycle, but an awareness of the presence of evil in the world. My world.

My playground, as you may have guessed, my six-year-old's garden of earthly delights, was a bombed-out section of residential Frankfurt, not yet rebuilt in those years following the Second World War. The walls and slabs I ran on and jumped from were what were left of the houses families had lived in. Raspberries and currants and gooseberries grew there because years before hands had planted, pruned, and tended them. The globs of glass I collected were windows which melted in the fires, windows mothers had watched their children from and waved at them as they played. The little blue motorcycle I rolled across my palm had rolled in the hands of some little boy who had lived in one of these houses that were no more.

What happened to that little boy, what happened to those families, I did not and could not know. What I came to know in that moment was that terrible things happened in this world, that evil had also played across my playground.

In this garden there were weeds.[29]

This incident from Willson's own life could serve as a synecdoche-style illustration. If Willson had been discussing the idea of coming to an awareness of the presence of evil, this experience would be a good example of the thing itself. Wilson, however, was not trying to illustrate just one idea. Rather, he was attempting to evoke a world of many meanings, a world in which good and evil are both present—indeed, a world in which it is impossible to determine always what is good and what is evil. He conveyed all this and more by employing this illustration metaphorically. His text was the parable of the wheat and the weeds (Matt. 13:24–30), and the sermon invited the hearers to live simultaneously in the complexity of the parable and the complexity of our life.

The danger in using metaphor-style illustrations is that they may create confusion rather than illumination. These illustrations must be so well-chosen and crafted that listeners can mine their insights and forge the relationships between them and the rest of the sermon. If we have to stop and explain them, they lose their power. On the other hand, if the listeners miss the connections, such illustrations evoke a bewildered shrug of the shoulders rather than an "Aha!"

OPENING DOORS

A sermon illustration is like a doorway opening into a larger room of understanding and experience. A preacher must always ask about any illustration, "Is this doorway wide enough for *all* the listeners to pass through?" Suppose, for example, we choose to relate the story of a person struggling to be ethically responsible amid the pressures, constant demands, and competitive environment of life in the corporate world. How will such an illustration be heard—indeed, can it

be heard at all?—by a ninth-grader or by an unemployed person who
would welcome the "constant demands" of a decent full-time job?

We are tempted to say no to this question; ninth-graders worrying
about algebra and people concerned about the source of their next
paycheck simply cannot recognize themselves in the world of a
corporate decision maker. There is a measure of truth in that, but
only a measure. As a matter of fact, people have a rather remarkable
capacity to enter imaginatively into the experiences of others and
then to take what they have seen and heard and learned into their
own lives. Indeed, it would be a serious mistake to become so concerned about speaking to every hearer's need all at once that we drain
the blood out of illustrations, making them bland descriptions of life
in general. There is no such thing as life in general; ironically, illustrations depend upon the honest ring of particularity—*this* life, *these*
circumstances—for their ability to speak powerfully to a wide range
of hearers.

We do, however, want to be sure that the range of our illustrative
material reflects the rich variety of experiences present among the
hearers. Sometimes this will mean that a section of a sermon will
require not one illustration but two or three, each embodying a
different kind of life circumstance: several doorways instead of only
one. On other occasions, instead of a single complete illustration, we
may choose to employ a series of images or vignettes. For example:

> But how do we handle the problem of unanswered prayer? We
> pray for rain, but the drought continues. We pray for peace, and
> the headlines still shout of war. We pray for healing, but the
> dark stain remains on the X-ray. We pray for our children, and
> the crises continue. We pray for inner calm, but the anxiety does
> not diminish. We pray for light, but the shadows lengthen. How
> do we handle the problem of unanswered prayer?

This preacher, instead of providing a single full illustration about
someone's struggle with unanswered prayer, has briefly named a
series of such experiences. Not every hearer, of course, will have
prayed for healing or for their children, but the chances are good that
most listeners will find themselves somewhere on this list.

We must also be concerned about the cumulative effect of our
illustrations. An illustration in this week's sermon about the ethical
struggles of a corporate executive may well be effective, but to draw
upon that world week after week soon closes the door to those on
the outside. Unless we work intentionally at increasing the range of
our illustrative repertoire, we will gravitate toward illustrations that
reflect only the experiences of people like ourselves, who see the
world the way we do. A young minister noted for her engaging
sermons once asked a few trusted members of her congregation for

an evaluation of her preaching. She was surprised to discover that, among their many words of praise, their one common criticism was that her illustrations were almost always about the struggles, issues, and experiences of young adults. That was, of course, the world she knew best, but cumulatively this illustrative world was taking its toll on the effectiveness of her preaching.

Just so, if most of our illustrations are about individuals wrestling with their concerns, we underline an individualistic distortion of the faith. If most are about family life, we communicate that being single is outside the Christian norm. If we never include the experiences of children, the gospel becomes adult-oriented. If most of our illustrations are laden with feeling and emotion, we imply that loving God with the mind and the will is not as important as loving God with the heart. If there are often stories about men helping troubled women, we reinforce sinister gender stereotypes. Over time, the illustrative material in our sermons creates a worldview, and we must be careful to ensure that this worldview reflects the life we have been given in the gospel and not merely the culture close at hand.

SEARCHING FOR THE SOURCES

Where do we find illustrations? The pulpit is a hungry place. How do we collect the quantity of illustrative material we need for weekly preaching? There are four primary sources: the preacher's own life, the preacher's imagination, the world around us, and the media.

The preacher's own life

Occasionally the best illustrative material we can find comes from our own life experiences. But is it appropriate to talk about ourselves from the pulpit? Contemporary homileticians and other students of preaching have given several answers to that question, ranging from an enthusiastic yes ("The best help we can offer is our own woundedness and a description of what has saved and healed us"—Salmon[30]), through a cautious "sometimes" ("Self-disclosure in moderation is appropriate to preaching"—Craddock[31]), to a horrified no ("To be blunt, there are virtually no good reasons to talk about ourselves from the pulpit"—Buttrick[32]).

Most homileticians occupy the middle ground, recognizing both the power and the danger in self-disclosure. Some important rules have been devised: Don't always make yourself the hero; don't reveal pastoral confidences; don't embarrass a child or a spouse; don't turn the pulpit into a confessional; do tell experiences with which the hearers can identify, rather than "minister stories"; and so on.

These are good rules, but far more important than a list of rules is the matter of intent. Listeners are surprisingly savvy about discerning not only what we are saying about ourselves but also why we are saying it. If we are trying to come across as powerful or charming, if we are trying to win their sympathy or to get them to take care of us, if we are straining to say, "I may be a minister, but look, I'm really human, too," if we are simply indulging ourselves in autobiographical egotism, most of the congregation will read us like a book. If, on the other hand, we are saying, "Here is how it is to encounter some aspect of life and the gospel; let me use my own life as an example," then our hearers can be helped, through our illustrations, to name their own experiences.

An important distinction can be made between those personal experiences in which we are the primary subject and those in which we are simply the observer. An illustration that begins, "Last week, while I was waiting in the check-out line at the grocery store, I overheard a conversation between a father and his daughter," is a personal experience, but one in which we are not one of the primary actors. In such illustrations it is usually better to keep ourselves on the periphery, to maintain a stance as the narrator. Rather than intruding into the middle of the incident, telling the hearers that we were touched, dismayed, angered, saddened, or whatever by this father-daughter conversation, it is generally more effective to recount the experience in a manner that allows the listeners to be affected themselves.[33]

The preacher's imagination

It is certainly permissible to make up sermon illustrations, so long as we adhere to one strict rule: The preacher must always signal to the hearers that the illustration is a piece of fiction. We do not have to be clumsy about this, saying, "Now beware, I made up this next story." An introductory phrase like "Suppose," "Imagine that," or "What if" will usually suffice.

Why is this rule necessary? What is the difference, for example, in telling a true account of a man who comes to us for counseling because he is depressed and telling as true a fictional story of a man in another town who seeks counseling for depression. The latter story *could* have happened, and no confidences are broken in its telling. The reason we must always let the congregation know when we are relating fictional illustrations is that our only resource in preaching is the truth. We may have many flaws in our preaching. We may be less than exciting, somewhat disorganized, or even honestly mistaken about matters. All these flaws can be forgiven, but the one unpardonable sin for a preacher of the gospel is to lie. Concealing the fact that an illustration is fiction may seem like a small deception, but it makes a tear nonetheless in the essential fabric of truthfulness upon which our preaching depends.

The world around us

The accomplished preacher Ernest T. Campbell zealously urges preachers to carry a small note pad at all times so they can record the wealth of illustrative material encountered in the course of every day. His advice has a double value: The note pad ensures that illustrative material is not lost, and the very habit of carrying it causes preachers to be more alert and watchful about the disclosive power of everyday life.

The main problem with most published collections of sermon illustrations is that the canned and stylized stories they contain are generally remote from the world of our hearers ("Gladstone and the Duke of Wellington stories" one preacher calls them). It is far better to populate our sermons with images, phrases, and experiences drawn from ordinary life: the message on the bank sign, a line from a song on the radio, a scene from the shopping mall, a conversation in the stands at the high school game. Part of what preaching does is help Christian people to see life around us through the eyes of our faith, and the including of artifacts from the world around us serves as dress rehearsal for that kind of envisioning.

It would be a dreary way to live, of course, if we were condemned to go out the front door every day in search of sermon illustrations. There is also something sadly utilitarian, perhaps even unethical, about asking about every experience, "Can I use this in a sermon?" The principal way to avoid turning our entire lives into homiletical mills is to know very specifically what it is that we are looking for. If, for example, we are working ahead on a sermon in which the concept "kindness" will appear, some hard advance thinking about "kindness" will implant that idea in the creative area of our minds. Then, as we go about our business, small, otherwise unnoticed events—a gesture of a department store clerk, a hand offered on a bus, an extra plate at a table—will attach themselves to the concept. If we know what we are looking for, the chances are improved that we will find it (and, as Campbell would remind us, the chances are good that we will promptly lose it if we don't write it down).

The media

Television, movies, plays, newspapers, magazines, books, and other media provide broad access to the world around us. It is especially important for a minister to develop the habit of regular reading of both theological and nontheological materials. This is a matter of frustration for many ministers, since the crushing demands placed upon them tend to crowd out time for "nonessential" reading and reflection. In fact, though, the reading of novels, plays, short stories, cultural analysis, and other types of literature is not a nonessential for contemporary ministry. Some cultures still communicate their crucial ideas orally, but most of us do our ministry in a world that thinks in print. A preacher in our time and place who does not read widely is like a physician, an attorney, or a teacher who does not read: quickly obsolete. Wise preachers view their reading as a part of their ministerial work load, build reading time into their schedules, and protect it.

Reading informs and invigorates ministry in a variety of ways, and it has several specific benefits for preaching. First, reading gives us access to scenes in plays, episodes in novels, news accounts, and other materials that can be employed as illustrative matter. Second, reading heightens our own creativity and sharpens our language and compositional skills. Scenes in good plays, for example, can be very instructive regarding the effective use of dialogue, since playwrights and preachers share at least one task: placing evocative human experience in concise oral form. Short-story writers and preachers share another task: shaping effective communication in a brief span. Reading plays and short stories can improve our preaching, even when we do not quote them in a sermon.

Even the most diligent preachers cannot read everything they would like to be able to read. Most congregations, however, have people who read widely, and they can become active partners in the ministry of preaching. If we will identify those people and let them know the sort of material we need, they can keep us supplied with a rich variety of illustrative material.

9
From Desk to Pulpit

*Question: Why do you actors seem to make such impressions upon
your audiences, while we preachers frequently leave our
congregations cold?*
*Answer: Actors speak of things imaginary as if they were real, while
you preachers too often speak of things real as if they were
imaginary.*
   *—An exchange between the Archbishop of Canterbury
and English actor Thomas Betterton*

A "written sermon" is a contradiction in terms. Of course, many
sermons are written down *before* they are preached, and some sermons are written up *after* they are preached, but a sermon itself
occurs not in the writing but in the preaching. A sermon, by definition, is a spoken event. This is an important distinction, since speaking and writing are not merely two separate but equal channels of
communication. The effects of the spoken word are markedly different from those of the written word.

One difference is that speaking can be addressed to a group,
whereas writing implies an individual reader, or at most a series of
individual readers. The apostle Paul wrote one of his letters "to all
the saints in Christ Jesus who are at Philippi," yet that letter, in its
written form, could not be read by "all the saints" at once, only by
individuals. However, when that letter was read aloud—that is,
spoken—to the Philippian congregation, the hearing of it became a
community experience. Indeed, the spoken word has the power to
create community. "Preaching" and "congregation" are reciprocal
terms. It is true that we preach *to* a congregation, but it is also true
that, through our preaching, the hearers *become* a congregation. As
Walter J. Ong has said,

When a speaker is addressing an audience, the members of the audience normally become a unity, with themselves and with the speaker. If the speaker asks the audience to read a handout provided for them, as each reader enters into his or her own private reading world, the unity of the audience is shattered, to be re-established only when oral speech begins again. Writing and print isolate. There is no collective noun or concept for readers corresponding to "audience." The collective "readership"—this magazine has a readership of two million—is a far-gone abstraction.[1]

Moreover, the act of speaking, unlike writing, takes place in the active presence of those who receive the communication. Even if I am "talking to myself," I have to pretend that I am two people.[2] Writers can imagine those who will eventually read their words, but speakers do not need to imagine the hearers. They are present in the moment of speaking, and their presence exerts a shaping force on the communication. This means that preachers do not "own" their sermons in quite the same way that authors "own" their manuscripts. When we stand up to preach, we already know most of what we will say, and we may even place on the pulpit a complete script of our words, but we do not really *have* the sermon in our hands or in our minds. A sermon happens only when we open our mouths and the hearers open their ears. People may call it "our sermon," but it does not belong to us alone. It belongs as well to those who help create it by their listening. To put it theologically, a sermon is a work of the church and not merely a work of the preacher.

FROM WRITTEN TO ORAL

In earlier chapters we explored the crucial steps a preacher takes in moving toward a sermon: interpreting a biblical text, creating a form, deciding about the use of illustrative material, and so on. Even though these activities have traditionally been thought of as "preparing the sermon," it would be more accurate, given the orality of preaching, to describe these steps as preparing *for* the sermon. Since most of these preliminary activities have involved reading and writing, one final step must be taken as we go from the desk to the pulpit: the move from writing to speaking.

The first decision we must make as we prepare to speak the sermon is the choice of what, if any, written materials to take with us into the pulpit. There are three broad options: a full manuscript, notes or an outline, or nothing written at all. Many people have cast their ballots for one or another of these methods, alleging its superiority, but the fact is that all three are quite acceptable and can be equally effective. The way to begin thinking about this decision is not by weighing the intrinsic merits of this or that method but by keeping our overall purpose in view. In preaching, we seek to say something important to other people, and whatever written helps we take with us into the pulpit should be designed to support that action. If you are to say something important to other people, three vital elements must be brought into cooperative interaction. *You* must be present in the speaking; some significant *message* must be spoken; and the *listeners* must be active partners in the event. How can written materials enhance or impede this interplay among speaker, message, and hearers?

The use of a full manuscript obviously places the emphasis on the sermon content, ensuring that the message will be intact, and that is no small virtue. The careful advance selection of apt words, phrases, and images for sermons is an act of ministry and much to be preferred over the sloppy and haphazard use of language that can result when we search for wording on our feet. The thoughtful composition of our sermons, heedfully selecting the language best suited for this congregation's hearing, is a way of taking seriously our responsibility to the listeners.

On the other hand, the cumbersome reading of a manuscript can strain the interaction between preacher and hearers to the vanishing point. The experience of hearing a preacher preach to a stack of papers rather than to the hearers is deadly. Many preachers, though, have learned how to read sermon manuscripts with energy and skill, minimizing the loss of presence often associated with this method. Also, manuscript pages can be composed so that they can be used much like a set of notes. The lines can be printed like stanzas of a poem, spaces can be allocated between the sections of the sermon, brackets can be drawn around illustrative material, key phrases can be underlined or highlighted, headings or marginal notes can be attached to various portions, or other markings made to render the manuscript more a picture of the sermon's movement and less an unbroken sea of print.

Moving to the other end of the spectrum, using no written materials whatsoever places the emphasis on the presence of the preacher and, to some degree, on the participation of the hearers. Preaching without written aids is a difficult skill to master, but there is an undeniable sense of authenticity and immediacy involved when the preacher speaks directly to the listeners with no written "screen" between them. This advantage is squandered, however, if the sermon seems recited from rote memory, on the one hand, or loose, rambling, and content-starved, on the other. Some preachers attempt to develop the ability to preach without notes because of the amazed approval often given to this method by congregations, but the oratorical nimbleness of the preacher is a pseudovalue in the Christian context. The church finally does not need to experience the presence of the preacher, it needs rather to hear the claims of the Christian faith *through* the preacher. If the avoidance of written materials causes the content of the sermon to be lost, ultimately all is lost.

The use of notes or a schematic outline represents a middle choice and an attempt to balance the competing needs for careful content, presence of the preacher, and hearer interaction. This method can involve something as simple as a list of key words or as elaborate as a full sentence outline. Some preachers create notes or an outline as their only written preparation; others prepare a full manuscript and then distill it into the briefer form. Again, the main risk in this method is the possible loss of precision in the use of language.

Which method you choose will depend on you and your skills, the kind of sermon being preached, and the nature of the specific preaching occasion. For some preachers, a manuscript acts like a magnet, drawing their energy and presence down into the pulpit and away from the congregation. For others, anything less than a manuscript produces vain repetitions and inappropriate ad-libs. Or again, a preacher who usually brings a full manuscript into the pulpit may want to have only a few notes, or nothing written at all, for a sermon preached at a graveside or at a camp communion service. In preaching we are trying, today and in this place, to bear witness to the gospel in such a way that these people know they are directly addressed by it. So long as we remain clear about this purpose, we are free to experiment with notes, manuscripts, and the like in various settings until we find the best methods to support our preaching ministry.

AND I QUOTE . . .

Quotations from books, essays, songs, and plays are often very helpful in sermons, but their use creates a special problem because quotations represent an intrusion of the written form into a spoken event. Before we decide to employ a quotation in a sermon, we should consider whether or not a quotation is the best means to accomplish our goal. Generally speaking, there are only two good reasons for using a quotation: the credibility of the person who said it or the power of the language in which it is said. Consider, for example, this quotation from a hymn:

> Should it be ours to drain the cup of grieving
>   even to the dregs of pain, at thy command,
> we will not falter, thankfully receiving
>   all that is given by thy loving hand.[3]

Those words possess their own power, but they gain even more strength when we know they were composed by Dietrich Bonhoeffer in a German concentration camp only months before his execution. Who said them is as important as what they say. Or again, consider this brief portion of a sermon on the opening verses of the Gospel of John:

> If we were to search for the most beautiful and moving passage in the New Testament, we would certainly have to consider the beginning lines—the Prologue—of the Gospel of John. These verses form a hymn which soars with majestic poetic power, and its images press deeply into our minds. Speaking of these verses, the New Testament scholar Raymond Brown observed, "If John has been described as the pearl of great price among the [New Testament] writings, then one may say that the Prologue is the pearl within this gospel. . . . The choice of the eagle as the symbol of John the Evangelist was largely determined by the celestial flights of the opening lines of the Gospel."[4]

Here the preacher quotes a well-known student of the Gospel of John as a way of saying, "The view I am describing is also held by biblical scholars—Raymond Brown, for example." One caution about this matter of quoting authorities: No words have more immediate credibility in a sermon that those of the truthful preacher. If our implied message is, "You may not accept this coming from me, but Augustine said it, Luther said it, Barth said it, and Einstein said it too," then we sadly underestimate, even cheapen, the gift of authority the Christian community grants to us in the act of preaching.

Sometimes it is the wording of the quotation, more than the person quoted, that most makes a statement effective. Here is an example:

> It is a mistake to sharpen our minds by narrowing them. It is a mistake to look to the Bible to close a discussion; the Bible seeks to open one. . . . The Bible is no oracle to be consulted for specific advice on specific problems; rather, it is a wellspring of wisdom about the ambiguity, inevitability, and insolubility of the human situation. . . . The Bible makes us comfortable with struggle but uneasy in success. . . . [T]he Bible is a signpost, not a hitching post.[5]

The power of that quotation lies in the way it is stated and not primarily in the fact that William Sloane Coffin happened to be the one who said it. When we employ a quotation like this, our responsibility to the hearers is to let them know, in the least disruptive way possible, that we are using the words of someone else. If the listeners would recognize Coffin's name, or if we wish to give the statement a personal ring, or if we simply desire to credit the source, we may introduce the quotation with a brief phrase like, "William Sloane Coffin has observed. . . ." Otherwise we can just say, "As one minister has said," "someone has pointed out," or the like. Elaborate oral footnotes (such as "William Sloane Coffin, in his collection of sermons entitled *The Courage to Love,* said . . .") tend to clutter the air and undermine the power of the quotation itself.

One rule about quotations: They almost always lose some of their effectiveness as they move from the page to the pulpit. They are seldom as evocative for the hearers as they were for us when we first read them. Because of this, sermon quotations should be sparingly used, and they should always be distilled to their essence. If, for example, we wish to quote a provocative statement of a character in a novel, instead of reading a whole page of the novel to give the background, we can set the scene ourselves, in our own words, and then provide the quotation.

FINDING THE RHYTHM

Should sermons be rehearsed aloud? That question never fails to provoke a squirm of embarrassment among preachers, since the language of rehearsal smacks of performance and play-acting. If we know the content of our sermon and believe what we are going to say in the sermon, why should we practice it? Would it not be more authentic simply to stand up and preach it "for real" the first time?

The primary purpose of practicing a sermon aloud, however, is not to polish our role as performer. To the contrary, it is to place ourselves in the role of the listener. Indeed, as we speak our sermon out loud, we become its first hearer. Listening to our own sermon being spoken makes us aware of the rhythms, movements, and intrinsic timing of the sermon in ways that studying notes or a manuscript can never do. We realize, perhaps, that a sentence that looks good on paper sounds convoluted in speech. If the hearers are to understand what we are saying, that sentence will need to be broken into shorter oral phrases. Or a description ("the many problems of our town") suddenly sounds dull and bloodless and cries out for sharper images (the abandoned factory with the rusting gate, the homeless child curled sleeping beside her mother under the highway bridge, the vodka bottle hidden in the laundry closet).

We discover in the speaking aloud of our sermon places where pauses will be necessary to allow the hearers time to reflect, where our speech will need to be more rapid, or slower, if the power of that part of the sermon is to be felt. We hear ourselves describing "Goliath, whose height was six cubits and a span" in a tiny, unamazed voice that would give the impression he was really only five feet four inches tall.[6] We recognize that if the hearers are to find themselves in a story we are telling, we must learn the story well enough to say it without reading it. As we practice the sermon aloud, we see in our imaginations the faces of the people who will hear it, and our language becomes more immediate, more directed to life, more rich with grace.

Practicing the sermon also enables us to absorb it. We do not memorize it, but we learn it "by heart" and, thus, can be more present with and for the hearers in the actual event of preaching.

SPEAKING THE TRUTH

The time has come for the sermon. We are standing there, and the congregation waits and listens. How should we speak? Should we be firm and convincing, or gentle and inviting? Shall we let our bodies be caught up in the energy of our message, or should we restrain our movements, letting our words speak for themselves? Should we make plenty of eye contact with the congregation, or will that only make them feel scrutinized and uncomfortable? Should we worry about our accents or our nasalization or how we always stumble over the word "Nebuchadnezzar" or the way our glasses slip down on our noses as we speak?

Obviously it would be foolish to say that the mechanics of voice and body do not matter in preaching. They do, and there are excellent manuals available to assist preachers in the techniques of body and voice control.[7] It is encouraging to know, however, that flaws and idiosyncrasies in our delivery are not nearly so damaging as one might suspect. Obviously, if our voice is too soft to be heard, our speech too slurred to be understood, or our gestures violent contradictions of our message, these are serious problems and need firm attention. Hearers soon learn, though, to live with the majority of hitches and halts in delivery that most of us have. They grow to love some of them, enjoy with amusement some others, and filter out the rest. It is called grace.

Sometimes preachers are given the rather lame advice to "be natural" in the pulpit. Such advice, Robert Kirkpatrick wryly notes, "is of no more help to the preacher than is the same advice when spoken by the photographer to the over-tense or over-relaxed individual on whom his camera is trained."[8] We cannot "be natural" when we are not "feeling natural." Preachers are not immune from nervousness, tenseness, or moodiness, and these conditions affect us when we preach. It is part of the human condition to which we, and our hearers, can and will learn to adjust.

There is an even deeper truth to learn, however, about sermon delivery and the preacher's physical presence in preaching. If we are faithfully exercising our ministry of preaching, if we are honestly bearing witness to the gospel, for and with people whom we love, over time it will show. If we are fundamentally bored by what we are doing, feel contempt for or superior to the hearers, are cynical toward what we are preaching, try to be impressive or charming, or wish we were in some other vocation, that will also show. A person who, week after week, is speaking the truth in love, looks and sounds like a person lovingly telling the truth; there is finally no hiding it.

10

Conversation
Along the Pilgrim Way

Each of us is moving, changing, with respect to others. As we discover, we remember; remembering, we discover; and most intensely do we experience this when our separate journeys converge.
— Eudora Welty,
One Writer's Beginnings

In times gone by, when many Christians made pilgrimages to holy shrines, they talked together as they journeyed. They told wonderful, sad, and even raucous stories. They disclosed their fears and their ambitions, their faith and their failings, their secret joys and hidden doubts as they broke bread at table and drank the harsh wine of wayside inns. When pilgrims embarked on their journey, they held in common only a destination; when they reached journey's end, they shared a common life.

We have now come to the final stretch of our mutual journey. Along the way I have imagined that you and I, and the others who have gone with us, were talking together as we traveled. I hope you have heard my voice and the voices of many others who have taken up the ministry of teaching those who preach. I also hope you have heard your own voice—questioning, probing, challenging, demurring, becoming your own teacher.

One of the well-traveled medieval pilgrim roads led through perilous regions of Spain to the great Cathedral of Saint James in Compostela. It is said that as the pilgrims approached the city they would focus their eyes on the horizon, straining to see the towers of the cathedral, the object of their long journey. The one who first spotted the cathedral in the distance would cry, "My joy!" and would promptly be named the "king" of the pilgrim band. In fact, many people today who have last names "King," "Leroy," "Koenig," or "Rex" owe their surnames to the sharp eyes of some pilgrim ancestor.[1]

Perhaps, as we have walked together on our pilgrim road toward a deeper understanding of the ministry of preaching, you have been casting your own eyes toward the distant horizon in the direction of our destination. Indeed, it would be gratifying to me to think that you were the first to have it in view, the one to cry, "My joy!"

PREACHING LORE

Whenever preachers gather to talk shop, certain perennial topics arise. There are some questions about preaching, large and small, practical and theoretical, that must constantly be reopened and examined anew. These questions have no permanent answers but rather an evolving "preachers' lore" which has grown up around them. "What do you do about . . . ?" "My experience has been . . ." "Have you tried . . . ?" "Do you find that . . . ?" "Whatever you do, don't . . ." These are the sounds of preachers talking with each other about the lore of their craft as they walk together along the pilgrim way. This last portion of our journey together will be spent exploring some of those recurring questions and entering into the ongoing conversation.

How much advanced planning should we do for our sermons?

Preachers vary widely in their planning habits. Some preachers have well-organized minds, and with the aid of a calendar and a lectionary they plan their preaching months in advance. A few even take a week or so of study leave to sketch out a general preaching scheme for the coming year. Most of us are less disciplined, beginning the next sermon only after the present one has been delivered.

The best wisdom is that every preacher can be actively at work on five or six sermons at once. A good method is to create separate file folders for, say, the next half dozen sermons. The biblical texts should be chosen and enough of the exegetical work done on these texts to know the general direction of each of the sermons. The preacher can then browse through these files periodically to keep the upcoming sermon themes in mind. Clippings from the newspaper, quotes from novels, pastoral experiences, and other ideas can then be placed into the files so that, when the time comes to create a sermon, its folder will already contain some working material. As soon as a sermon is complete, a new file is made to take its place at the end of the line. Older homileticians called this method a "homiletical garden." The big task is in setting up the system, since exegetical work on several sermons is required. Once the garden is planted, however, it can be tilled and cultivated as a matter of routine.

How do you save illustrative material for future use?

Again, customs differ among preachers. Some have elaborate filing systems (a growing number on computer). Whenever they encounter a story or an incident that shows promise as preaching material, they make a judgment about its subject matter and file it accordingly. This is an orderly way to proceed, but the problem lies in the fact that good preaching material can seldom be easily categorized. It is difficult to classify, for example, a newspaper story about a wealthy man who, weary of the burdens of his riches, tossed his fortune in $100 bills onto a busy freeway, causing motorists to abandon their cars and chase wildly after the money. A story like that can be "about" many things, and it is hard to know where to file it.

Thus, other preachers do not file illustrative material at all; rather, they keep it in a single place and sort through it for every sermon, allowing unexpected connections to be made between the sermon content and the collected bits and pieces. A compromise solution is to file the material in its most likely slot but also to make a one-phrase record of each item on an index card. The files keep the material in order; the cards can be used for random searches.

Should sermons have titles? If so, what kind?

Nowhere is it written in stone that sermons must have titles. Indeed, a great deal of distorted preaching has been generated by preachers assigning titles to sermons before the work on them is done (for the sake of the newspaper, church newsletter, or printed church bulletin), only to find that careful exegesis of the biblical text demands that the sermon move in another direction. In a tug-of-war between a text and a previously announced title, the title almost always wins, and the sermon is the poorer for it.

Nevertheless, most sermons do have titles, and that means we need to think through the purpose of a title. Some people argue that titles have a semievangelistic purpose, since church wanderers and other seekers survey the Saturday newspaper for a tempting sermon title. I am dubious about that, but even if a small number of people scan the church ads for alluring titles, it would be unfortunate if preachers created glitzy sermon titles to snare curiosity-seekers.

The main function of a title is to serve as an advance introduction to the sermon. When people read the title, they immediately begin guessing what the sermon will be about. Just like the regular sermon introduction, then, a sermon's title makes an implied promise. If we entitle a sermon "God's Answer to Suffering," we are promising nothing less than to supply that answer. Homer K. Buerlein, a lay critic of preaching, complains that some sermon titles tell too much.

They don't make promises about the sermon; they "give the sermon away." Commenting on a title like "Practicing Christianity Through Love of God and Man," Buerlein writes:

> From that title, you know exactly what the preacher is going to say. You know, for instance, that a true Christian cannot love God without loving people, and vice versa. No doubt, numerous examples of each type of love will be present in the sermon.[2]

The best sermon titles, then, are probably those that orient people to the sermon and prepare them to be active listeners, without either promising too much or revealing too much of the sermon content. A simple title, like "Repentance" or "Learning to Forgive," is good, and so are titles that are intriguing yet honest, like William Muehl's "God Has No Pride"[3] or Ernest T. Campbell's "Locked in a Room with Open Doors."[4] Such titles create a sense of anticipation and readiness on the part of the hearers.

How long should a sermon be?

It is tempting to say that each sermon should be long enough to get its task done—no more, no less—but the matter is not that simple. Preaching is not just putting messages of various sizes into spoken form; preaching is ritual activity as well, and a ritual has its own internal pacing and timing. A sermon is an oral genre, and there are community expectations about its length. To illustrate, imagine that a neighbor runs into you on the street, opens the conversation by saying, "Got time for a good joke?" You are in the mood for a laugh and not in a hurry, so you nod your head, and the neighbor begins, "There were these two sailors on shore leave. . . ." An hour and a half later, the neighbor is still not finished telling the joke. Think how perplexed you would be. When you said you had time for this, you were expecting a brief, funny story. Now there is no law stating that a joke cannot last for an hour—or a week, for that matter—but in our culture the oral genre called "joke" means a short, humorous story. Anyone who takes on the ritual role of joke-teller must abide by those limits or suffer the consequences of listener mutiny.

Congregations have ritual expectations about the range of time a sermon should last. These expectations are the product of many forces, including their past experience with preaching, the specific nature of the service of worship, and the larger view of time in their culture. Some congregations expect a sermon to last only ten minutes; others expect forty-five minutes or an hour. If the preaching is too brief, the congregation will not perceive that they have heard a "real" sermon, regardless of its content. If the sermon far exceeds the expected length, the congregation will almost surely grow restless, will perhaps even shut down their listening altogether.

Preachers should take these congregational expectations seriously but not legalistically. Indeed, a congregation's ritual regarding preaching is strong but not inflexible. If, for example, the previous preacher was a person who did not value preaching very much and for twenty-five years presented two-minute "thoughts for the day" instead of sermons, we are not locked into that format even though the congregation has grown to expect it. If we choose to preach sermons of, say, eighteen or twenty minutes in length, we should not be surprised to receive some initial resistance, but the congregation will almost surely gradually adjust its expectations accordingly.

A different sort of problem is posed by the occasional sermon that falls outside the range of time expected by the hearers. Suppose we decide that a certain sermon needs an extra fifteen minutes beyond the normal length. The chances are good that, if we simply preach that long without doing anything to prepare the congregation, they will find the extra time to be a struggle. We could, of course, announce at the beginning, "The sermon today will be a long one, so be prepared," but that would almost surely send up a groan and precipitate a sit-down strike. It is generally more effective to send a more subtle signal to the hearers that this sermon is an exception to the rule. Presumably, we have a good reason for making this particular sermon longer than usual, and, instead of merely warning them that "this will be a long one," we can offer the reason.

In the gospel lesson for today, Jesus told the rich ruler, "Sell all that you have and distribute it to the poor." Most of us would be happy to consider that command as applying to the ruler, but surely not to us. But is this so? Are we, too, commanded to "sell all"? What responsibility do we have toward our possessions? Those are not easy questions, and there are no easy answers. We will have to think carefully and deeply about them, and today, even more than usual, we will have to put on our thinking caps and look seriously at what our faith demands of us.

This preacher has said nothing about the length of the sermon, but a clear signal has been given that this sermon will be unusually demanding. This does not guarantee, of course, that the hearers will not become restless, but it does honestly inform them of the reason why this day's sermon will be extended.

Some homileticians believe that attention spans have been seriously eroded by television and that, as a result, sermons need to be briefer, more episodic, and more visually oriented. There is surely a measure of truth in this, but the destructive effects of the electronic media on preaching have probably been exaggerated. In fact, the shallowness of communication in our time generates a hunger for an urgent and important word. If our sermons begin to imitate the flashy, superficial style of the media, we relinquish the great opportunity we have been given to speak that word.

Are children's sermons a good idea?

Some argue that children's sermons are the unfortunate result of a modern mentality that dotes on the cuteness of children. There is no more reason, the argument goes, to create a special sermon for children than there is to create one for people over sixty-five. Moreover, children's sermons tend to be banal, moralistic, and indulgent of some children's desire to perform in front of adults.

That is a harsh opinion but worth considering, nonetheless. It is true that the ideal is to construct the whole of worship, including the sermon, in such a way that the entire congregation, including the children, can be involved in every element. This does not mean that the language of worship is reduced to a child's level but rather that the needs and capacities of children are taken into account throughout. A sermon, for example, can and should include some material that speaks to the world of children. The children in the congregation can participate directly in those portions of the sermon and listen more rhythmically and intuitively to other parts that are beyond their understanding.

The practical problem is that this ideal is quite difficult to achieve. Children represent perhaps the hardest group to incorporate into the full span of worship, and the best way to consider a children's sermon is as a frank admission of our failure to create genuinely multigenerational worship. So, yes, children's sermons are, for many congregations, a good idea, so long as they do not serve as a substitute for the continuing search for more embracing forms of worship. Moreover, special attention can be given to children in worship other than through a children's *sermon.* Indeed, it reinforces a misunderstanding about worship to imply that the sermon is the only crucial element. Including children's prayers, hymns, responses, or offerings, instead of only children's sermons, overcomes this narrowing of liturgical focus.

If we do decide to preach children's sermons, however, there are some cautions we should consider:

1. They should be real sermons: that is to say, they should be proclamations of the gospel and not lessons on conventional morality.

2. They should be addressed to the children, and not through the children to the overhearing adults.

3. We should not assume that children are a monolithic group.

Cognitive abilities change rapidly during childhood, and there is no such thing as "speaking at the level of a child." There are many such levels. The widespread custom, for instance, of giving "object lessons" ("these eyeglasses, children, are like the Bible") depends on the child's capacity to think abstractly, an ability very young children simply do not have. Some children's sermons should just be the telling of stories, including Bible stories, without any attempt to make a point. Understanding a "point" again requires the capacity for abstract thought.

4. We should be cautious about the practice of asking open-ended questions of the children, not only because this sends their parents into anxiety but also because of the potential for embarrassing the child. A child's serious response may amuse the congregation, whose unexpected laughter can be perplexing or even frightening.

How do we handle the dry periods in our preaching?

Preachers inevitably experience periods of drought in their preaching, times when sermons come even more painfully than usual and creativity ebbs. These times should neither surprise nor dismay us. In some ways, the best counsel is to acknowledge that all preachers have them, to expect them, and to allow them to run their course.

Many times, though, dry periods in our preaching signal empty moments in our own growth in faith. The best response, then, is not to fret about sermon technique but rather to set out in some new direction in our understanding of and commitment to the gospel. Some preachers, when they sense that their preaching is losing vitality, set themselves to the task of preaching a series of sermons on issues, doctrines, or biblical texts with which they are less familiar. This forces them onto new ground, where they must read, study, wrestle, and pray as they prepare to preach.

How do we get out of stylistic ruts in our sermons?

If we are not careful and diligent, our sermons may begin to sound alike. We may find ourselves employing similar, and thus predictable, forms for every sermon or using characteristic formulas of speech. Some preachers almost always begin their sermons with a contemporary story; others overuse rhetorical questions as means for engaging the hearers ("So what does this ancient text have to say to us today?"); still others have their pet phrases ("dear friends," "peace and justice concerns," "spirit-filled Christians").

Because these patterns are ours and reflect the ways we think and speak, they are usually difficult to spot. Sometimes we can become aware of them by reviewing, several weeks after the fact, manuscripts or tapes of sermons that we have preached. The delay in time provides the sense of distance we need to cast a critical eye on our own work. Far better, though, is to ask some impartial observer with an editorial knack (generally a trusted friend or colleague outside of our congregation) to comb through a sample of our sermons looking for oft-repeated techniques and clichés of form and language. This can be a threatening exercise, of course, but the reward of vitality in our preaching is worth the risk.

Should we balance pastoral sermons with prophetic ones?

Preachers recognize that some sermons are addressed more to personal needs and issues, while others apply more to public issues and the concerns of the larger society. They believe, accurately, that the Christian faith addresses both kinds of issues, and so they seek to keep their preaching in balance.

It would be a mistake, however, to make too sharp a distinction between "pastoral" and "prophetic" sermons, as if personal issues could be separated from their placement in the social context, and vice versa. The gospel does not speak to isolated individuals and then swivel to speak another word to the world of politics and social systems. The gospel speaks to the totality of human life, to people as they strive to be faithful among the many and complex interconnections of their lives.

In chapter 2 we learned that when preachers go to scripture they take the people with them, and that what is heard in the text is affected by the circumstances of those who will hear the sermon. It is absolutely crucial that preachers understand that we are standing before scripture on behalf of the people in the full realities of their lives—personal and political. Consider, for example, what Allan Boesak, the South African minister who has worked, suffered, and preached eloquently against the government policy of apartheid, heard when he listened, on behalf of his congregation, to the text in Revelation 13:11–18 that describes the beast that looks like a lamb but speaks like a dragon:

> It looks like a lamb, John warns, but it speaks like a dragon. It says peace! peace! where there is no peace. It speaks about reconciliation without the confrontation and the cost. The dragon which looks like a lamb is full of compassion for the anguish of the oppressor as he makes yet another "unavoidable" decision to kill the innocent. And yet it cannot hear the voice of God in the cries of the poor and the needy. It is the voice of those who believe that the sins of the church should be buried by history instead of confessed and forgiven. It is the voice of those who are so concerned about what may happen to white

> South Africans *one day,* after apartheid will have come to its inevitable
> end, that they show no concern at all about what is being done to black
> South Africans *right now.* It looks like a lamb, but its voice is the voice
> of a dragon. It is the voice that protests, even now, as the blood of our
> children stains the streets, "Apartheid is a Christian policy!" But the
> truth is out and cannot be suppressed: apartheid is not Christian, it
> is a blasphemy, an idolatry, and a heresy.[5]

Because of the place in history occupied by Boesak and his congregation, he heard the text speaking a true and powerful word against the
oppressive powers of the government. This is clearly a political,
prophetic word, but it is not a nonpastoral word. It is an inspiring,
encouraging word to lift the hearts and nourish the souls of those
who must live each day in the terrors of that situation.

Here is what a preacher in another context heard when he stood
on behalf of the people before the parable of the Unforgiving Servant
(Matt. 18:23–35):

> We forget that sin is what you and I do, too. That we too owe a debt.
> Take a moment right now, and think back over just the past month
> in your life. Think about the times you have spoken sharply to your
> husband or wife or parent or child. Think about the things you have
> done you really don't want anybody else to know about. The things
> out of pure selfishness. Remember taking that shortcut at work? En-
> joying somebody else's embarrassment [or] pain? And then multiply
> the month's failure by twelve for the months of the year and that again
> by the number of years in your life. And you begin to understand what
> Jesus meant by giving the unmerciful servant such an enormous,
> unmanageable debt.[6]

Now this hearing of scripture is admittedly far more inward and less
sharply political than the word Boesak heard. The sermon portion
is populated by images of personal analysis and self-reflection. And
yet even here there are forces pushing beyond the merely private life
of an individual into the more systemic worlds of family, work, and
social responsibility.

So rather than arbitrarily dividing our preaching into pastoral and
prophetic categories, we take the fullness of the life of the people into
the encounter with scripture and then tell the truth about what we
hear. Sometimes our sermons will take a more pastoral tone, sometimes a more prophetic one, but these are not two distinct kinds of
preaching. Even so, we must constantly guard against our inevitable
tendency to silence the full witness of scripture. For many of us—let
us admit it—this means a tendency to force the gospel in personal,
inward, and individualistic directions. As Walter Brueggemann has
observed,

a tendency to which good preaching is opposed is a kind of subjectivity that assumes we are free or able to conjure up private worlds that may exist in a domesticated sphere without accountability to or impingement from the larger public world. Such a powerful deception among us seems to offer happiness, but it is essentially abdication from the great public issues that shape our humanness.[7]

What that means, among other things, is that even if we are preaching in a suburban context where the immediate concerns are job, home, school, and personal crises of one kind or another, we cannot pretend that we do not participate in the same world in which Allan Boesak lives. We are involved in the struggles against the principalities and powers, both through our faithfulness and through our sinful cooperation with those forces of evil. We must take that circumstance with us as we go to the text, and then we must bear witness to the fullness of the gospel even though the cost be great.

A PARTING WORD ON THE PILGRIM WAY

That which was from the beginning,
  which we have heard,
  which we have seen with our eyes,
  which we have looked upon
    and touched with our hands,
  concerning the word of life—
the life was made manifest,
  and we saw it,
  and witness to it.

1 John 1:1–2

Notes

Introduction

1. Jürgen Moltmann, *The Church in the Power of the Spirit: A Contribution to Messianic Ecclesiology* (New York: Harper & Row, 1977), p. 303.

2. Ibid., p. 206.

3. Craig Dykstra, "The Formative Power of the Congregation," *Religious Education* 82(4):532 (Fall 1987).

4. Ibid., p. 537.

5. Ibid., p. 540.

6. William H. Willimon, *What's Right with the Church* (San Francisco: Harper & Row, 1985), p. 121.

7. Moltmann, *The Church,* p. 303.

8. Karl Barth, *The Doctrine of Reconciliation, Church Dogmatics,* IV/2, trans. G. W. Bromiley (Edinburgh: T. & T. Clark, 1958), pp. 124–125.

9. Moltmann, *The Church,* p. 110.

Chapter 1: What Does It Mean to Preach?

1. William H. Willimon, *What's Right with the Church* (San Francisco: Harper & Row, 1985), p. 107.

2. Jürgen Moltmann, *The Church in the Power of the Spirit* (New York: Harper & Row, 1977), p. 303.

3. Karl Barth, *The Doctrine of the Word of God, Church Dogmatics,* I/1, trans. G. T. Thomson (Edinburgh: T. & T. Clark, 1936), p. 57 (emphasis mine).

4. D. W. Cleverley Ford, *Ministry of the Word* (Grand Rapids: Wm. B. Eerdmans Publishing Co., 1979), p. 104.

5. Karl Barth, in Emil Brunner and Karl Barth, *Natural Theology,* trans. Peter Fraenkel (London: Centenary Press, 1946), p. 127.

6. Dietrich Ritschl, *A Theology of Proclamation* (Richmond: John Knox Press, 1960), pp. 132, 133.

7. Ford, *Ministry of the Word,* p. 103.

8. William McAdoo, in Gene E. Bartlett, *Postscript to Preaching* (Valley Forge, Pa.: Judson Press, 1981), pp. 60–61.

9. Moltmann, *The Church,* p. 303.

10. Robert C. Tannehill, *The Sword of His Mouth: Forceful and Imaginative Language in Synoptic Sayings* (Philadelphia: Fortress Press, 1975), p. 1.

11. Amos N. Wilder, *Early Christian Rhetoric: The Language of the Gospel* (London: SCM Press, 1964), p. 26.

12. Ford, *Ministry of the Word,* pp. 107–108.

13. On the relationship of preaching to culture, see Daniel Patte, *Preaching Paul* (Philadelphia: Fortress Press, 1984). Patte observes that Paul, as a preacher, faced a situation similar to that of the contemporary preacher: His message, the *kerygma,* was couched in Jewish apocalyptic terms, but his hearers were participants in a culture, Hellenistic, for which those terms were alien. Patte argues that Paul's preaching neither avoided the Hellenistic context nor reduced the *kerygma* to culturally amenable concepts. Rather, Paul repeated the *kerygma* in its Jewish vocabulary but accompanied this with the declaration that this *kerygma* was being fulfilled in terms of the hearers' own experience. Paul's preaching, then, occurred at the intersection of two languages, two "worlds": the kerygmatic and the specifically cultural-experiential.

14. Heinz Zahrnt, *The Question of God: Protestant Theology in the Twentieth Century,* trans. R. A. Wilson (New York: Harcourt, Brace & World, 1969), p. 118.

15. Ibid., p. 117.

16. Karl Barth, *The Preaching of the Gospel,* trans. B. E. Hooke (Philadelphia: Westminster Press, 1963), p. 74.

17. J. Randall Nichols, *The Restoring Word: Preaching as Pastoral Communication* (San Francisco: Harper & Row, 1987), p. 16.

18. Clement Welsh, *Preaching in a New Key: Studies in the Psychology of Thinking and Listening* (Philadelphia: Pilgrim Press, 1974), pp. 15–16.

19. Nichols, *The Restoring Word,* p. 6.

20. J. Randall Nichols, *Building the Word: The Dynamics of Communication and Preaching* (San Francisco: Harper & Row, 1980), ch. 2.

21. Edmund Holt Linn, *Preaching as Counseling: The Unique Method of Harry Emerson Fosdick* (Valley Forge, Pa.: Judson Press, 1966), pp. 15–16.

22. Gary D. Stratman, *Pastoral Preaching: Timeless Truths for Changing Needs* (Nashville: Abingdon Press, 1983).

23. Nichols, *The Restoring Word,* p. 189.

24. Joseph Sittler, *The Anguish of Preaching* (Philadelphia: Fortress Press, 1966), p. 38. See also the discussion of this point in Morris J. Niedenthal, "Focusing the Listener's Story," in Edmund A. Steimle, Morris J. Niedenthal, and Charles L. Rice, *Preaching the Story* (Philadelphia: Fortress Press, 1980), pp. 78–80.

25. George A. Lindbeck, *The Nature of Doctrine: Religion and Theology in a Postliberal Age* (Philadelphia: Westminster Press, 1984), p. 118.

26. Ibid.

27. Steimle et al., *Preaching the Story,* pp. 12–13, 15.

28. Peter Berger as quoted in Clyde E. Fant, *Preaching for Today,* rev. ed. (San Francisco: Harper & Row, 1987), p. 45.

29. A phrase David Kelsey applies to Barth's view of the Bible. Quoted in Lindbeck, *The Nature of Doctrine,* pp. 120–121.

30. David Buttrick, *Homiletic: Moves and Structures* (Philadelphia· Fortress Press, 1987), p. 12.

31. For examples of proponents of sermons with narrativelike structures, see Eugene Lowry, *The Homiletical Plot* (Atlanta: John Knox Press, 1980), and my own

earlier work, "Shaping Sermons by Plotting the Text's Claim Upon Us," in *Preaching Biblically*, ed. Don M. Wardlaw (Philadelphia: Westminster Press, 1983), pp. 84–100.

32. Stanley Hauerwas, *A Community of Character: Toward a Constructive Christian Ethic* (Notre Dame, Ind.: University of Notre Dame Press, 1981), p. 66.

33. H. Richard Niebuhr, *The Meaning of Revelation* (New York: Macmillan Co., 1941, 1960), p. 35.

34. Hendrikus Berkhof, *Christian Faith: An Introduction to the Study of the Faith* (Grand Rapids: Wm. B. Eerdmans Publishing Co., 1979), p. 17.

35. Paul Ricoeur, "The Hermeneutics of Testimony," in *Essays on Biblical Interpretation*, ed. Lewis S. Mudge (Philadelphia: Fortress Press, 1980), p. 131.

36. Ibid., pp. 128–129.

37. Lindbeck, *The Nature of Doctrine*, p. 121.

38. Ricoeur, "The Hermeneutics of Testimony," p. 131.

39. Richard K. Fenn, *Liturgies and Trials* (New York: Pilgrim Press, 1982), p. 27.

40. Buttrick, *Homiletic*, p. 451.

41. Moltmann, *The Church*, p. 224.

Chapter 2: The Biblical Witness in Preaching

1. Yngve Brilioth, *A Brief History of Preaching*, trans. Karl E. Mattson (Philadelphia: Fortress Press, 1965), p. 9.

2. George Arthur Buttrick, "The Bible and Preaching," in *The Interpreter's One-Volume Commentary on the Bible*, ed. Charles M. Laymon (Nashville: Abingdon Press, 1971), p. 1255.

3. James Barr, *The Scope and Authority of the Bible* (Philadelphia: Westminster Press, 1980), p. 55.

4. Cf. David Kelsey, *The Uses of Scripture in Recent Theology* (Philadelphia: Fortress Press, 1975), p. 208.

5. Barr, *The Scope and Authority of the Bible*, p. 55.

6. J. Christiaan Beker, *Suffering and Hope* (Philadelphia: Fortress Press, 1987), p. 25.

7. Walter Brueggemann, *The Bible Makes Sense* (Atlanta: John Knox Press, 1977), p. 34.

8. Leander E. Keck, *The Bible in the Pulpit* (Nashville: Abingdon Press, 1978), p. 62.

Chapter 3: Biblical Exegesis for Preaching

1. Cf. John H. Hayes and Carl R. Holladay, *Biblical Exegesis: A Beginner's Handbook* (Atlanta: John Knox Press, 1982), pp. 23–28. This guide to biblical study is one of the best available, and the reader will find here a full description of the standard exegetical approaches plus a rich bibliography of resources.

2. Actually, modern biblical scholarship is becoming increasingly aware of how the "social placement" of the exegete affects the exegetical results. Even so, discussions in biblical studies of the relationship of social setting to hermeneutics are usually focused upon broad ideological and class categories, rather than upon the more finely tuned congregational situations that are so important for preaching.

3. Fred B. Craddock, *Preaching* (Nashville: Abingdon Press, 1985), p. 99.

4. Cf. William H. Todd, Jr., "Protagonist Corner: A Word for the Fashion Conscious, or the Limits of the Lectionary," *Journal for Preachers* 11(1):35–37 (Advent 1987).

5. For a more general discussion of the apparent bias of some lectionaries, see Justo L. González and Catherine G. González, *Liberation Preaching: The Pulpit and the Oppressed* (Nashville: Abingdon Press, 1980), pp. 38ff., and William D. Thompson, *Preaching Biblically* (Nashville: Abingdon Press, 1981), p. 20.

6. Cf. Joseph A. Fitzmyer, *The Gospel According to Luke I–IX*, The Anchor Bible, vol. 28 (Garden City, N.Y.: Doubleday & Co., 1981), especially pp. 134, 800; and E. E. Ellis, ed., *The Gospel of Luke*, in The Century Bible Commentary (London: Thomas Nelson & Sons, 1966), p. 36.

7. Cf. John H. Hayes and Carl R. Holladay, *Biblical Exegesis: A Beginner's Handbook* (Atlanta: John Knox Press, 1982), p. 24.

8. For a fine treatment of the exegetical role of the liturgical seasons, see Walter J. Burghardt, *Preaching: The Art and the Craft* (New York: Paulist Press, 1987), especially ch. 7.

9. See the discussion about polarities in biblical texts in Thompson, *Preaching Biblically*, pp. 54–56.

10. J. Randall Nichols, *Building the Word: The Dynamics of Communication and Preaching* (San Francisco: Harper & Row, 1980), p. 128.

11. Ibid.

12. Ibid., p. 129.

13. Craddock, *Preaching*, p. 123.

14. Hayes and Holladay, *Biblical Exegesis*, p. 45.

15. Ibid., p. 46.

16. Craddock, *Preaching*, p. 118.

17. O. C. Edwards, Jr., *The Living and Active Word: One Way to Preach from the Bible Today* (New York: Seabury Press, 1975), p. 22.

18. For a fine introduction to the sociological analysis of biblical texts, see Richard L. Rohrbaugh, *The Biblical Interpreter: An Agrarian Bible in an Industrial Age* (Philadelphia: Fortress Press, 1978). Rohrbaugh gives numerous examples of foolish preaching that resulted from a blindness to the social setting of biblical texts or, worse, from a stubborn twisting of those texts to make them fit comfortably into the social conventions of the preacher's own time.

19. Walter Brueggemann, "The Social Nature of the Biblical Text for Preaching," in *Preaching as a Social Act: Theology and Practice*, ed. Arthur Van Seters (Nashville: Abingdon Press, 1988), p. 131.

20. Walter Brueggemann, *The Bible Makes Sense* (Atlanta: John Knox Press, 1977), pp. 45–58.

21. Ibid., p. 52.

22. Ibid., p. 53.

23. For specific guidance on the relationship between the biblical genres and preaching, see Thomas G. Long, *Preaching and the Literary Forms of the Bible* (Philadelphia: Fortress Press, 1989).

24. Nichols, *Building the Word*, pp. 126–127.

25. Bernhard W. Anderson, "The Problem and Promise of Commentary," *Interpretation* 36(4):342, 343 (Oct. 1982).

26. Elisabeth Schüssler Fiorenza, "Response (to Walter J. Burgnardt)," in *A New*

Look at Preaching, ed. John Burke, Good News Studies 7 (Wilmington, Del.: Michael Glazier, 1983), p. 52.

27. See Brueggemann, "The Social Nature of the Biblical Text," pp. 127–165.

Chapter 4: The Focus and Function of the Sermon

1. Fred B. Craddock, *As One Without Authority* (Nashville: Abingdon Press, 1971), pp. 124–125. At the heart of Craddock's argument is the distinction between "inductive" and "deductive" movement in sermons. A similar distinction was made a generation earlier by W. E. Sangster in *The Craft of the Sermon* (London: Epworth Press, 1954), pp. 71–79.

2. Craddock, *As One Without Authority*, p. 105.

3. Ibid., p. 100.

4. Richard L. Eslinger, *A New Hearing: Living Options in Homiletic Method* (Nashville: Abingdon Press, 1987), pp. 124–125.

5. Ronald E. Sleeth, *God's Word and Our Words: Basic Homiletics* (Atlanta: John Knox Press, 1986), p. 44.

6. Eugene L. Lowry, *Doing Time in the Pulpit: The Relationship Between Narrative and Preaching* (Nashville: Abingdon Press, 1985), pp. 79, 80.

7. David H. Kelsey, *The Uses of Scripture in Recent Theology* (Philadelphia: Fortress Press, 1975), p. 91.

8. Ibid., p. 208.

9. Lowry, *Doing Time in the Pulpit*, p. 80.

10. David G. Buttrick, "Interpretation and Preaching," *Interpretation* 25(1):58 (Jan. 1981).

11. O. C. Edwards, Jr., *Elements of Homiletic: A Method for Preparing to Preach* (New York: Pueblo Publishing Co., 1982), p. 63.

Chapter 5: The Basic Form of the Sermon

1. Halford E. Luccock, *In the Minister's Workshop* (New York: Abingdon-Cokesbury Press, 1944), p. 118.

2. The sermon outline is an expanded version of one described in Harold T. Bryson and James C. Taylor, *Building Sermons to Meet People's Needs* (Nashville: Broadman Press, 1980), p. 94.

3. Merrill R. Abbey, *Communication in Pulpit and Parish* (Philadelphia: Westminster Press, 1973), pp. 161–164.

4. Fred B. Craddock, *As One Without Authority* (Nashville: Abingdon Press, 1971), p. 56.

5. See, for example, Craddock, *As One Without Authority* and *Overhearing the Gospel* (Nashville: Abingdon Press, 1978); Milton Crum, Jr., *Manual on Preaching* (Valley Forge, Pa.: Judson Press, 1977); Eugene L. Lowry, *The Homiletical Plot: The Sermon as Narrative Art Form* (Atlanta: John Knox Press, 1980) and *Doing Time in the Pulpit: The Relationship Between Narrative and Preaching* (Nashville: Abingdon Press, 1985); Richard A. Jensen, *Telling the Story: Variety and Imagination in Preaching* (Minneapolis: Augsburg Publishing House, 1980); Edmund A. Steimle, Morris J. Niedenthal, and Charles L. Rice, *Preaching the Story* (Philadelphia: Fortress Press, 1980); Richard L. Eslinger, *A New Hearing: Living Options in Homiletic Method* (Nashville: Abingdon Press, 1987); Don M. Wardlaw, ed.,

Preaching Biblically (Philadelphia: Westminster Press, 1983); and David Buttrick, *Homiletic: Moves and Structures* (Philadelphia: Fortress Press, 1987).

6. Craddock, *As One Without Authority,* p. 53.

7. Ibid., p. 156.

8. Ibid., p. 66.

9. Lowry, *The Homiletical Plot,* p. 76.

10. Ibid., pp. 29–30.

11. Ibid., p. 31.

12. Ibid., p. 50.

13. Fred B. Craddock, *Preaching* (Nashville: Abingdon Press, 1985), pp. 173–174.

14. David G. Buttrick, "Interpretation and Preaching," *Interpretation* 25(1):55–56 (Jan. 1981).

15. Buttrick, *Homiletic,* p. 294.

16. Ibid., pp. 320–321.

17. This description of Buttrick's move system is adapted from my review of *Homiletic* in *Theology Today* 45(1):109–110 (April 1988).

18. Richard Lischer, "Preaching and the Rhetoric of Promise," *Word and World* 8(1):69 (Winter 1988).

19. Ibid., p. 70.

20. Edmund A. Steimle, "The Eye of the Storm," in Steimle et al., *Preaching the Story,* pp. 121–125.

Chapter 6: Refining the Form

1. For a more complete discussion of systemic sermon unity, see Thomas G. Long, "Pawn to King Four: Sermon Introductions and Communicational Design," *Reformed Review* 40(1):27–35 (Autumn 1986).

2. William H. Willimon, "Love in Action," a sermon preached at the Duke University Chapel, 14 February 1988.

3. Henry H. Mitchell, "To Think on These Things," a sermon preached on the National Radio Pulpit in the July–September 1978 series (New York: National Radio Pulpit, 1978), p. 53.

4. Barbara K. Lundblad, "Growing Old and Passing On," a sermon preached on the Lutheran Series of the Protestant Hour, 19 May 1985 (New York: Lutheran Church in America, 1985), pp. 34–35.

5. Edmund A. Steimle, "Last Call," a sermon preached on the Lutheran Series of the Protestant Hour, 1 July 1973 (New York: Lutheran Church in America, 1973), pp. 14–16.

6. Thomas G. Long, "Sermon: Figs Out of Season," in *Preaching Biblically,* ed. Don M. Wardlaw (Philadelphia: Westminster Press, 1983), pp. 99, 100.

7. John Vannorsdall, "A Day Far Spent," a sermon preached in the Lutheran Series of the Protestant Hour, 3 May 1981 (New York: Lutheran Church in America, 1981), p. 10.

8. Probably the best of these, in many ways the classic treatment of "standard" forms, was Halford E. Luccock's, "Some Types of Outline," a chapter in his excellent homiletical text, *In the Minister's Workshop* (Nashville: Abingdon-Cokesbury Press, 1944), pp. 134–147.

9. This list borrows from similar lists in Luccock; in Fred B. Craddock, *Preaching*

(Nashville: Abingdon Press, 1985), p. 177; and in John Killinger, *Fundamentals of Preaching* (Philadelphia: Fortress Press, 1985), pp. 50–59.

10. James Sanders, *God Has a Story, Too* (Philadelphia: Fortress Press, 1979), pp. 20–21.

Chapter 7: Beginnings, Connections, and Endings

1. Gerald Kennedy, *His Word Through Preaching* (New York: Harper & Brothers, 1947), p. 58.

2. George E. Sweazey, *Preaching the Good News* (Englewood Cliffs, N.J.: Prentice-Hall, 1976), p. 95.

3. J. Randall Nichols, *Building the Word: The Dynamics of Communication and Preaching* (San Francisco: Harper & Row, 1980), pp. 102–103.

4. Ilion T. Jones, *Principles and Practice of Preaching* (Nashville: Abingdon Press, 1956), p. 153.

5. Nichols, *Building the Word,* p. 101.

6. David Buttrick, *Homiletic: Moves and Structures* (Philadelphia: Fortress Press, 1987), p. 85.

7. See also Thomas G. Long, *The Senses of Preaching* (Atlanta: John Knox Press, 1988), pp. 65–68.

8. Robert McAfee Brown, "Freedom and Political Responsibility," in *Proclaiming the Acceptable Year: Sermons from the Perspective of Liberation Theology,* ed. Justo L. González (Valley Forge, Pa.: Judson Press, 1982), p. 117.

9. John R. Fry, "Blindness," in his *Fire and Blackstone* (Philadelphia: J. B. Lippincott Co., 1969), p. 45.

10. Cynthia A. Jarvis, "Let Us Pray: Why Do We Pray?" an unpublished sermon preached 4 August 1985 at Nassau Presbyterian Church, Princeton, N.J.

11. John Killinger, *Fundamentals of Preaching* (Philadelphia: Fortress Press, 1985), p. 84.

12. Adapted from Edmund A. Steimle, "Do Not Cling to Me," a sermon preached in the Lutheran Series of the Protestant Hour, 22 April 1973 (New York: Lutheran Church in America, 1973), pp. 13–14.

13. Walter J. Burghardt, "Who Touched Me?" in his *Sir, We Would Like to See Jesus: Homilies from a Hilltop* (Ramsey, N.J.: Paulist Press, 1982), p. 99.

14. Buttrick, *Homiletic,* p. 90.

15. Killinger, *Fundamentals of Preaching,* p. 83.

16. Buttrick, *Homiletic,* pp. 84–85.

17. See the excellent discussion of "connective logic" in Buttrick, *Homiletic,* pp. 70–74.

18. Some contemporary homileticians would add a third question to the set: *Who?* Who provides the conclusion, the preacher or the hearer? In his presentation of the inductive method of preaching, Fred Craddock suggests that the hearer may well be the better choice, that "the listener completes the sermon. . . . What is here suggested . . . is that the participation of the hearer is essential, not just in the post-benediction implementation but in the completion of the thought, movement, and decision-making within the sermon itself. The process calls for an incompleteness, a lack of exhaustiveness in the sermon." Fred B. Craddock, *As One Without Authority* (Nashville: Abingdon Press, 1971), p. 64.

Craddock is pointing to the possibility, even the desirability, of a certain open-endedness in sermon conclusions. If the preacher resists the temptation to wrap everything up, the hearers are given the freedom to finish the sermon for themselves and to "make it their own." This is a valuable suggestion, so long as we do not insist on it for all sermons and also remember that the preacher still bears responsibility for providing both the resources and the guidance for the hearers' completion of the sermon. An open-ended conclusion, in other words, is different from dumping a box of sermonic tinker-toys into the middle of the sanctuary and telling the hearers, "Make what you want to out of this."

19. John Vannorsdall, "A Small Parade," a sermon preached in the Lutheran Series of the Protestant Hour, 31 March 1985 (New York: Lutheran Church in America, 1985), p. 8.

20. Barbara K. Lundblad, "Longing for Breath," a sermon preached in the Lutheran Series of the Protestant Hour, 26 May 1985 (New York: Lutheran Church in America, 1985), p. 40.

21. Henry H. Mitchell, "To Run and Not Be Weary," a sermon preached on the National Radio Pulpit in the summer of 1978 (New York: National Radio Pulpit, 1978), p. 45.

22. Richard John Neuhaus, "Change for the Kingdom's Sake," in *Preaching in the Witnessing Community,* ed. Herman G. Stuempfle, Jr. (Philadelphia: Fortress Press, 1973), pp. 53–54.

23. Baron von Hugel, as quoted in Robert E. C. Browne, *The Ministry of the Word* (London: SCM Press, 1956), p. 50.

Chapter 8: Images and Experiences in Sermons

1. See, for example, the remarks of the fourteenth-century homiletician Robert of Basevorn on "the winning-over of the audience" in the essay "Ornamentation," in *Theories of Preaching: Selected Readings in the Homiletical Tradition,* ed. Richard Lischer (Durham, N.C.: Labyrinth Press, 1987), pp. 219–223.

2. See, for example, Ilion T. Jones, *Principles and Practice of Preaching* (Nashville: Abingdon Press, 1956). This typical textbook of the 1950s speaks confidently of preaching as "a redemptive deed" with the purpose of persuading others "to know and feel the gospel truth." The practical sections of the book, however, embody an almost exclusively ideational, rationalistic approach to sermon construction.

3. W. E. Sangster, *The Craft of the Sermon* (London: Epworth Press, 1954), p. 208.

4. George E. Sweazey, *Preaching the Good News* (Englewood Cliffs, N.J.: Prentice-Hall, 1976), p. 194.

5. Jones, *Principles and Practice,* p. 139.

6. At least one recent homiletical textbook—John Killinger, *Fundamentals of Preaching* (Philadelphia: Fortress Press, 1985), pp. 107–110—provides a list of the purposes of illustrations clearly dependent on similar lists in earlier textbooks, except that the element of persuasion is omitted. It is characteristic of more recent homiletics to view persuasion in terms of manipulation and, thus, as a negative characteristic when applied to preaching. For an alternate view, see Ronald E. Sleeth, *Persuasive Preaching* (Berrien Springs, Mich.: Andrews University Press, 1981).

7. Jones, *Principles and Practice,* p. 137.

8. Sangster, *The Craft of the Sermon,* p. 206.

9. Sweazey, *Preaching the Good News,* p. 193.

10. Charles Haddon Spurgeon in *Lectures to My Students,* as quoted in John R. W. Stott, *Between Two Worlds: The Art of Preaching in the Twentieth Century* (Grand Rapids: Wm. B. Eerdmans Publishing Co., 1982), p. 240.

11. Stott, *Between Two Worlds,* pp. 240–241.

12. Some contemporary homileticians, convinced that the word "illustration" is irreparably tainted by its rationalistic past, advocate its banishment from the vocabulary of preaching. Others, like David Buttrick, continue to use it, but only in a restricted sense and along with other descriptive terms, like "image," "metaphor," and "example." See David Buttrick, *Homiletic: Moves and Structures* (Philadelphia: Fortress Press, 1987), pp. 113–151.

13. Fred B. Craddock, *Preaching* (Nashville: Abingdon Press, 1985), p. 204.

14. William Sloane Coffin, "The Courage to Love," in his *The Courage to Love* (San Francisco: Harper & Row, 1982), p. 9.

15. James S. Stewart, "Beyond Disillusionment to Faith," in *Best Sermons, 1962,* ed. G. Paul Butler (Princeton: D. Van Nostrand Co., 1962), p. 24. The full text of this illustration is cited as an example of a "Geographical or Topographical Illustration" by John Killinger in *Fundamentals of Preaching,* pp. 113–114.

16. Elizabeth Achtemeier, "Of Children and Streets and the Kingdom," in *Best Sermons 1,* ed. James W. Cox and Kenneth M. Cox (San Francisco: Harper & Row, 1988), pp. 288–289.

17. Buttrick, *Homiletic,* p. 133.

18. Ibid., pp. 133–134.

19. Ibid., p. 134.

20. Robert E. C. Browne, *The Ministry of the Word* (Philadelphia: Fortress Press, 1958), p. 39.

21. This account of Margie McCoy's death, as well as the quoted material, is found in Marjorie Casebier McCoy, *Frederick Buechner: Novelist Theologian of the Lost and Found,* with Charles S. McCoy (San Francisco: Harper & Row, 1988), pp. xiii, 156–157, 159–160, 158.

22. Jürgen Moltmann, *The Church in the Power of the Spirit: A Contribution to Messianic Ecclesiology* (New York: Harper & Row, 1977), p. 222.

23. Ibid., p. 220.

24. Ibid., p. 225.

25. Ibid., p. 191.

26. Wendell Berry, "A Dance," in *The Collected Poems of Wendell Berry, 1957–1982* (Berkeley, Calif.: North Point Press, 1985), p. 202.

27. C. H. Dodd, *The Parables of the Kingdom* (London and Glasgow: Fontana Books, 1961), p. 16.

28. Charles L. Rice, *Interpretation and Imagination: The Preacher and Contemporary Literature* (Philadelphia: Fortress Press, 1970), p. 126.

29. From Patrick J. Willson, "Weeds in Our Garden," an unpublished sermon preached on 19 July 1987 at Shades Valley Presbyterian Church, Birmingham, Ala.

30. Bruce C. Salmon, *Storytelling in Preaching: A Guide to the Theory and Practice* (Nashville: Broadman Press, 1988), p. 54.

31. Craddock, *Preaching,* p. 209.

32. Buttrick, *Homiletic,* p. 142.

33. Cf. Craddock, *Preaching,* pp. 208–209.

Chapter 9: From Desk to Pulpit

1. Walter J. Ong, *Orality and Literacy: The Technologizing of the Word* (London: Methuen, 1982), p. 74.

2. Ibid., p. 176.

3. Dietrich Bonhoeffer, "New Year, 1945," in *Letters and Papers from Prison*, ed. Eberhard Bethge, trans. Reginald H. Fuller (New York: Macmillan Co., 1953), p. 249.

4. Raymond E. Brown, *The Gospel According to John, I–XII* The Anchor Bible, vol. 29 (Garden City, N.Y.: Doubleday & Co., 1966), p. 18.

5. William Sloane Coffin, *The Courage to Love* (San Francisco: Harper & Row, 1982), pp. 7–8.

6. Charles L. Bartow, *The Preaching Moment* (Nashville: Abingdon Press, 1980), p. 37.

7. Some are Charles L. Bartow, *The Preaching Moment;* Al Fasol, *A Guide to Self-Improvement in Sermon Delivery* (Grand Rapids: Baker Book House, 1983); and an older but still valuable work, Robert White Kirkpatrick, *The Creative Delivery of Sermons* (New York: Macmillan Co., 1944).

8. Kirkpatrick, *The Creative Delivery of Sermons,* p. 11.

Chapter 10: Conversation Along the Pilgrim Way

1. James A. Michener, *Iberia: Spanish Travels and Reflections* (New York: Random House, 1968), p. 892.

2. Homer K. Buerlein, *How to Preach More Powerful Sermons* (Philadelphia: Westminster Press, 1984, 1986), p. 25.

3. William Muehl, *All the Damned Angels* (Philadelphia: Pilgrim Press, 1972), p. 15.

4. Ernest T. Campbell, *Locked in a Room with Open Doors* (Waco, Tex.: Word Books, 1974), p. 20.

5. Allan A. Boesak, *Comfort and Protest: Reflections on the Apocalypse of John of Patmos* (Philadelphia: Westminster Press, 1987), p. 105.

6. Ronald D. Sisk, "How to Forgive," in *Best Sermons 1,* ed. James W. Cox (San Francisco: Harper & Row, 1988), p. 312.

7. Walter Brueggemann, "The Social Nature of the Biblical Text for Preaching," in *Preaching as a Social Act: Theology and Practice,* ed. Arthur Van Seters (Nashville: Abingdon Press, 1988), p. 147.

Index of Names
and Subjects

Index
of Scripture References